I0812849

IMAGES
of America

JEFFERSON CITY
MISSOURI

Capitols Location Map

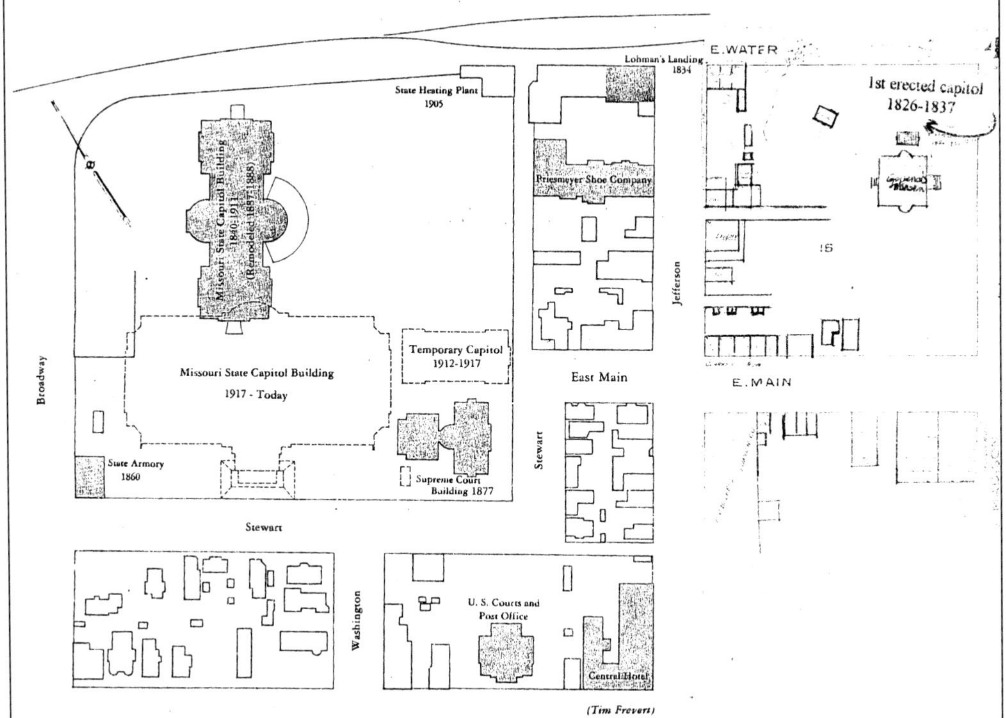

The Sanborn Insurance Maps of 1908 and 1916 owned by Dr. J. S. Summers, Jr. provided the locations of the 1840 Capitol, the temporary Capitol and the present Capitol.

This map of the capitol complex over time shows the placement of the first, second, and third capitol buildings in the City of Jefferson and the current executive mansion. The drawing is by Tim Frevert. (Summers Collection; Missouri State Archives.)

Cover Image: Friends of Miss Pauline Dallmeyer and Mr. Alvin Dallmeyer, seated far right, front, are pictured meeting a state official. The photo was taken about 1900. (Dottie Dallmeyer.)

IMAGES
of America

JEFFERSON CITY
MISSOURI

Dr. Joseph S. Summers and Dottie Summers Dallmeyer

ARCADIA
PUBLISHING

ISBN 978-0-7385-0834-4

Published by Arcadia Publishing
Charleston, South Carolina

Printed in the United States of America

Library of Congress Catalog Card Number: 00102919

For all general information contact Arcadia Publishing at:
Telephone 843-853-2070
Fax 843-853-0044
E-mail sales@arcadiapublishing.com
For customer service and orders:
Toll-Free 1-888-313-2665

Visit us on the Internet at www.arcadiapublishing.com

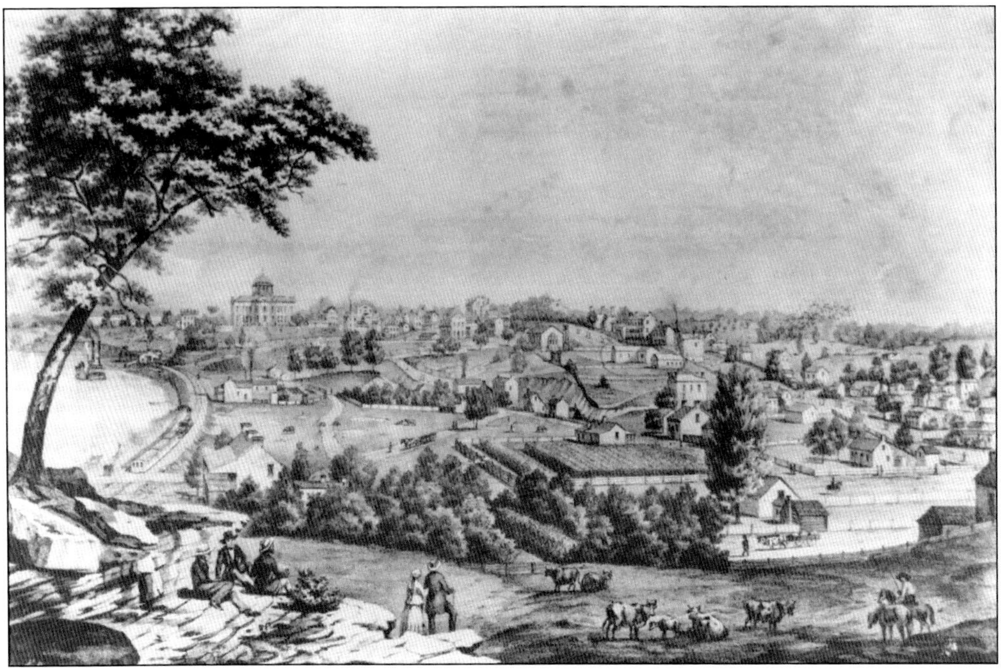

This sketch was made of the City of Jefferson in 1859. The second capitol, built in 1840, is located on the hill in the background. The first capitol burned in 1837. In the foreground is an area that became known as "Millbottom," with a few industries and some farming. To the left of the drawing is Missouri's first "highway," with a steamboat used as transportation. The railroad, next to the Missouri River, came to the City of Jefferson in 1856.(Summers Collection; Missouri State Archives.)

Contents

Acknowledgments 6

Introduction 7

1. The City of Jefferson is the Seat of State Government 9
2. Building a Community 27
3. The Importance of Transportation 43
4. The Growth of Local Business 53
5. Millbottom and Floods 83
6. City of Jefferson Street Scenes 93
7. The Evolution of the City 113
8. Life and Times in the City of Jefferson 121

ACKNOWLEDGMENTS

We would like to very gratefully thank Laura Jolley for all her support and hard work on this project. We would also like to thank Ken Winn, state archivist, for the excellent job he is doing at the archives, making it possible for us to do our work; and to Gary Kremer for his help, encouragement, and the work he has done to keep local history "alive." I would also like to thank Tracy Graves for the use of her computer.

INTRODUCTION

Missouri was the 24th state to enter the Union on August 10, 1821. The first governor was Alexander McNair. On December 31, 1821, legislation was passed enabling a commission to be appointed to select a site for the new state capitol. The act of Congress allotted four grants of land for this purpose. There were five commissioners chosen—one from each corner of the state and one from the middle of the state. It was required that the site be on the Missouri River, within 40 miles of the mouth of the Osage River.

A site near Howard's Bluff on the south side of the Missouri River was selected. Daniel M. Boone, son of the famous pioneer, and Major Elias Bancroft were commissioned to lay out and plan the capital city. They were to complete the task in 120 days and were paid the handsome sum of $4 per day. The streets were planned to be "not more than 120 feet wide or less than 80 feet," with alleys 20-feet wide between. Some of the old main streets and alleys still retain these dimensions. The original plan was for a thousand lots, each about half an acre, called in-lots, in the central city area. Larger lots, from 5 to 40 acres, called out-lots, were planned around the city core. The first sale of these lots occurred in May of 1823; the average price of the in-lots was $32.75.

On October 1, 1826, the first capitol building was completed, and the City of Jefferson officially became the capital of the State of Missouri. In November of 1826, the first legislative session convened in the City of Jefferson. The first capitol building was situated on a bluff above and facing the Missouri River. The first floor served as legislative, judicial, and executive headquarters, and the second floor served as living quarters for the governor. This building was on the site of the present Governor's Mansion. The first legislators were a rough-looking group of men in homespun buckskin and homemade shoes—only one owned a store-bought suit. There were only 31 families in the city at that time. The City of Jefferson was incorporated in 1839 and the first mayor was Thomas Lawson Price.

From this planned beginning, the City of Jefferson struggled through the 19th century to find a firm economic base. The city was defined as being the seat of government for the State of Missouri, but that position was always threatened by other cities who wanted to host the capital. This struggle with outside forces and the internal struggle to establish a city separate, but within the position as the capital city, colored many of the decisions of early town fathers and shaped the City of Jefferson of today.

The City of Jefferson was a river town first. The reason this site was chosen was because it was on the Missouri River. In 1833, a bill was passed to establish a penitentiary. It was completed and the first prisoner was incarcerated in 1835. The prison was the first of many efforts to keep the City of Jefferson the capital of Missouri.

The first erected capitol of Missouri burned in November of 1837. The second capitol was started in 1840. During this time, there came the first influx of German immigrants. Most of the early settlers were from the South—Virginia, the Carolinas, Kentucky, and Tennessee.

The Union Pacific Railroad arrived in 1856, and for a while, it was the railhead. The City of Jefferson became a railroad town. Later a roundhouse was built, so the railroad was an integral part of commerce in the community.

The Civil War, and all its conflicts, was hard on our city, with frequent clashes between pro-slavery southern sympathizers and anti-slavery German immigrants. There are several important Civil War sites in and around the City of Jefferson. After the war, in 1866, Lincoln Institute was established by several black soldiers and their white sergeant to educate African Americans. Reconstruction, with the issue of freed slaves and old emotional scars, was difficult.

Another wave of German immigrants brought on a construction boom in the 1870s. The present Governor's Mansion was built in 1871, as were a number of other homes and businesses still standing. The first high school graduation was in 1875. Electricity was first used in the city in 1887; the Capital City Water Company originated in 1888. The second capitol building was enlarged and remodeled in 1888.

The Commercial Club was evident in the early 1890s, although members were responsible for the establishment of the water company earlier. The Commercial Club was comprised of a group of business and professional men who had the common goal of keeping the capital in the City of Jefferson and making this a more commercially-viable city. Some of the members had factories within the prison walls—they had moved to town to take advantage of inexpensive prison labor, became very wealthy, and gave back to the community with their efforts in the Commercial Club. Commercial Club members pooled their resources to have a toll bridge constructed across the Missouri River. They encouraged the construction of schools and streets, and bought property for owners of shoe factories and other prison industries in order to encourage them to remain in the City of Jefferson. It is said that the prison factories were so productive that at one time, seven thousand shoes were made in them per day—more than any other place in the world at the time. The Commercial Club shaped the direction of the City of Jefferson coming into the 20th century.

By 1900, the Capital City Telephone Company was organized. Some of the other highlights of the 20th century that have continued to influence growth and development included: the burning of the second erected capitol on February 5, 1911; the construction and use of a temporary capitol; and the building of our present capitol, which was dedicated in 1924. Other influences and events included: the construction of other public buildings; in 1905, St. Mary's hospital; streetcar service from 1911 to 1934; and World War I and its impact on the German population in the City of Jefferson. The Depression of the 1930s was not as great of a problem because there were more state workers than industrial employees. During World War II, the economy remained fairly stable with more growth after the war. In 1954, a major prison riot occurred; in 1955, the second bridge across the Missouri River was constructed, there was a push for more industry, and state government expanded. In the 1970s, there was great destruction of older buildings in the name of urban renewal. In 1991, a third bridge was constructed, and in 1993, there was a major flood.

We will tell the story of the growth and development of the historic City of Jefferson through the photos in this book.

One

The City of Jefferson is the Seat of State Government

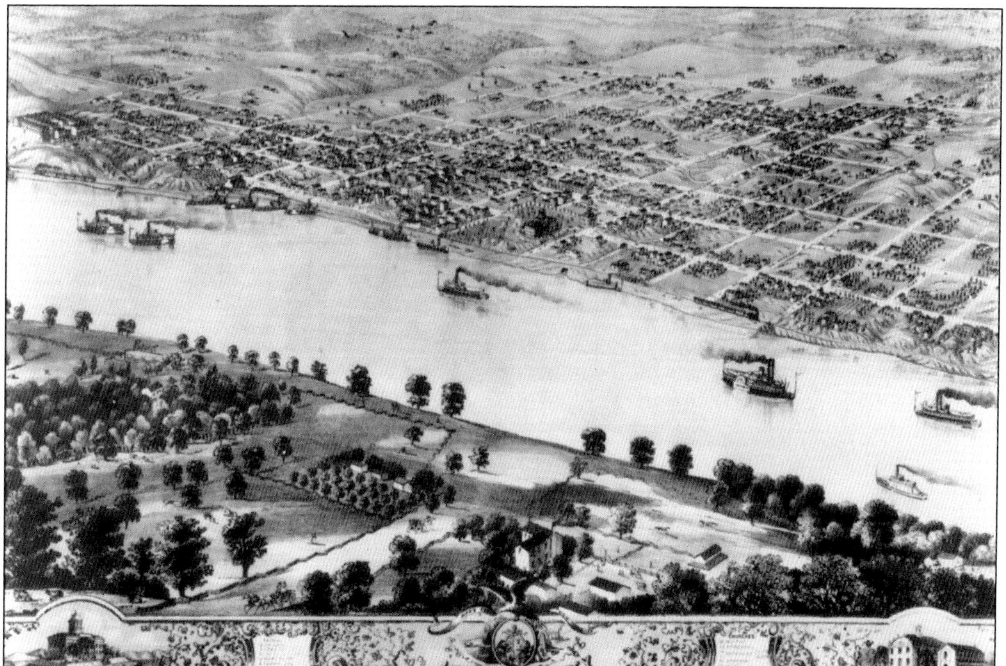

The City of Jefferson is the seat of state government. Some of the points of interest in this birds-eye-view sketch done in 1869 include: the second capitol built in the City of Jefferson; the Executive Mansion that preceded the current Governor's Mansion; the steamboat traffic on the Missouri River; the armory on the capitol grounds, built in 1860; the Missouri State Penitentiary; the fairgrounds in the upper left; and the women's college on the corner of Jackson and Water Streets. In the lower right corner is a sketch of the old courthouse and market house; the original State Seal as designed by Robert Wells is under the eagle.

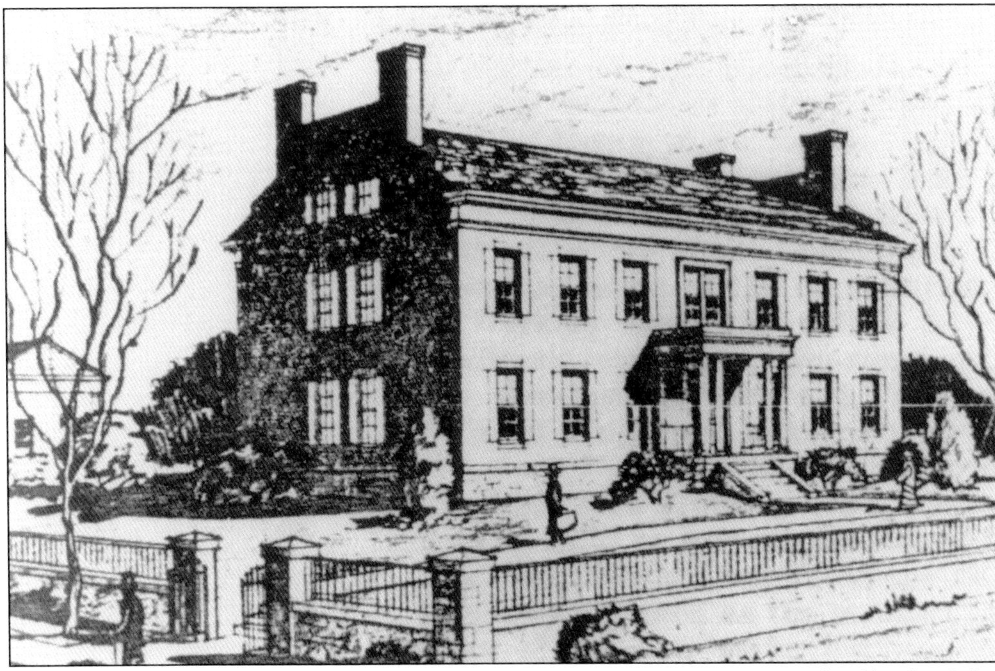

This is a sketch of the first capitol in the City of Jefferson. The structure was made of brick, 40 feet by 60 feet, facing the Missouri River. There are no photos or original sketches. This one was done in 1955 by a St. Louis architect, Marcel Boulicault. This building housed the legislature and served as the governor's residence. In 1837, a fire in the fireplace of the secretary of state's office was not banked properly, and the building burned down. (Cole County Historical Society.)

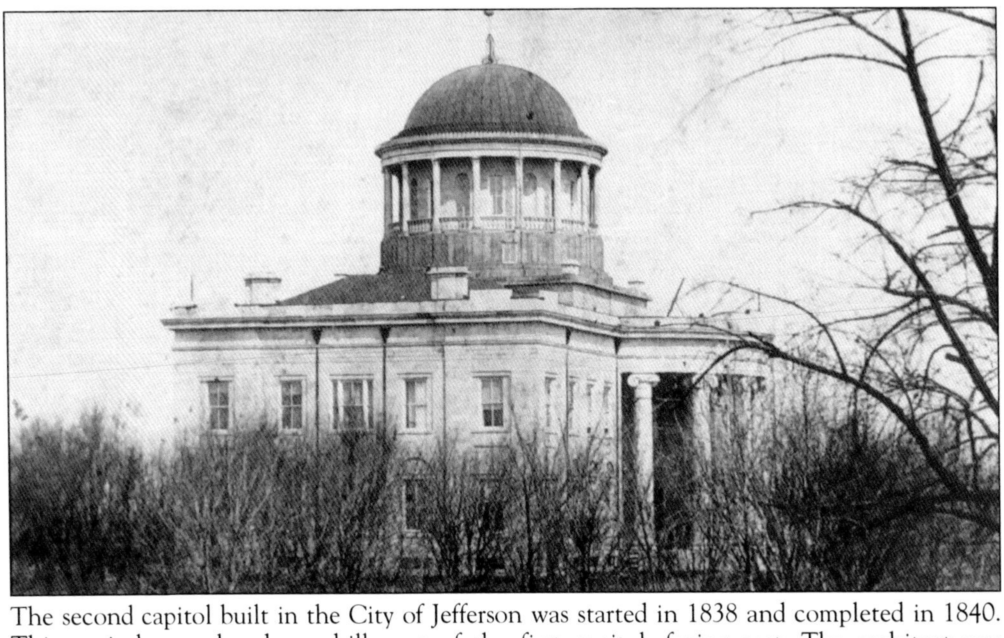

The second capitol built in the City of Jefferson was started in 1838 and completed in 1840. This capitol was placed one hill west of the first capitol, facing east. The architect was A. Stephen Hills. The interior was made of brick and the exterior of stone. This photo was taken about 1885. (Cole County Historical Society.)

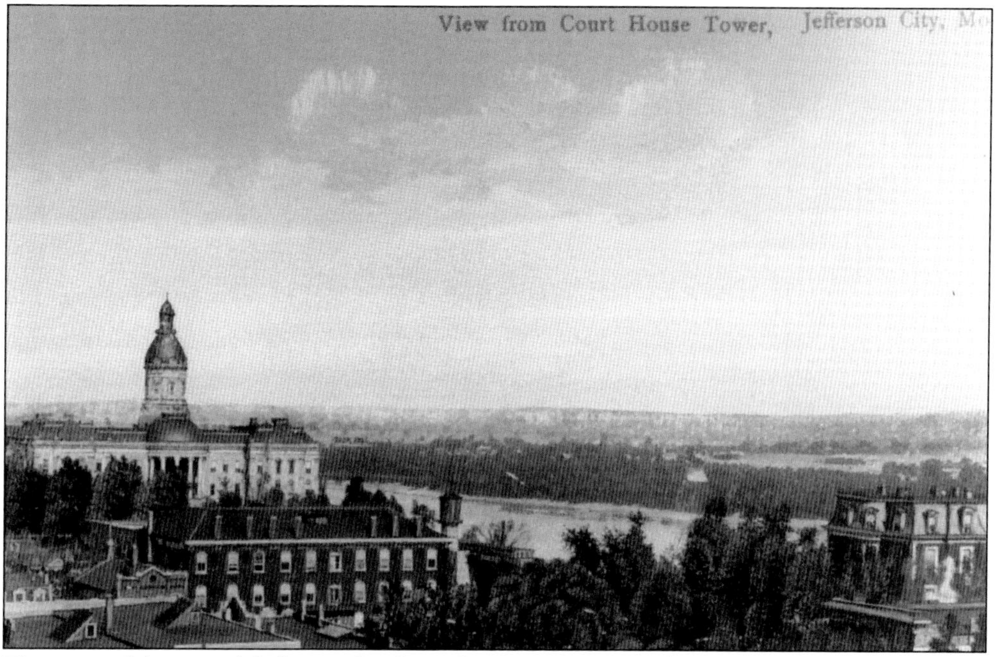

This view of the remodeled capitol is from about 1900. It was taken from the tower of the Cole County Court House. The Governor's Mansion, which is on the site of the first capitol, is seen by the Missouri River. The Madison House Hotel is pictured to the left in front of the capitol. (Summers Collection; Missouri State Archives.)

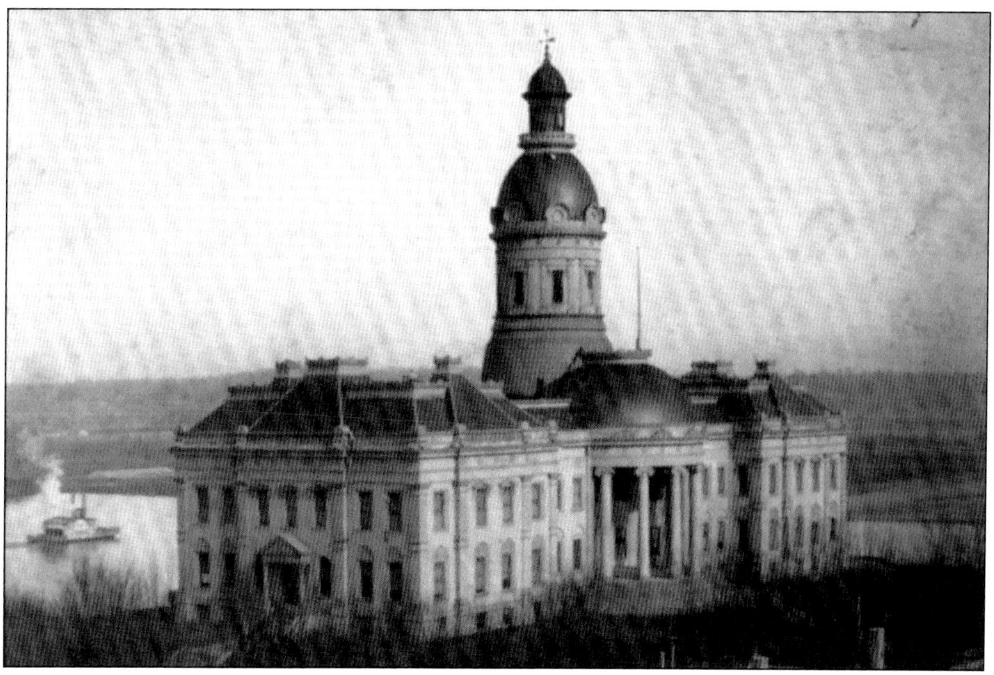

The second capitol was remodeled in 1887–1888. One wing was added to each side, north and south, and a new 185-foot-high dome was built. Note the steamboat on the river behind the capitol. This view was taken about 1900. (Summers Collection; Missouri State Archives.)

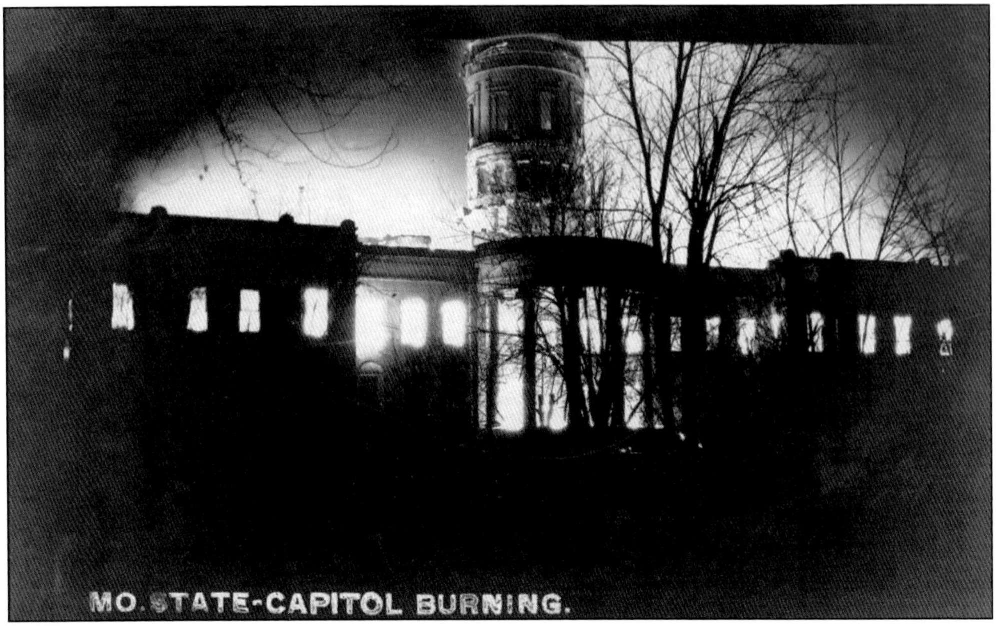

The second erected capitol burned as a result of being struck by lightning on February 5, 1911. (Summers Collection; Missouri State Archives.)

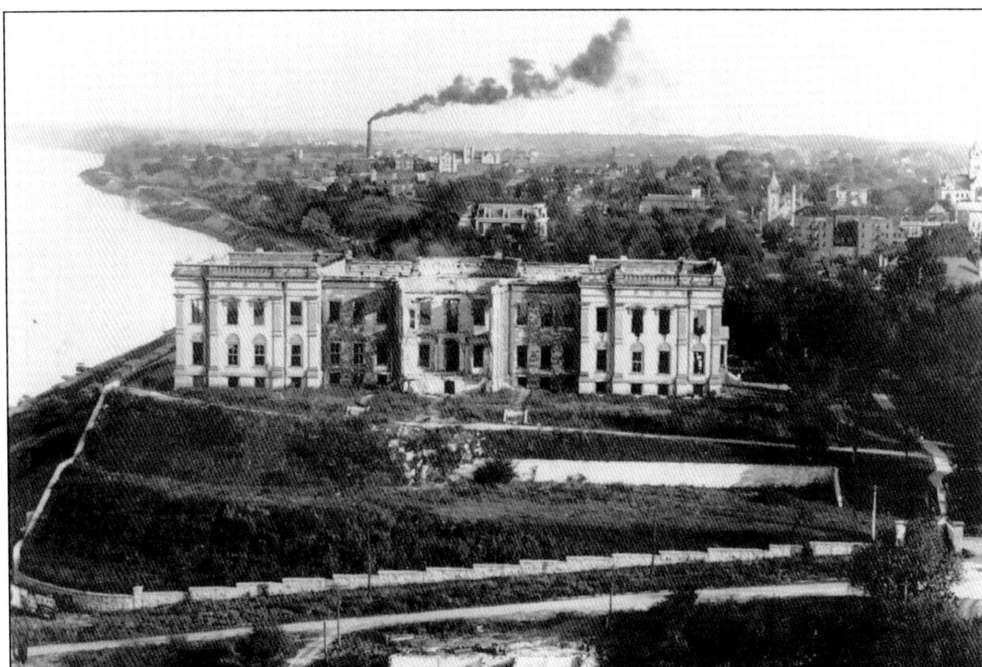
The ruins of the second capitol are pictured here after the fire. This view is from the west looking east. In the background is the Governor's Mansion, Madison House Hotel, Cole County Court House, Carnegie Library, Methodist Church, and the Missouri State Penitentiary with the smokestack. (Summers Collection; Missouri State Archives.)

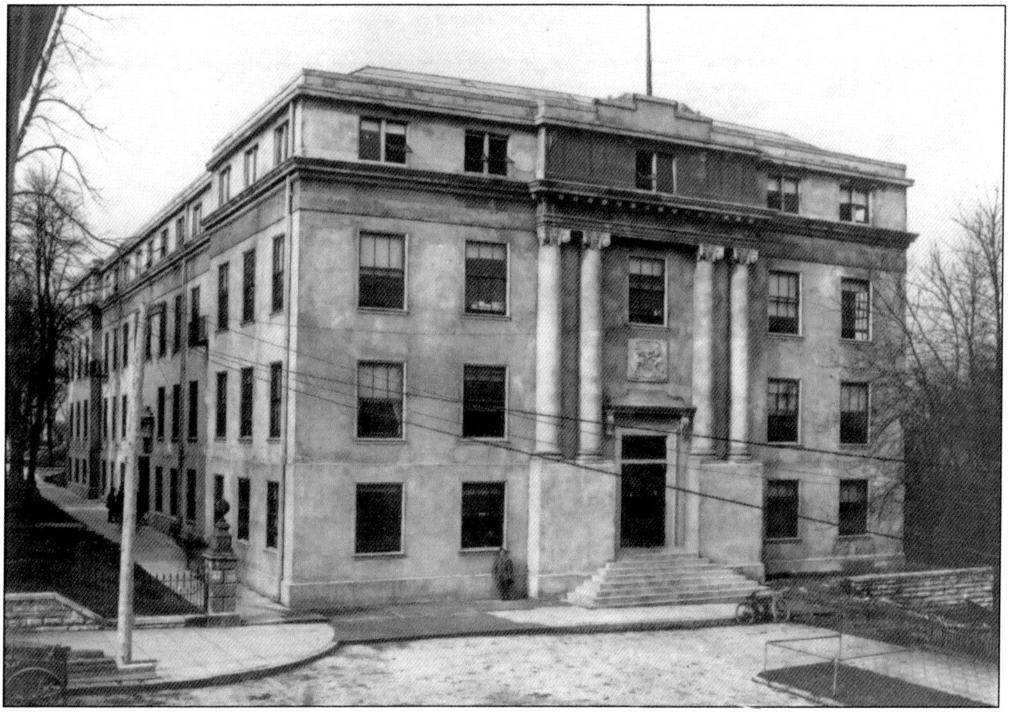

In 1912, this building was built as a temporary capitol. It took three months to build and was comprised of wood and stucco, smoothed to resemble stone. The leaky roof on the building was a constant problem. The temporary capitol was placed south of the present one and was used until October 1917, when the new capitol was complete enough to be moved into, then it was torn down. (Summers Collection; Missouri State Archives.)

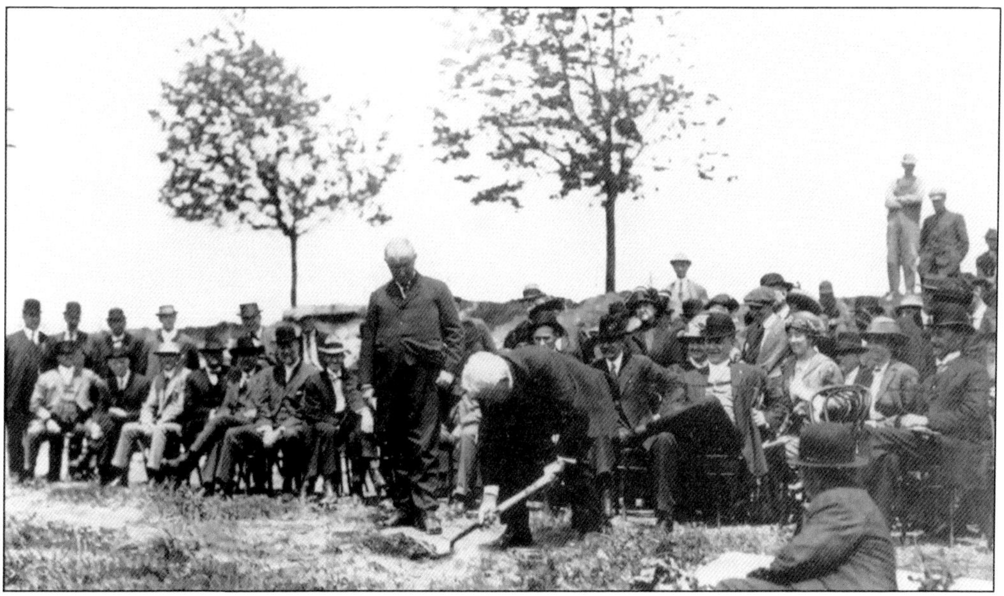

Capitol commissioners and state officers broke ground for the new capitol building on May 6, 1913. (Summers Collection; Missouri State Archives.)

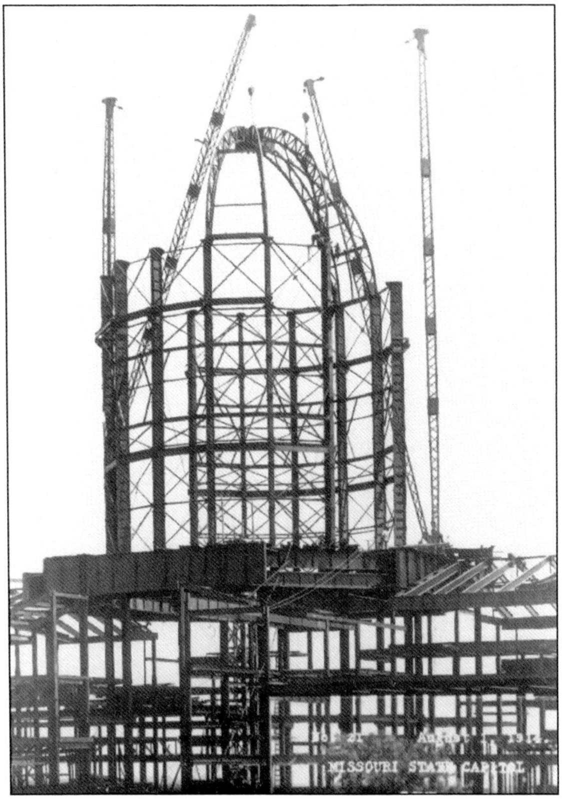

On August 1, 1914, the new capitol's superstructure looked like this as the steel girders of the dome were being completed. (Missouri State Archives.)

The south face of the current capitol is pictured under construction. This view was taken from the roof of the Supreme Court Building, across the street. The Senate Chambers are on the right, and the House of Representatives is on the left. (Missouri State Archives.)

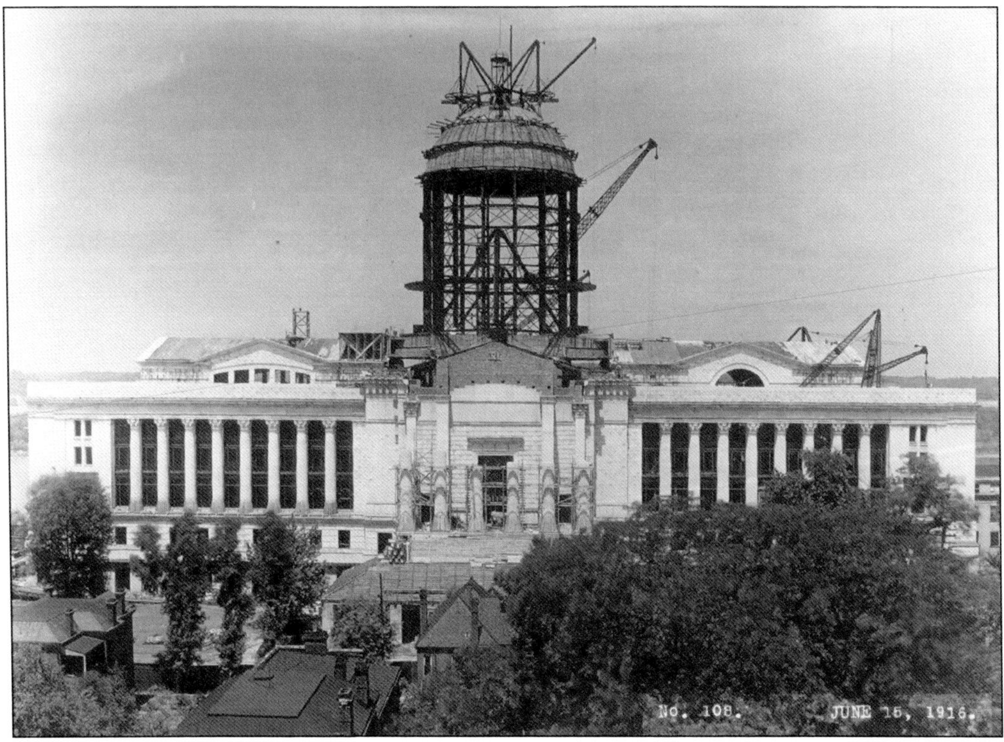

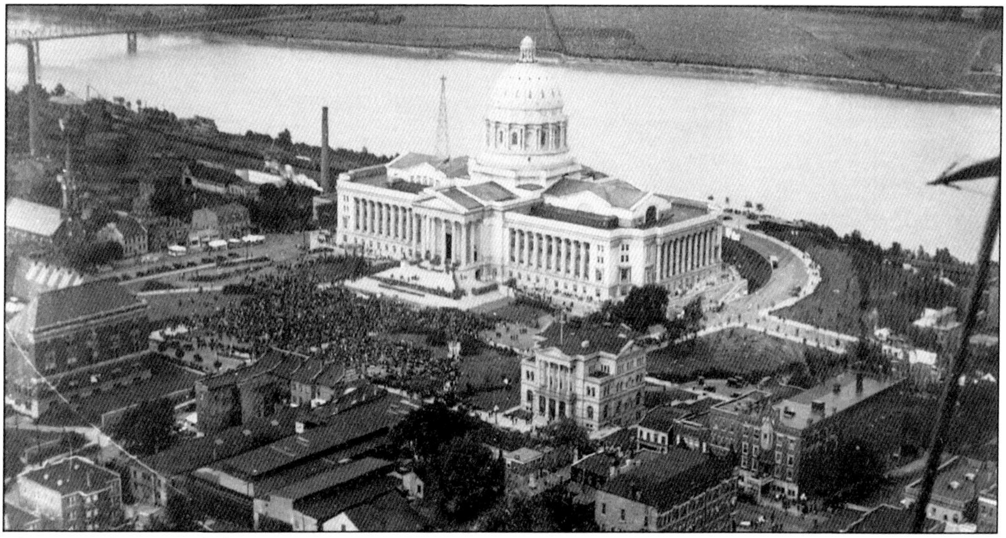

This aerial view of the present capitol was taken from a biplane on Capitol Dedication Day, October 6, 1924, when the building was completed. Work continued on interior and exterior decoration until about 1928. One-fourth of the budget for the building was allotted for decoration, which is exceptional. Some world-famous paintings and sculptures were used, and some were chosen through competitions. This photo shows the crowds and tent booths on the lower right, which sold food and cold drinks. As part of Dedication Day, there was a ballet from Stephens College and a pageant which included many of the children of the city. (Ron Arsenault.)

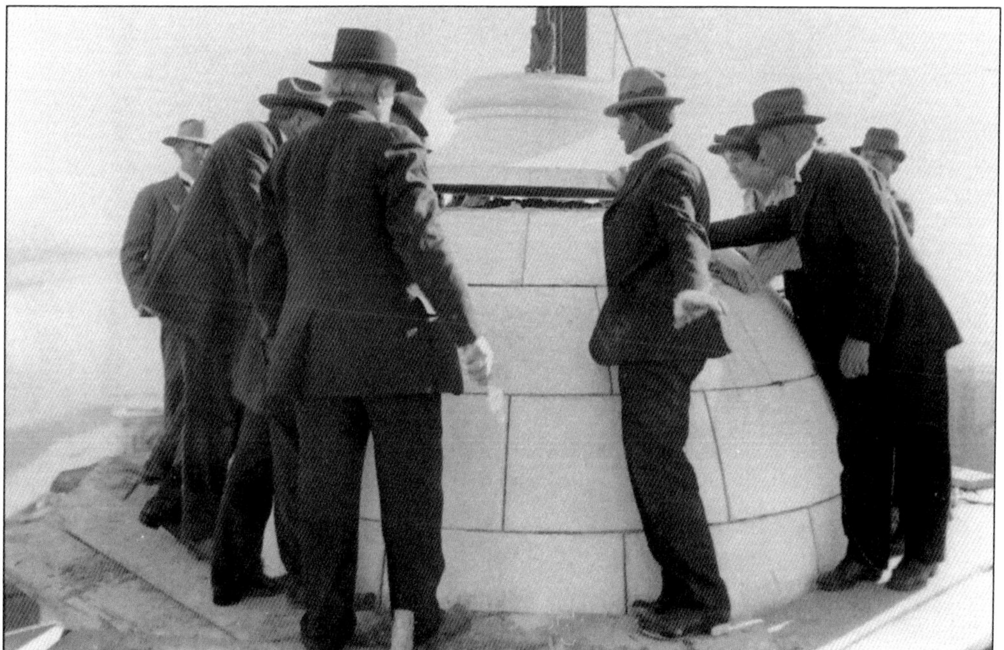

The dome capping ceremony was held on October 6, 1924, with the capitol commissioners and Miss Mathilda K. Dallmeyer, an important member of the women's suffrage movement, in attendance. Mathilda placed a dime in the concrete at the base of the statue *Ceres* in remembrance of her part of the ceremony. (J.J. Prost.)

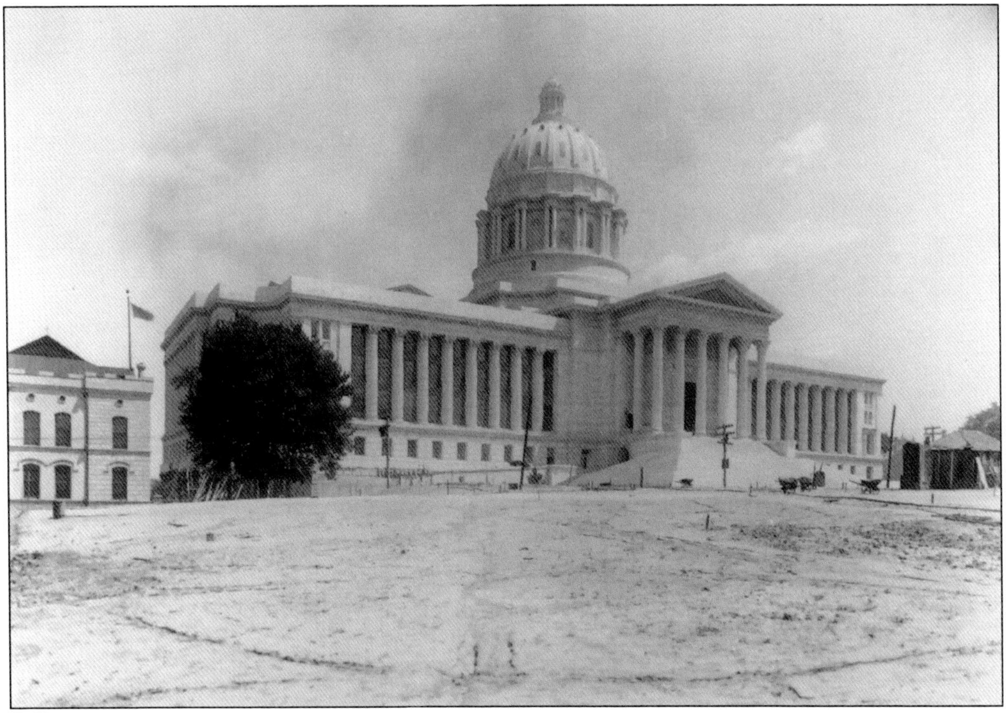

This is a 1917 view of the present capitol, while still under construction. To the left is the armory, and in the background, beyond the construction shack, are the state library and old Supreme Court Building. (Missouri State Archives.)

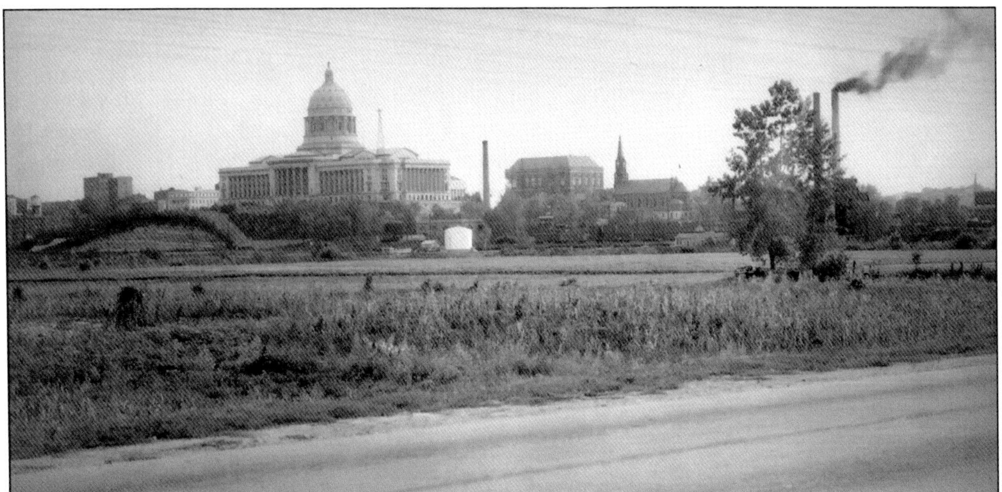

This is a view of the capital city from the north side of the Missouri River taken October 9, 1934. Points of interest, from the left, include: Madison House Hotel; the water tower for Tweedie Shoe Company; the Central Trust Building; the Missouri Highway Department building; the present capitol; the United States Post Office just behind; the tower for the first radio station—WOS, meaning "watch our state"—which was housed in the capitol dome; the smokestack for Missouri Power and Light; the Supreme Court Building; and St. Peter's Church. (Summers Collection; Missouri State Archives.)

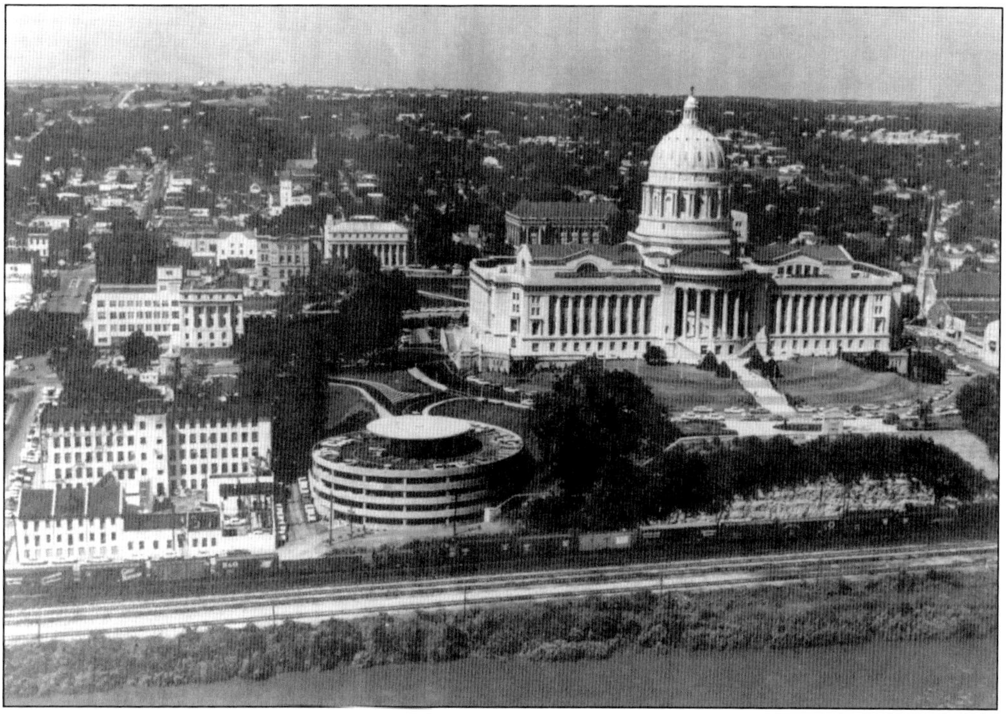

This aerial view from the north of the City of Jefferson was taken about 1969. Points of interest from the right on the river are: Tweedie Shoe Company, state parking garage—behind is the state highway department, the old United States Post Office, the new United States Post Office, the Supreme Court Building, the Capitol, and St. Peter's Church. (Bill Decker.)

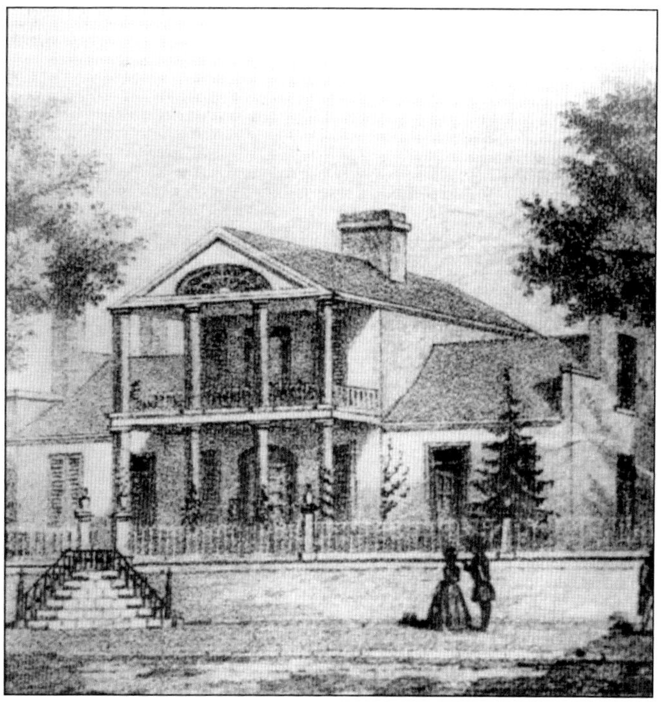

This is an artist's rendition of the first Governor's Mansion. (Cole County Historical Society.)

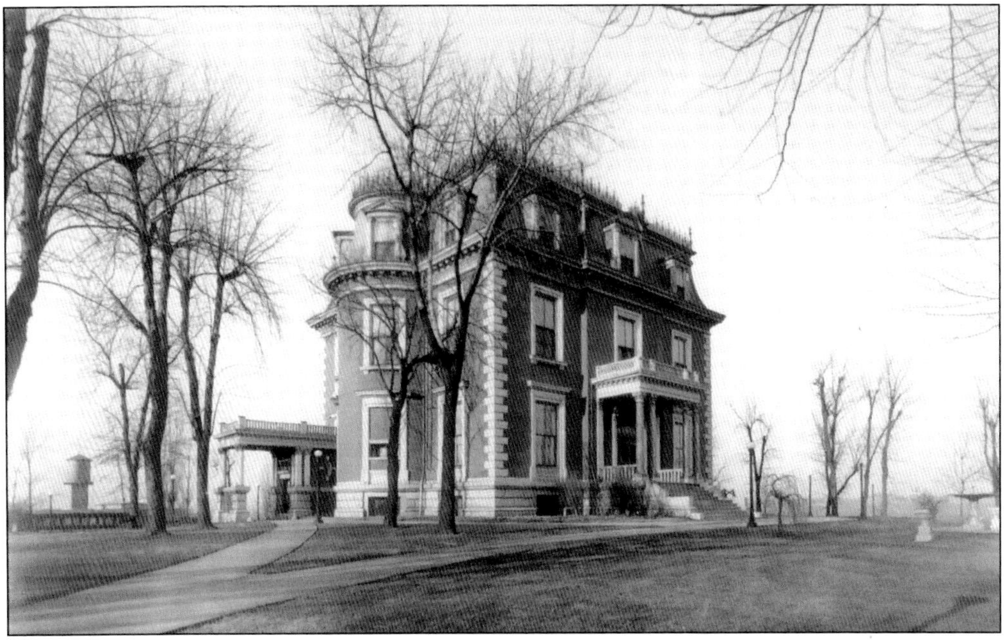

The Governor's Mansion was built in 1871, when Benjamin Gratz Brown was governor, with the carriage entrance located on the south side. This photo was taken about 1900. In the background is the water tower for A. Priesmeyer Shoe Company. (Jim Twyman.)

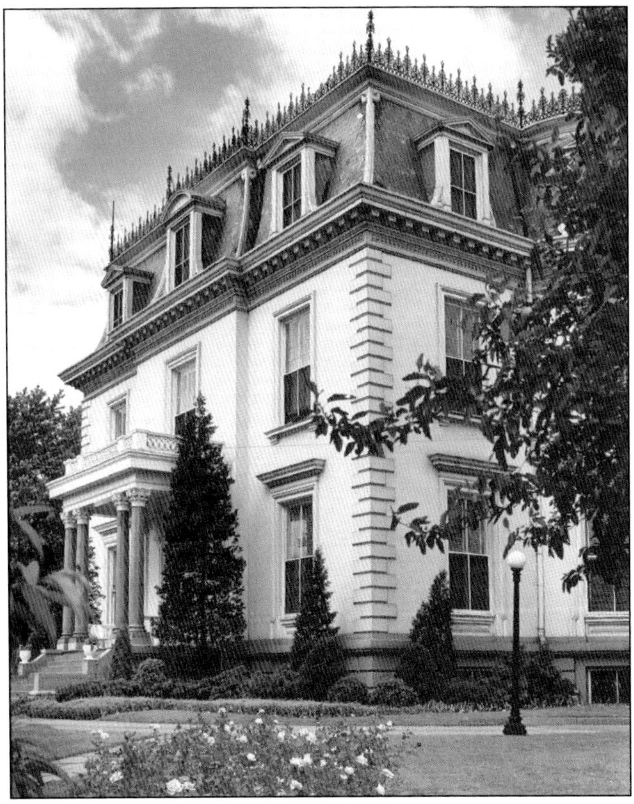

The front of the Governor's Mansion is pictured from the northeast in the 1950s, when it was painted white.(Gerald Massie.)

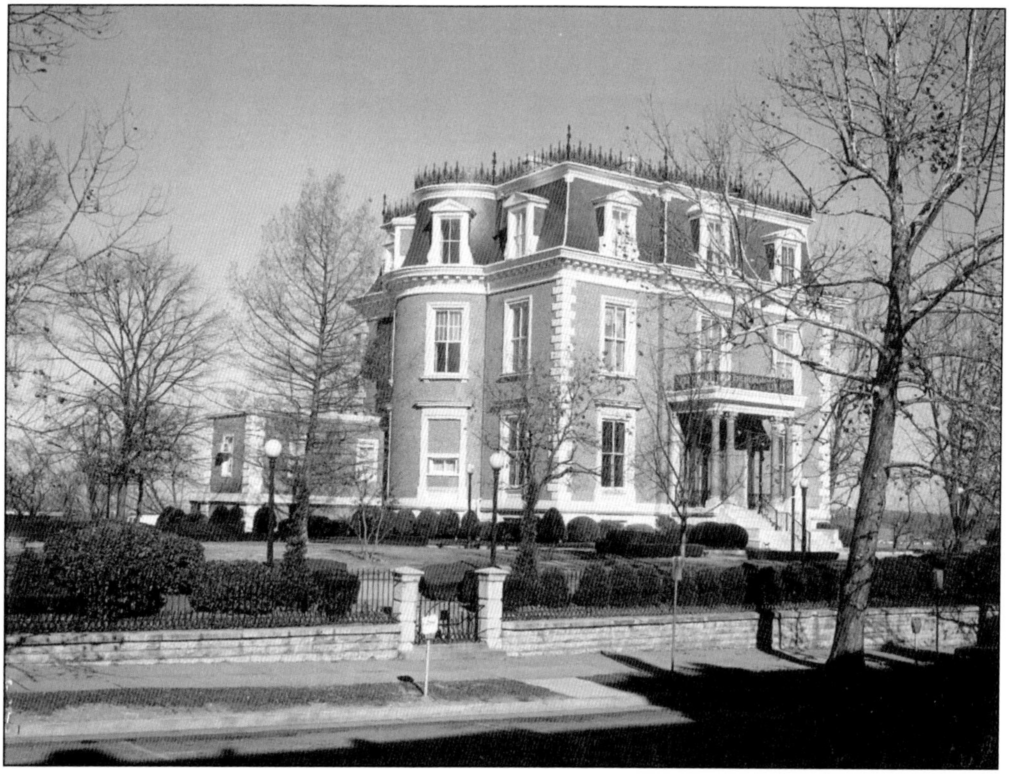

The Governor's Mansion is pictured here as it looks today, with its paint removed and restored to the original brick and stone. (Gerald Massie; Missouri State Archives.)

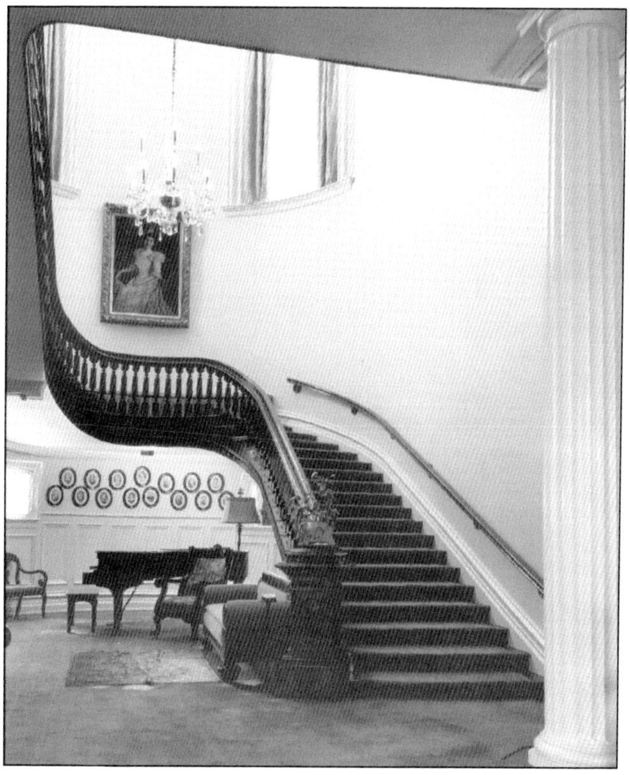

The grand stairway in the Governor's Mansion, pictured about 1961. (Gerald Massie; Missouri State Archives.)

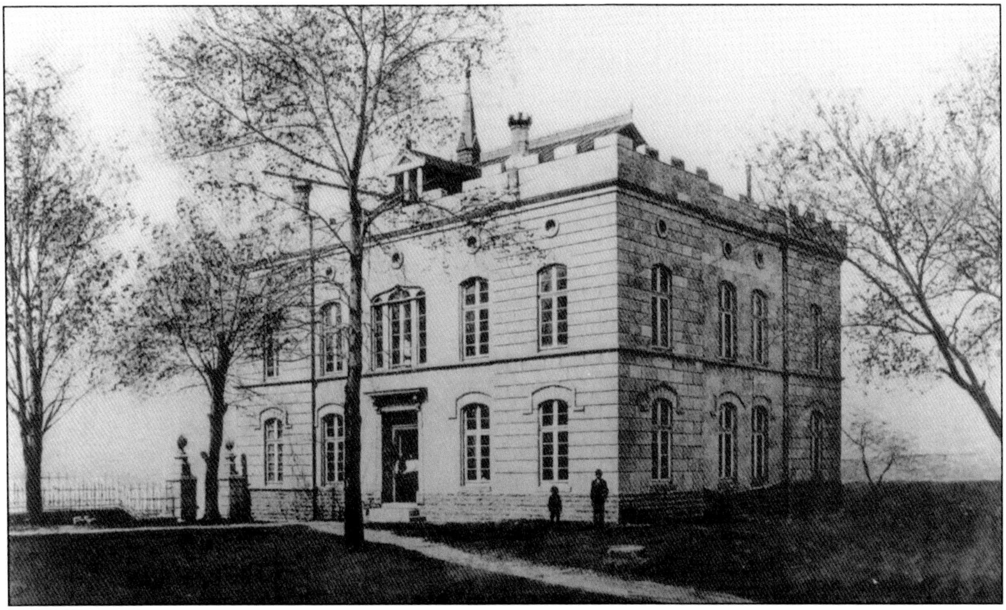

The state armory was built in 1861 on the southwest corner of the capitol grounds. This photo was taken in 1891, with the spire of St. Peter's Church behind. (Summers Collection; Missouri State Archives.)

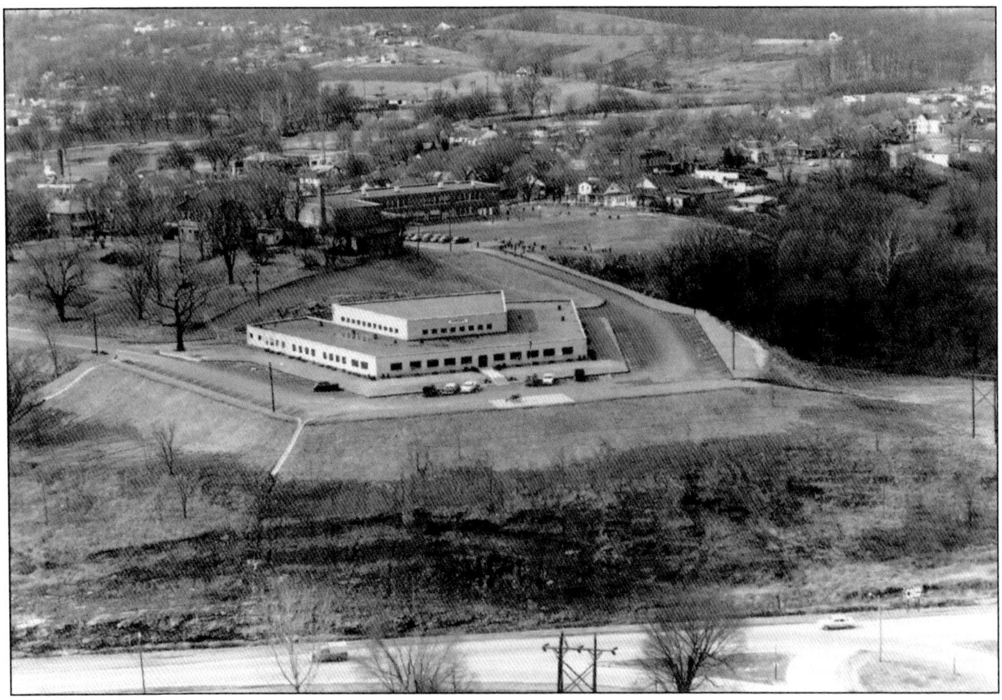

This aerial photo of the National Guard Armory was taken about 1960. Just behind are St. Mary's grade school, now Southwest School, and the Dulle home, known as headquarters of General John C. Fremont during the Civil War, in September 1861. (Summers Collection; Missouri State Archives.)

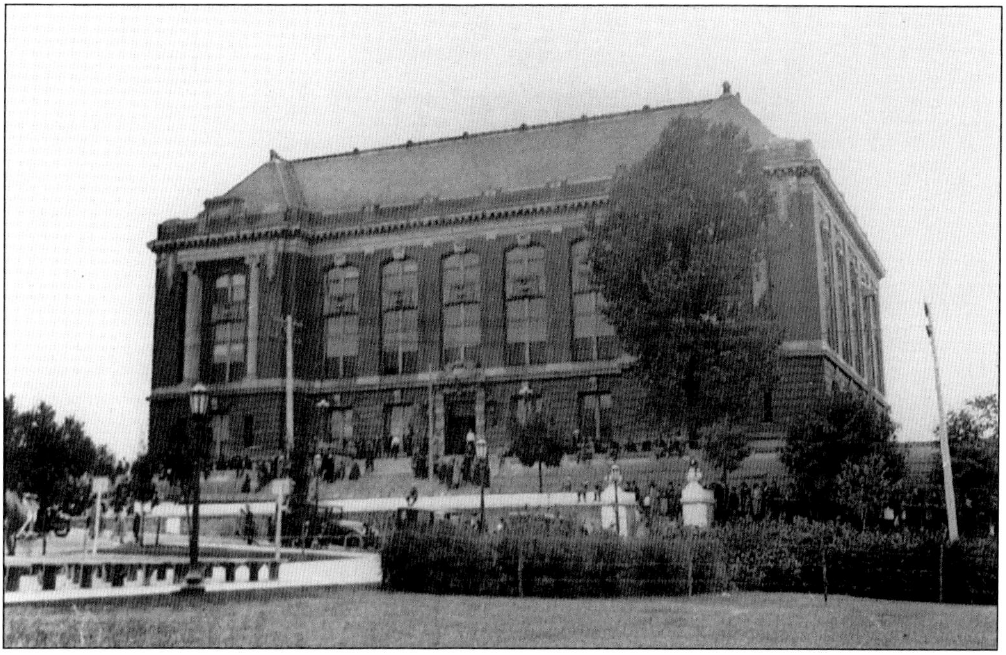

This is the north face of the Supreme Court Building across the street from the Capitol. This building was built in 1905, primarily with funds left over from the St. Louis World's Fair. This photo was taken about 1924. (Joe Kroeger.)

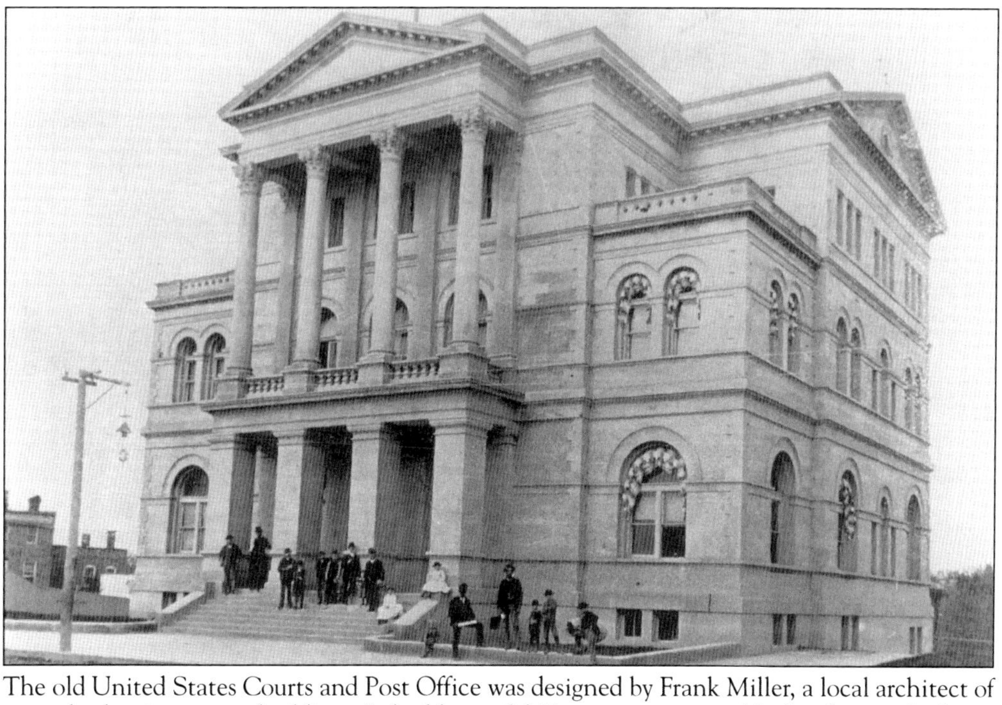

The old United States Courts and Post Office was designed by Frank Miller, a local architect of several other important buildings. It had beautiful Tennessee rose marble fireplaces, which are now in the Cole County Historical Society Museum. This photo was taken in 1897, and the building was torn down in the 1970s. (Summers Collection; Missouri State Archives.)

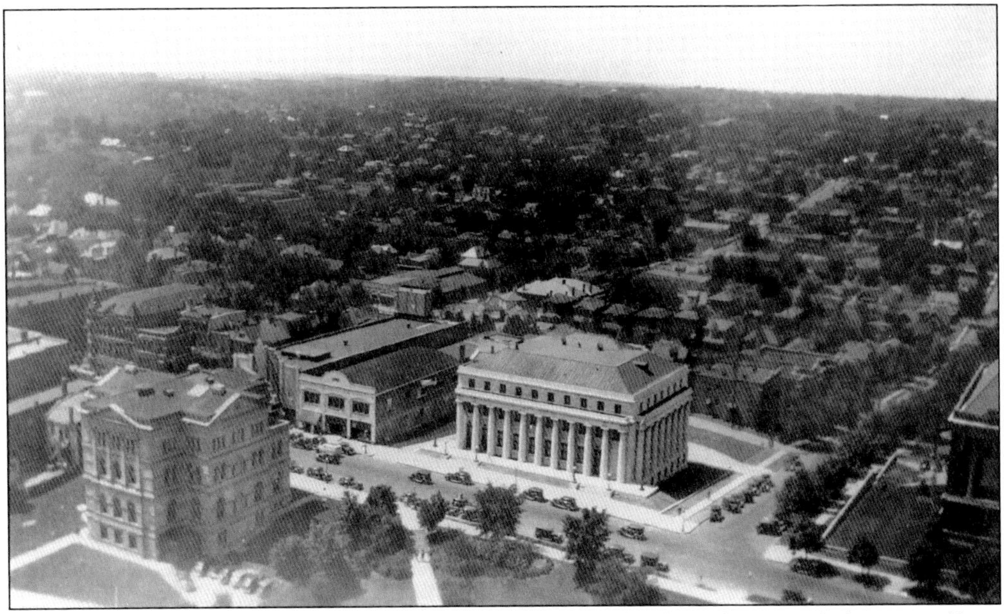

This is a view to the southwest from the dome of the capitol, taken about 1935, depicting (from the left edge): the Central Hotel, the old United States Courts and Post Office, Ott Lumber Company, the new United States Court and Post Office, and part of the Supreme Court Building. (Joe Kroeger.)

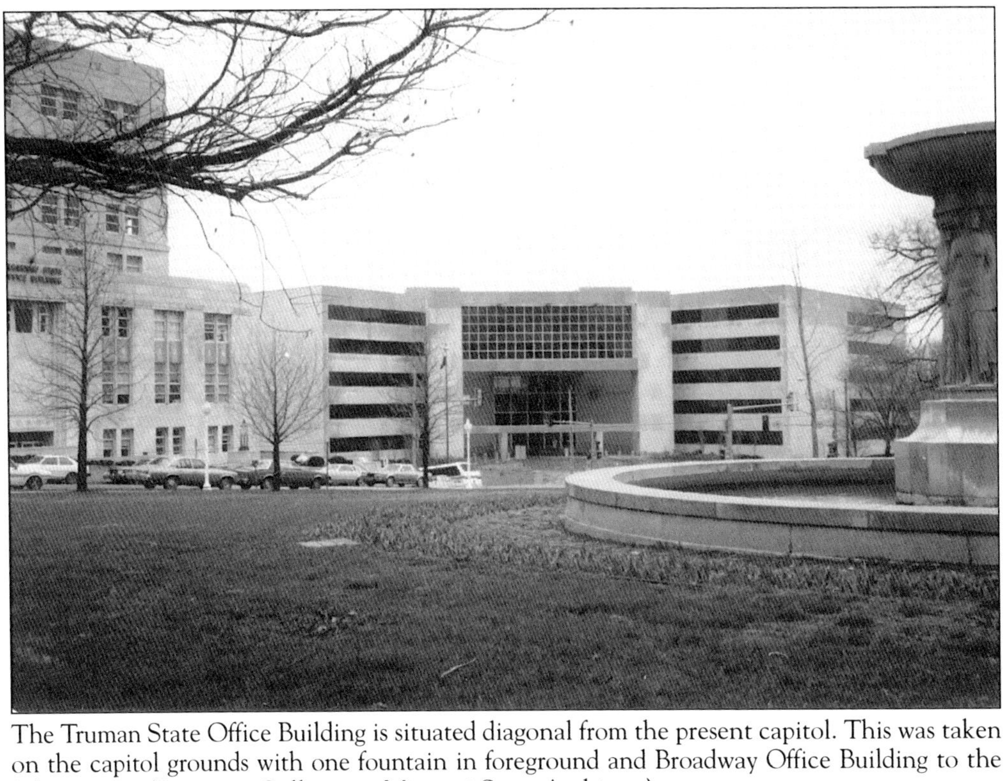

The Truman State Office Building is situated diagonal from the present capitol. This was taken on the capitol grounds with one fountain in foreground and Broadway Office Building to the left, c. 1984. (Summers Collection; Missouri State Archives.)

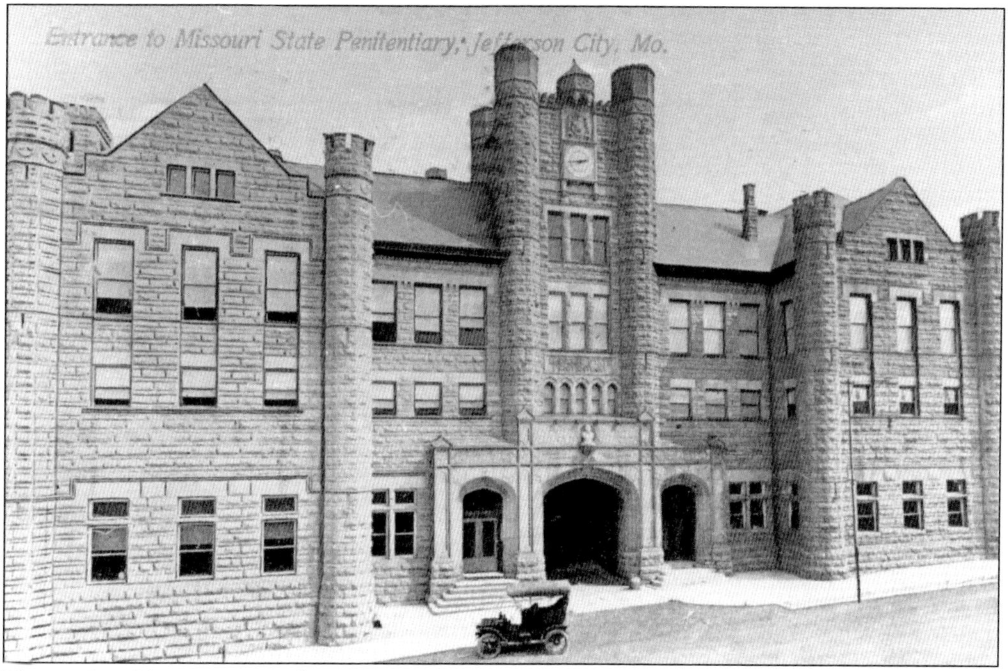

This is the old entrance to the Missouri State Penitentiary, facing Lafayette Street. The facade is rock, as are the walls around the penitentiary, giving it the nickname the "Walls." Notice above the entrance the bust of Governor Dockery. This photo was taken about 1910. (Summers Collection; Missouri State Archives.)

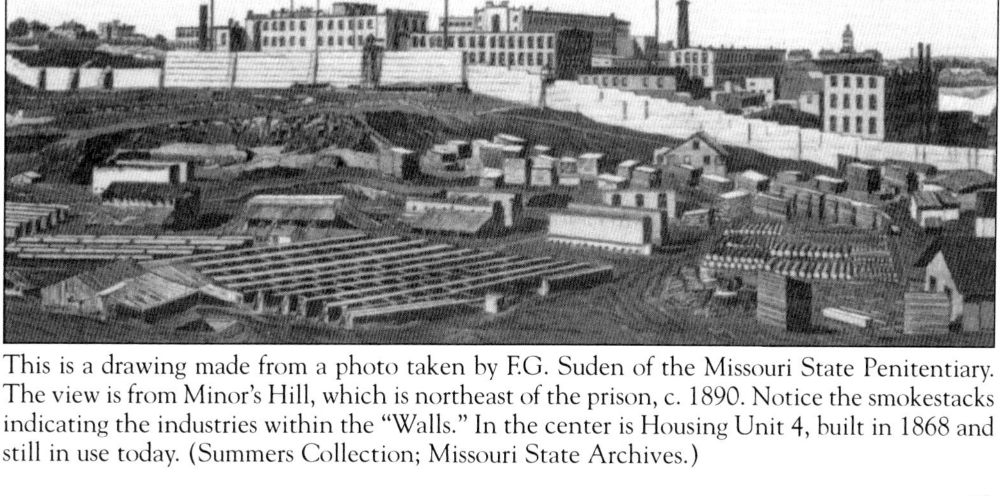

This is a drawing made from a photo taken by F.G. Suden of the Missouri State Penitentiary. The view is from Minor's Hill, which is northeast of the prison, c. 1890. Notice the smokestacks indicating the industries within the "Walls." In the center is Housing Unit 4, built in 1868 and still in use today. (Summers Collection; Missouri State Archives.)

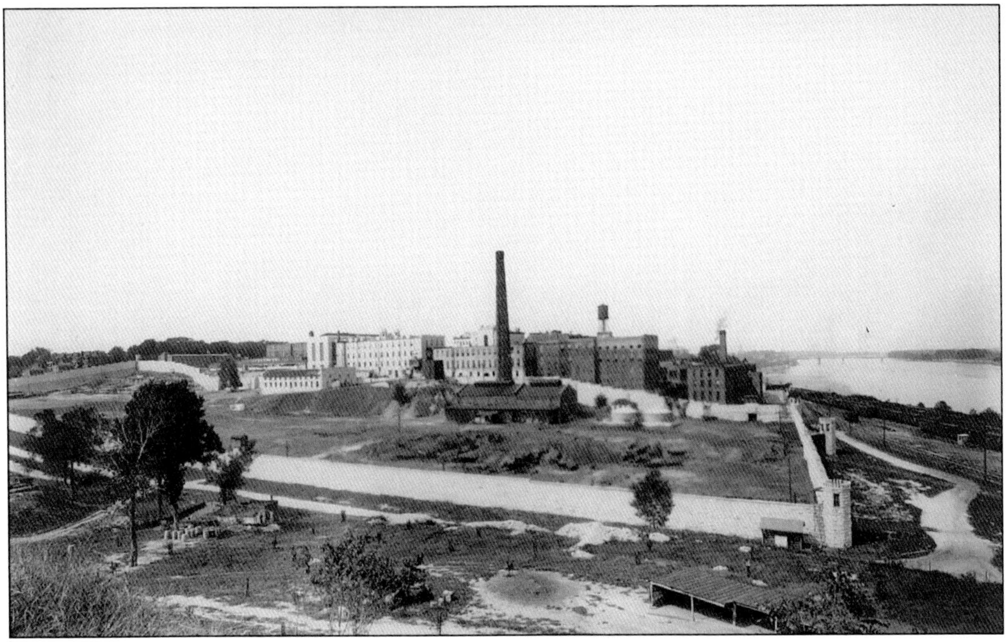

This photo was taken from Minor's Hill after the expansion of the penitentiary walls from Cherry Street east to Chestnut Street. There were three shoe factories, a broom factory, a saddle tree factory, and a pants factory within the "Walls." (Jim Twyman.)

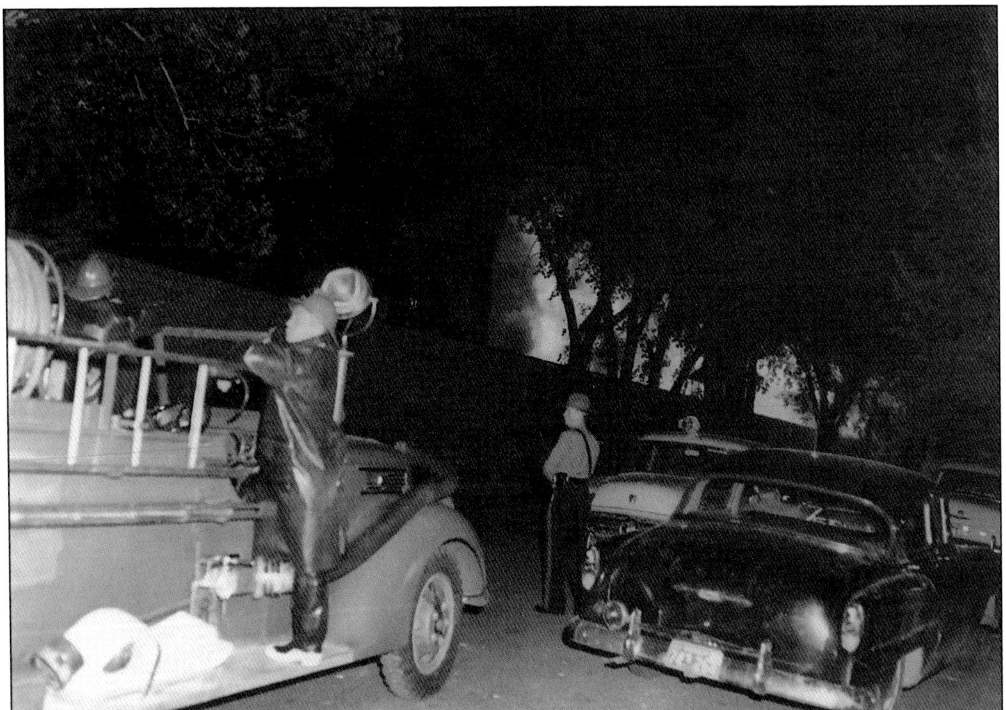

Pictured here are the fires from the Missouri State Penitentiary riot on September 22, 1954. It was so dangerous inside the prison that the firefighters could do little to help. (Joe Kroeger.)

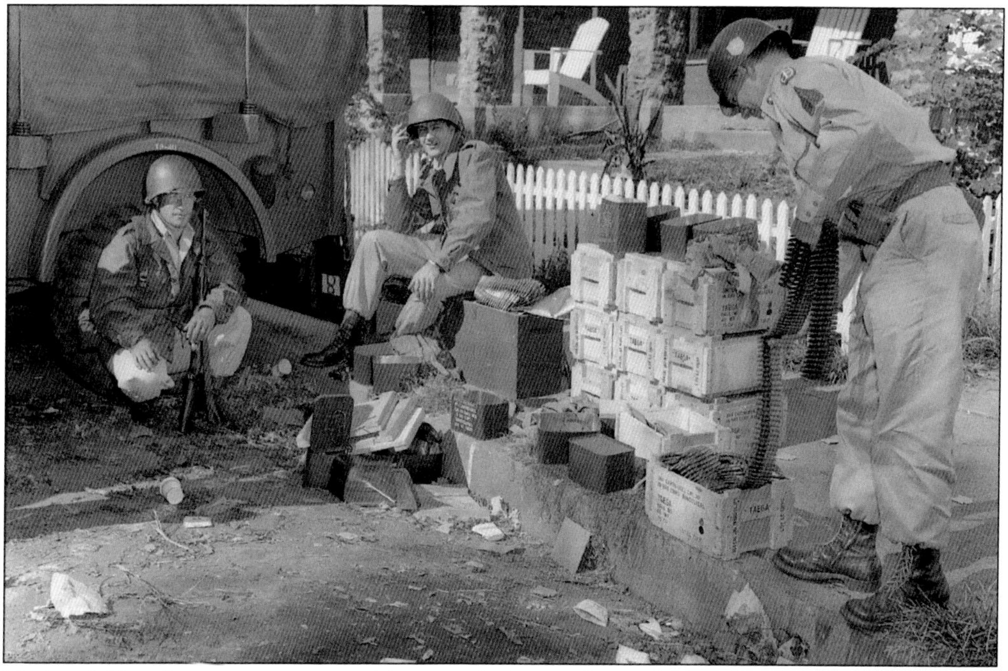

National Guard troops are pictured here on Lafayette Street September 23, 1954, across from the prison, ready to help in the aftermath of the worst riot in the history of the Missouri State Penitentiary. (Joe Kroeger.)

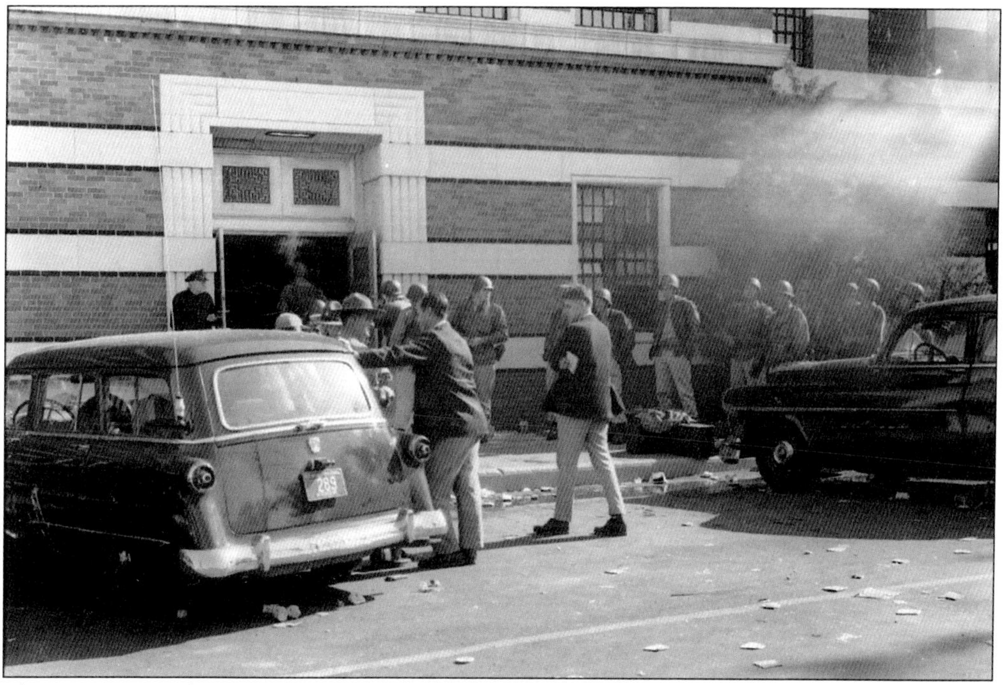

The entrance to the Missouri State Penitentiary is pictured here on September 23, 1954, after the riot, with National Guardsmen, highway patrolmen, prison guards, and residual smoke from the fires. (Joe Kroeger.)

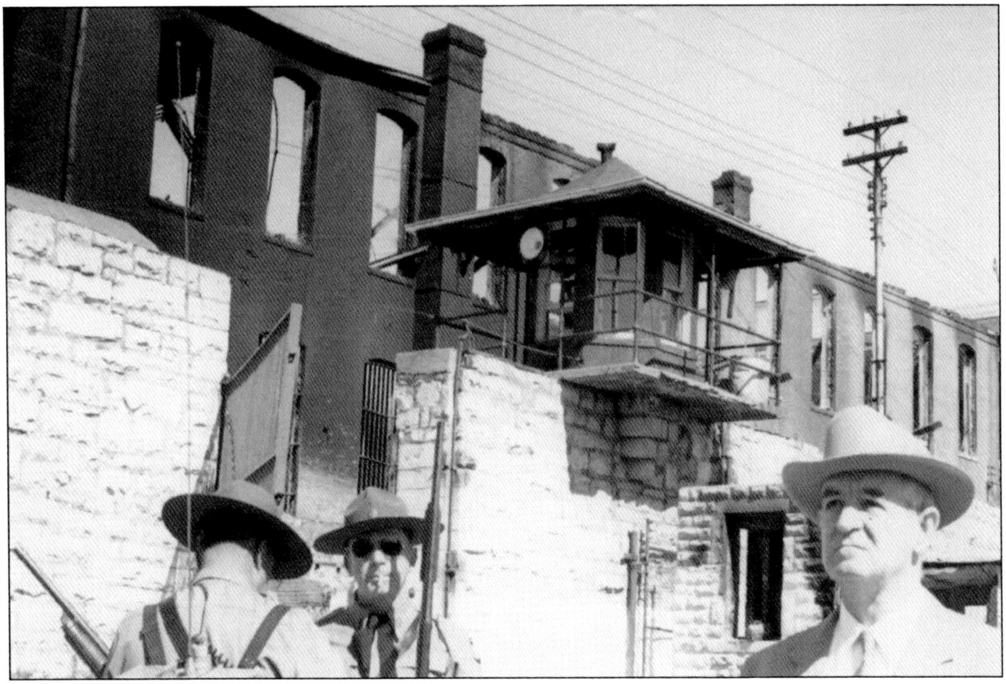

Governor Phil Donnelly is inspecting the damage after the prison riot on September 23, 1954, as a highway patrolman looks on. Hugh Waggoner, who was head of the highway patrol, anticipated a riot and had set up a key word to gather the troops to the City of Jefferson as quickly as possible. When he was informed of the riot, he put his plan into action, and troops from all over the state were in place within three hours—three hundred strong. (Zeal Wright.)

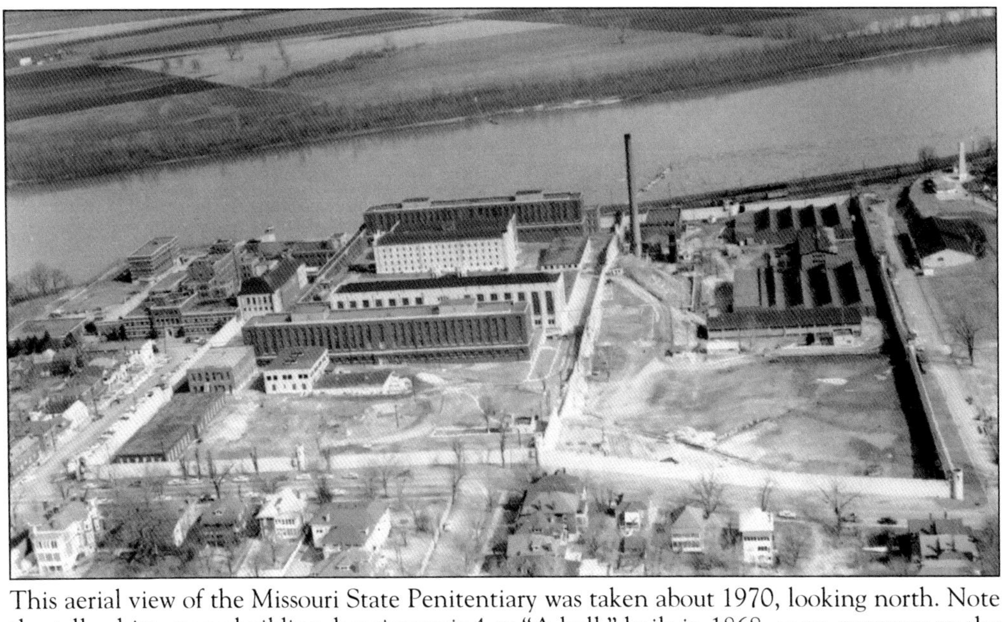

This aerial view of the Missouri State Penitentiary was taken about 1970, looking north. Note the tall, white, stone building, housing unit 4 or "A hall," built in 1868, as an entrance to the prison at the end of Lafayette Street and the white, rock, old entrance just east of it. (Summers Collection; Missouri State Archives.)

Two

Building a Community

The City of Jefferson was slow to build a community separate from the state government. There seemed to be a struggle to establish an economic base outside of the state business, which was always threatened as cities competed to remove the capital to a larger, more substantial city. By the late 1880s and 1890s, city fathers were beginning to work together to establish the commerce of the City of Jefferson separately, but within its role as the seat of state government. There was resistance by city fathers to invite industry, other than the prison industry, into the city until the 1930s. The prisoners supplied a cheap work force and made the owners quite wealthy.

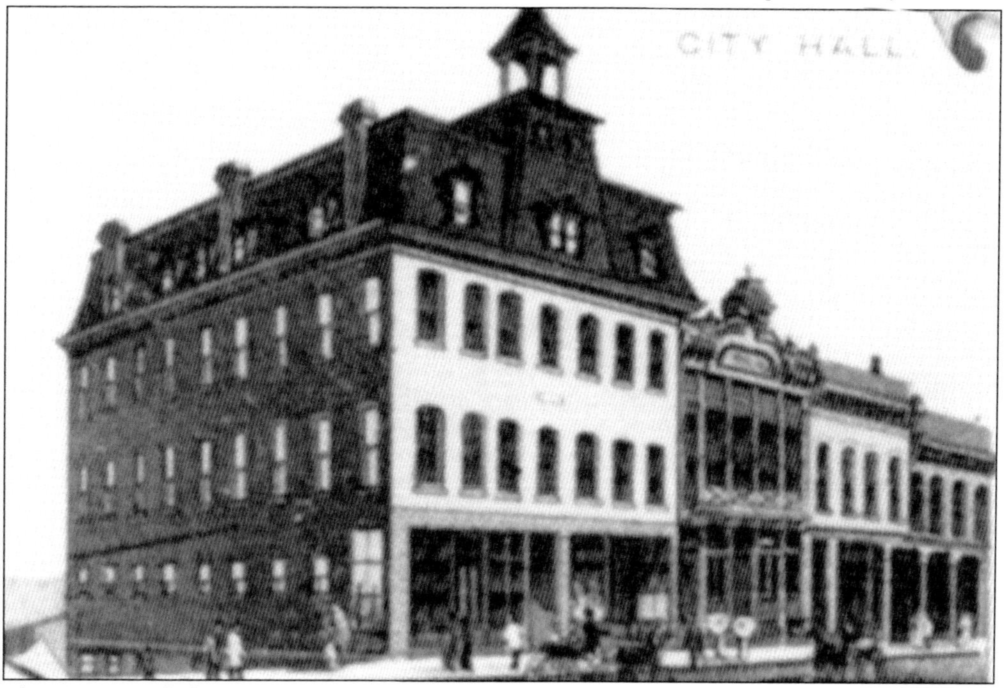

This Bragg Hall drawing is from F.G. Suden's 1891 photograph. The hall was built by H.A. Bragg in the 1870s. This building was a gift to the city to be used as city hall and a meeting place by Major Joseph M. Clarke, after the Market House meeting place was torn down. It was used as the city hall until 1983, when a new one was built. The bell on top was used to alert the volunteer fire department. (Summers Collection; Missouri State Archives.)

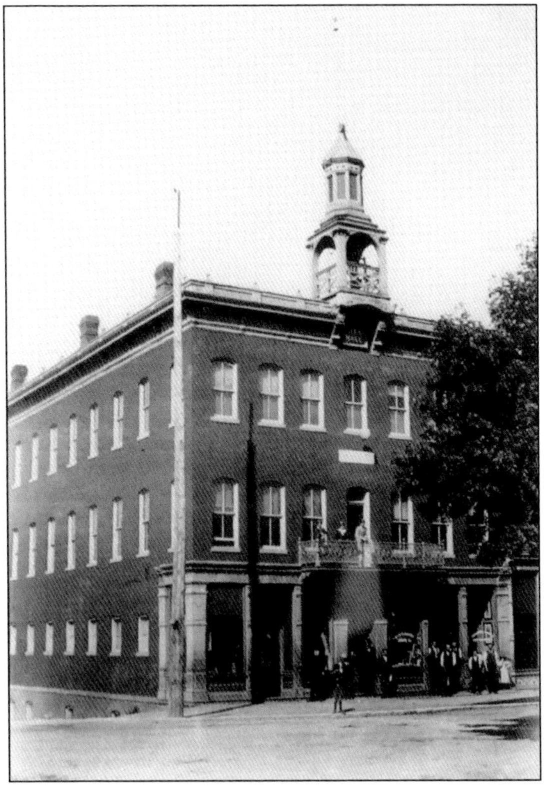

Bragg Hall is pictured here in 1897, with the fourth-floor meeting area removed and the bell for the volunteer fire department modified but in place. The *Tribune* newspaper was the first occupant of the first floor, and by the time of this photo, the Fleming and Company furniture store was in the building. In the 1920s, the fire department occupied the first floor. (Summers Collection; Missouri State Archives.)

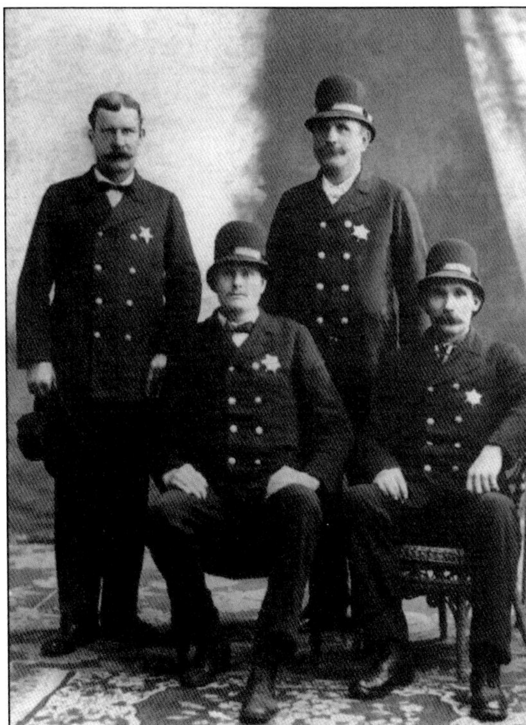

The first police force in the City of Jefferson is pictured here in the 1920s. The chief of police was called a marshal. This photo shows Marshal Charles R. Davis on the left with a soft felt hat. (Anna B. Davis Roedel.)

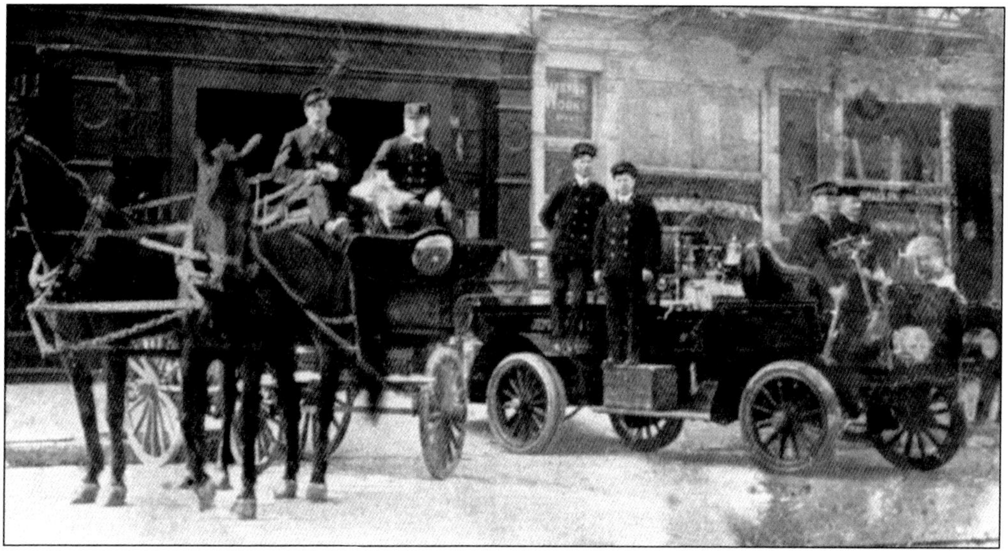

A year after the second capitol burned down, in 1912, the City of Jefferson purchased a motorized pumper for the fire department; it was the second one purchased in the state. (Bill and Mary Gamble.)

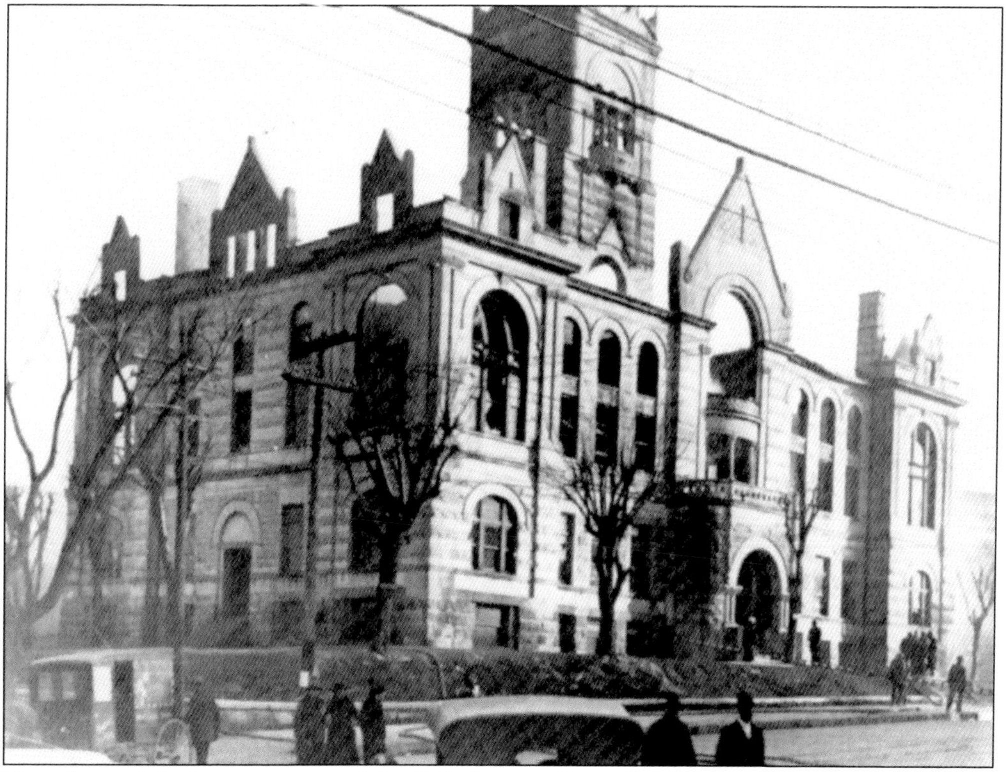

This photo of the burnt remains of the Cole County Court House was taken in May 1918, from the yard of 208 Monroe, Dr. Summers' childhood home. Note the touring car, Mueller Brothers' "Dandy Bread" wagon. There is now a sheriff's department and Cole County Jail on the north side of the court house. (Cole County Historical Society.)

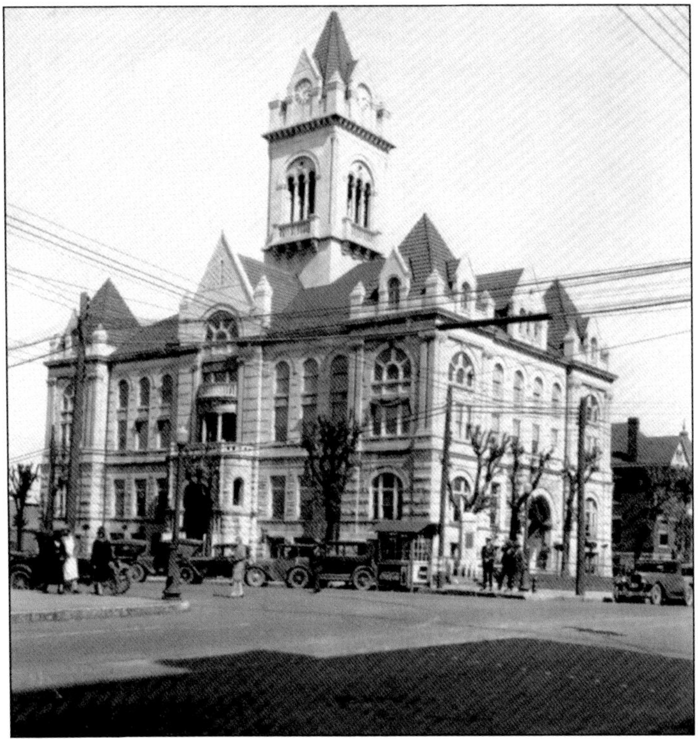

The restored Cole County Court House is pictured in the 1920s. The court house was designed by Frank Miller with lots of interesting detail, including gargoyles, using the talent of German stone masons in the community. (Cole County Historical Society.)

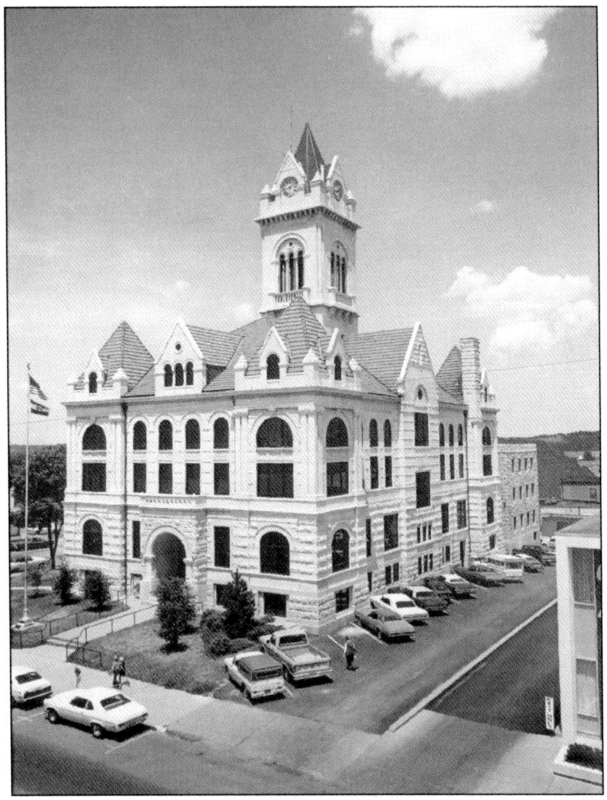

The Cole County Court House is pictured as it appears today. (Ralph Walker; Missouri State Archives.)

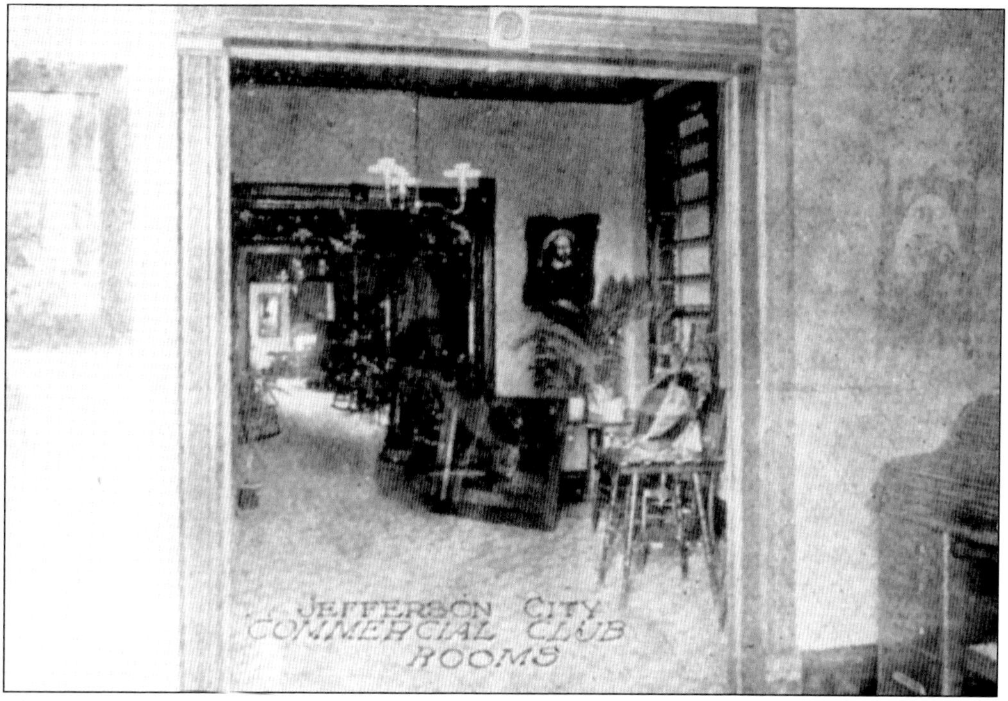

The Commercial Club meeting rooms on the second floor of the Merchants Bank Building are pictured about 1900. Many members of the Commercial Club were merchants who, after getting their businesses started in the morning, would leave their shops to their wives and children to run while they met with other merchants in the Commercial Club rooms, have a little social time, and discuss the direction they wanted to see the City of Jefferson take. (Summers Collection; Missouri State Archives.)

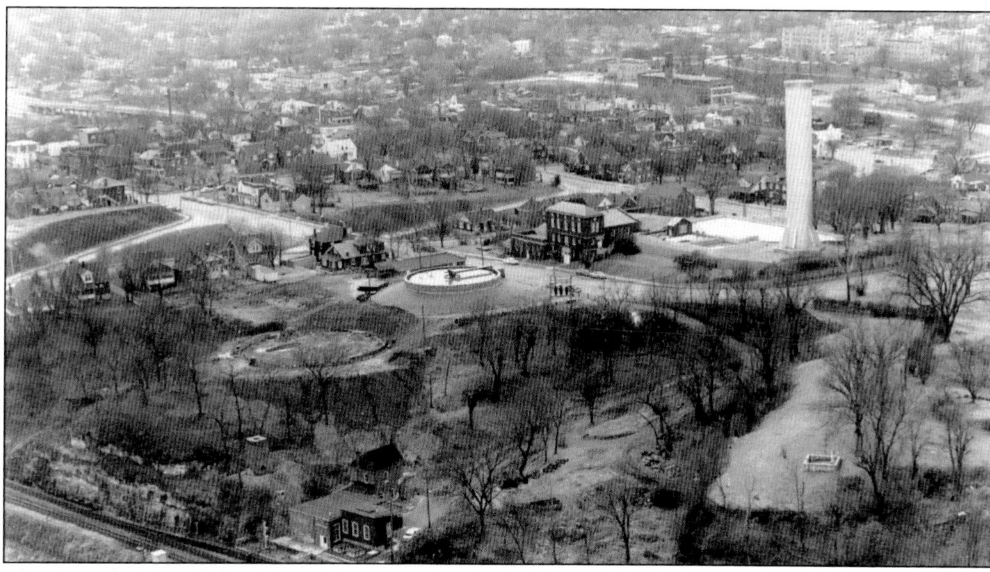

This aerial view of the Water Company was taken from the north, showing the pump plant when the settling basins were being constructed and revised in the 1920s. The water tower is from the 1880s. (Summers Collection; Missouri State Archives.)

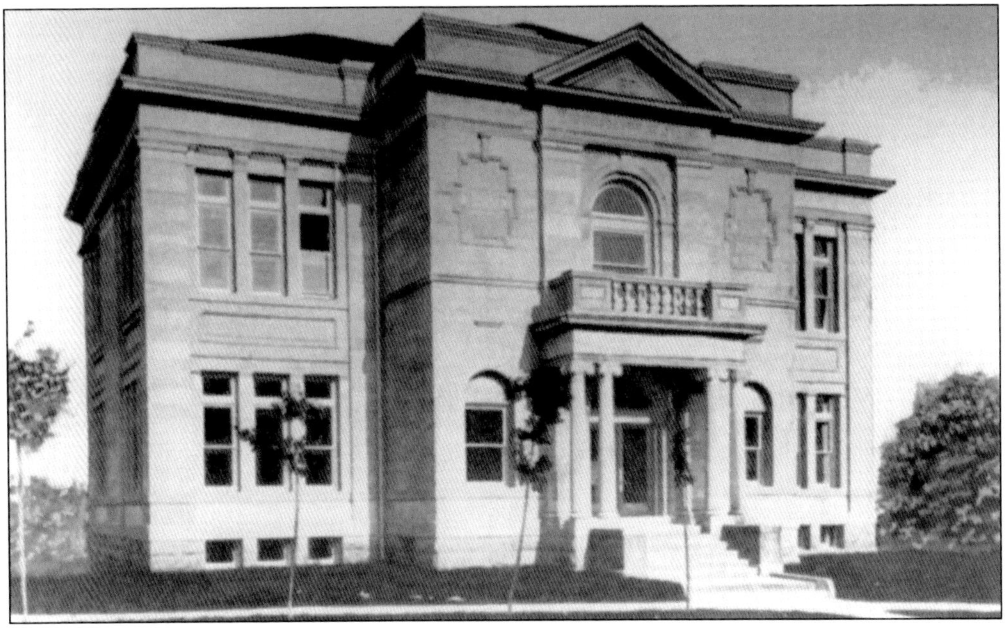

The Carnegie Public Library was built in 1901—the second one constructed in Missouri. It now houses Cole County offices. A new library was built just south of this one in 1967. (Summers Collection; Missouri State Archives.)

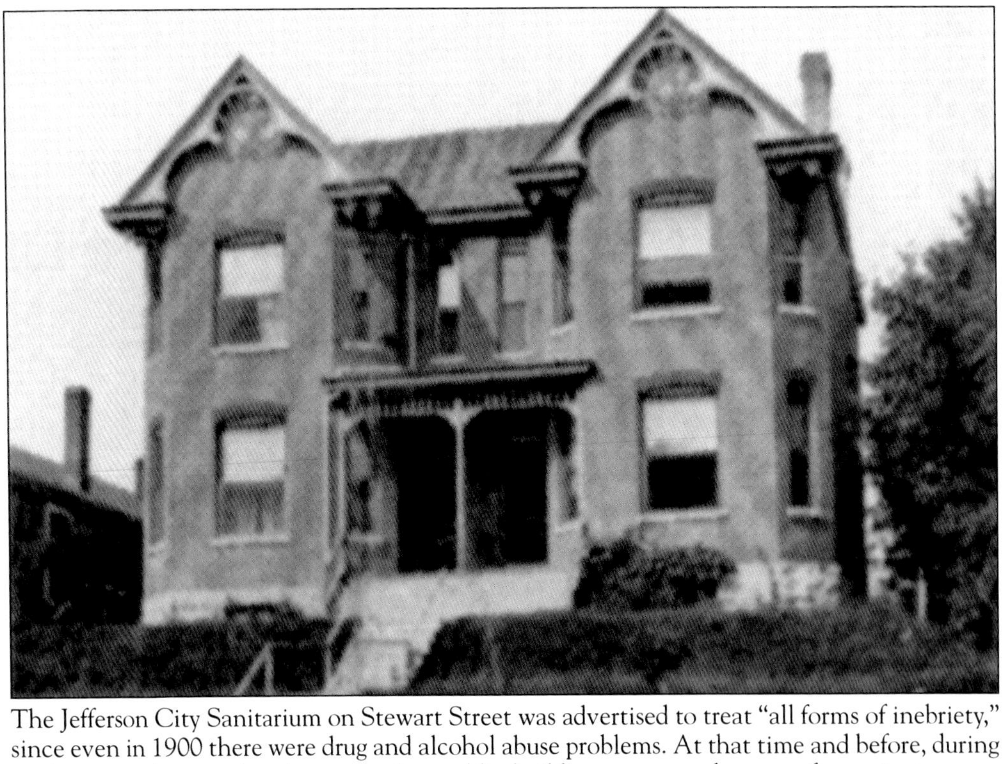

The Jefferson City Sanitarium on Stewart Street was advertised to treat "all forms of inebriety," since even in 1900 there were drug and alcohol abuse problems. At that time and before, during epidemics and wars, churches and other public buildings were used to care for patients, as no hospitals were available. (Summers Collection; Missouri State Archives.)

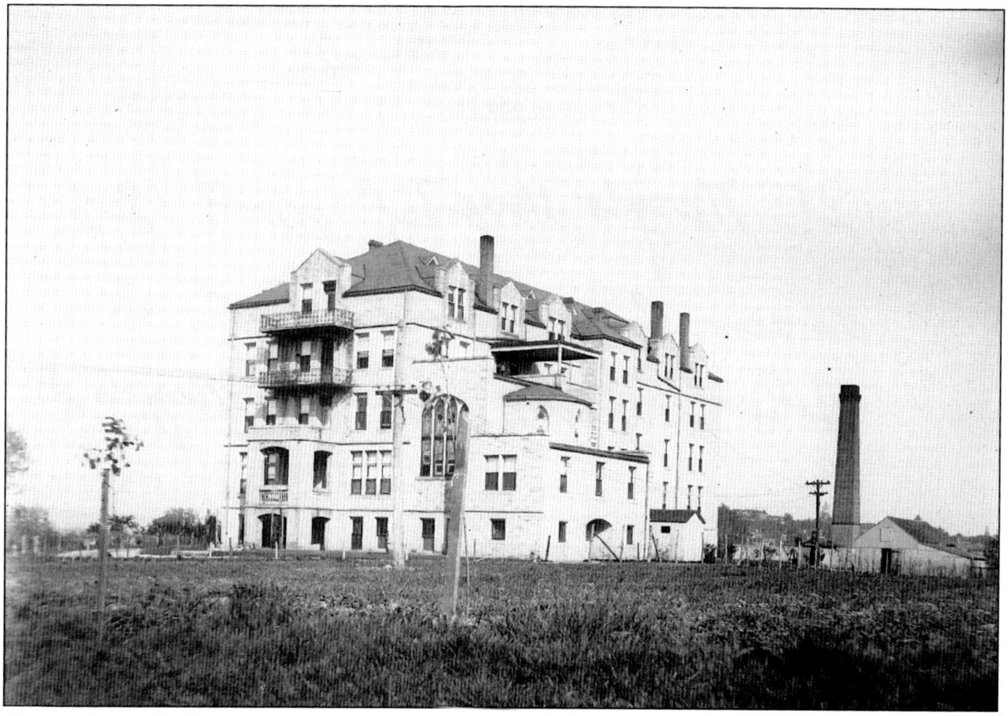

Sister Mary Odelia brought nuns to the City of Jefferson to create St. Mary's Hospital in 1905–1906. This view shows the beautiful chapel window, which no longer can be seen from the outside, and the power plant for the hospital. (Joe Kroeger.)

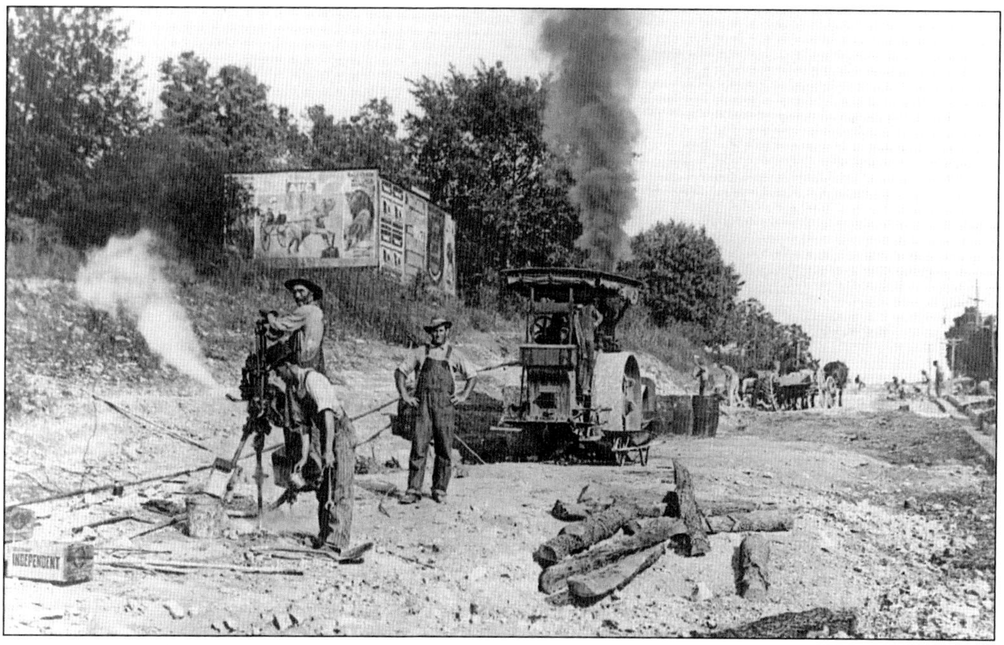

A crew at work on street construction is pictured here in the 1920s. Joe Pope, a German immigrant, had a street paving company, which was responsible for most of the early street construction in the City of Jefferson. (Bryan Pope.)

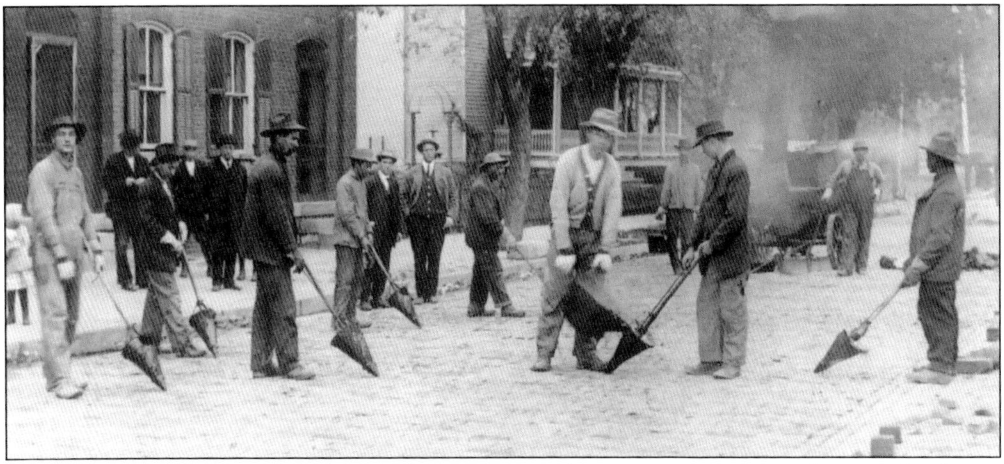

Joe Pope's street construction crew is depicted at work giving tar treatment between bricks on streets in the early 1920s. This was another effort to make the City of Jefferson a better place for a capital than rival Sedalia. They continued to make the streets even though city funds were scarce, so a deal had to be made between the contractor, a banker, and city officials. (Bryan Pope.)

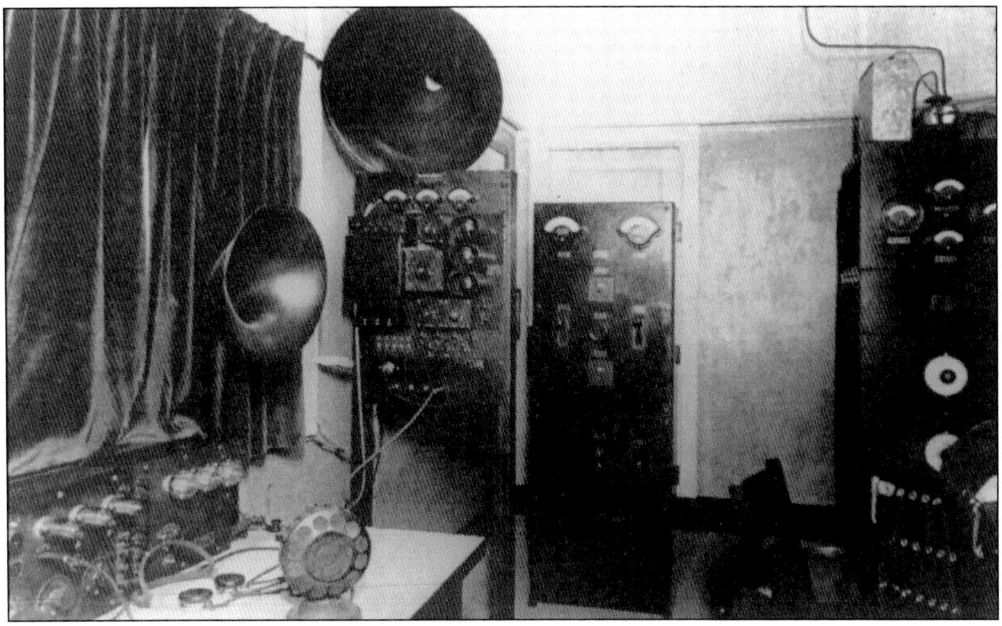

The State of Missouri Agricultural Department experimented with a radio station to send market reports to farmers. The state bought the seventh radio transmitter ever produced. It took a while to put the station together. It went on the air in 1922 and left the air in 1933, when the government discontinued ownership. This photo is of the transmitter room in the base of the dome of the capitol, with the curved amplifier and curtained, double-glass window that looked into the broadcasting room. A steel tower by the northwest corner of the capitol had a wire running from it to the dome in order to broadcast. There was a music show featuring the talent of prisoners—particularly Harry Snodgrass, who had a prison jazz band. Harry was called "King of the Ivories" and was paroled early because of his talent. In the 1940s, another radio station originated in the City of Jefferson, with the call letters KWOS, "Keep Watching our State." (Summers Collection; Missouri State Archives.)

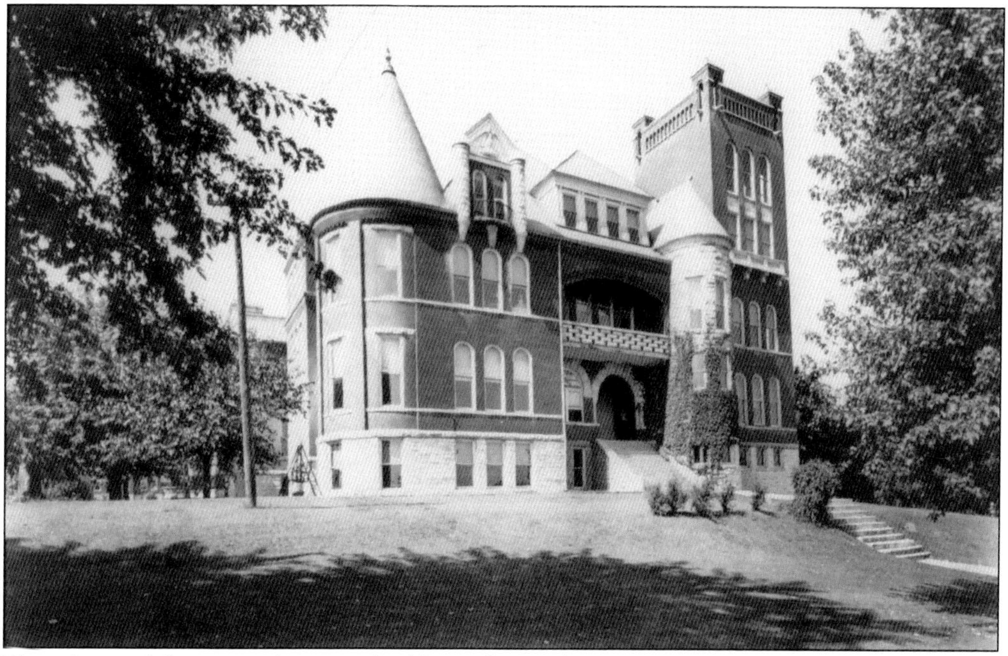

This photo of the main classroom building of Lincoln Institute was taken about 1920. It was illegal in Missouri to educate African Americans until after the Civil War. The idea of Lincoln University was conceived around a campfire on January 14, 1866, by the 62nd United States Colored Infantry at Fort McIntosh near Galveston, Texas. The school was incorporated on June 25, 1866. Lincoln Institute, later Lincoln University's, special mission was to educate African Americans. (Jim Twyman.)

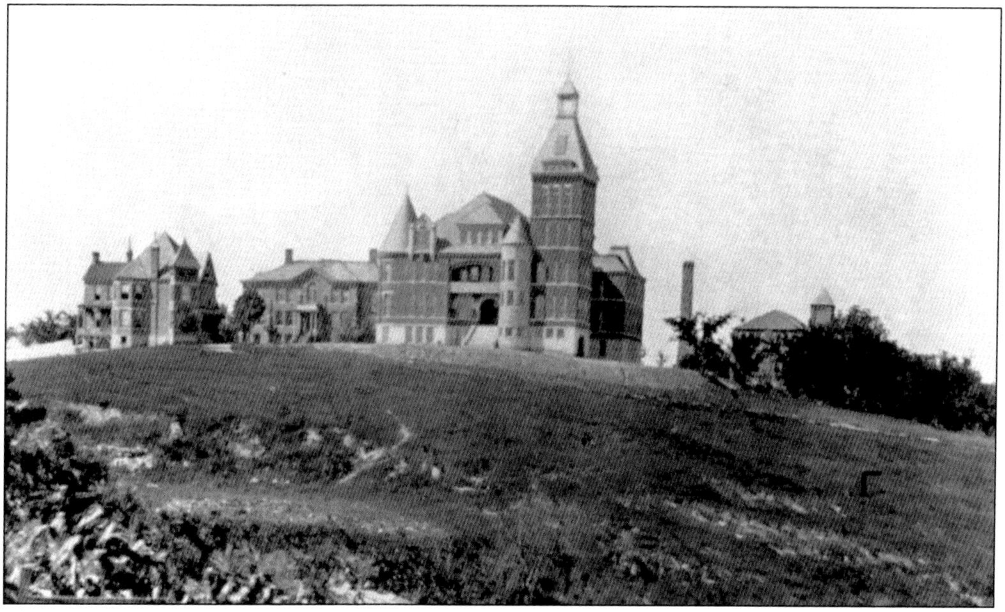

This view of the campus of Lincoln Institute was captured about 1900. The architect was Charles Opel. It was an all-black school until the late 1950s, when it became integrated. (Summers Collection; Missouri State Archives.)

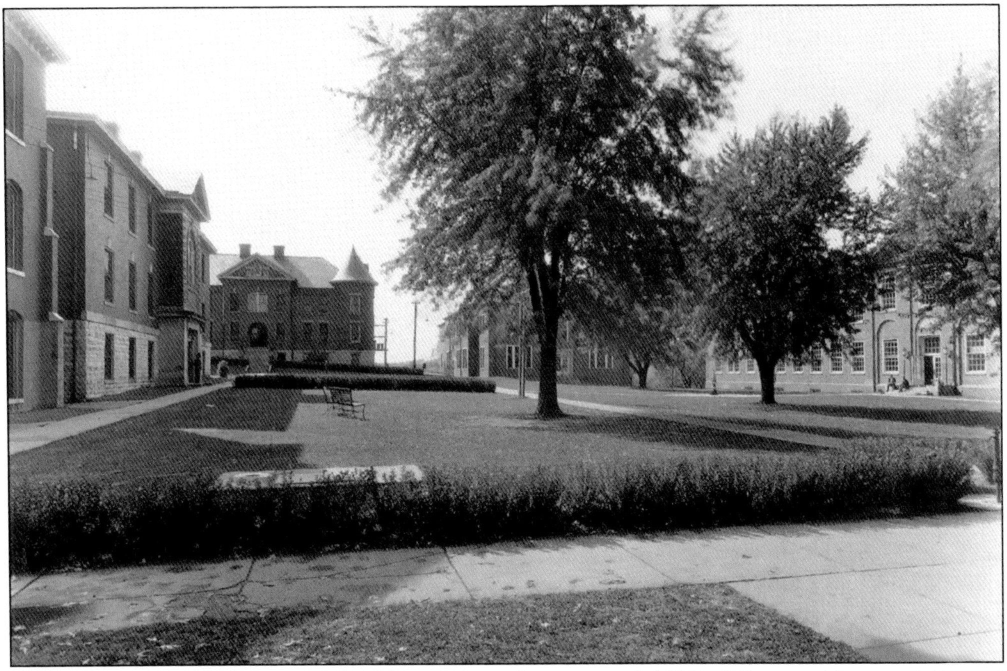

This is the quadrangle at Lincoln University, taken around 1920. (Thomas Cooper; Missouri State Archives.)

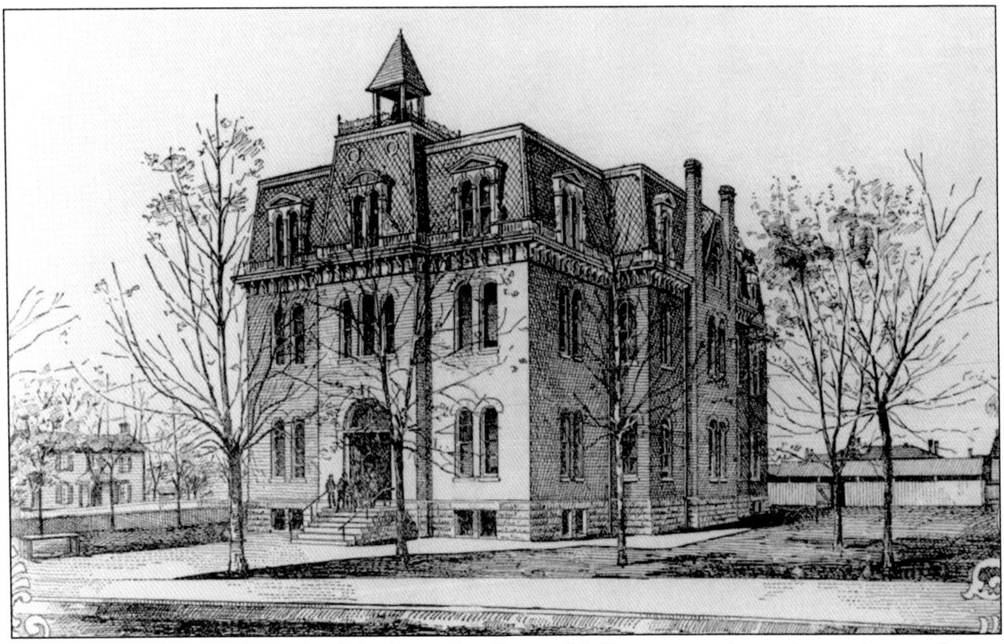

Probably the first public school built in the City of Jefferson was located on the northwest corner of Monroe and Miller Streets. The top floor became the high school. The school was sold to the Lutheran church to become the Lutheran School, and during this period, the top floor was torn down. In the early 1960s, a new Lutheran school was built and this building torn down and replaced by a hotel. (Summers Collection; Missouri State Archives.)

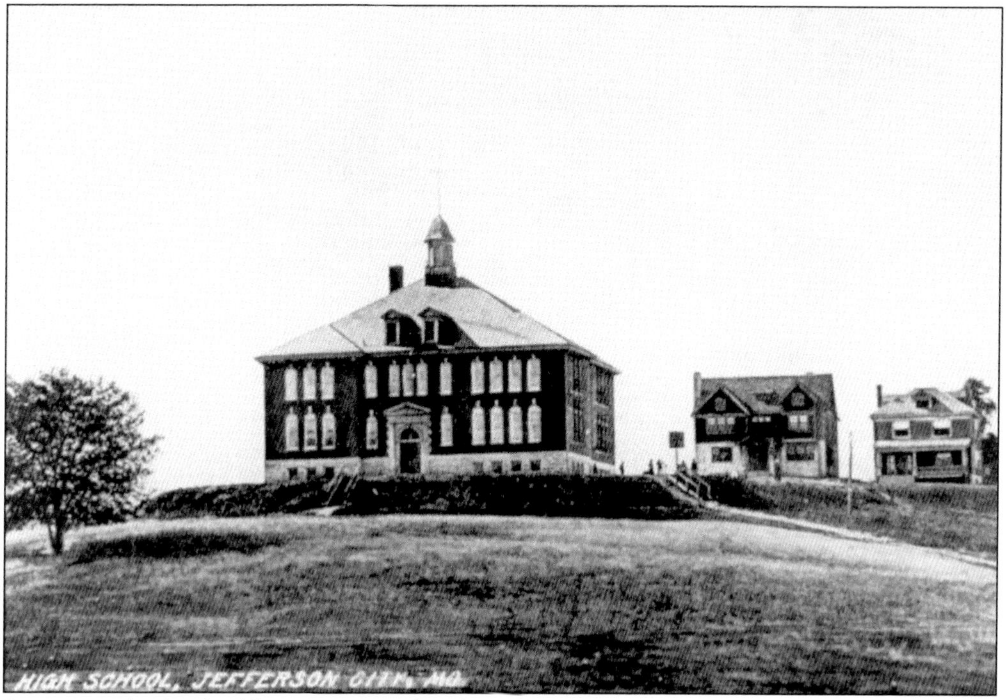

Simonsen, the first building constructed as the Jefferson City High School, was on "Hobo Hill," on Miller Street about 1900. (Summers Collection; Missouri State Archives.)

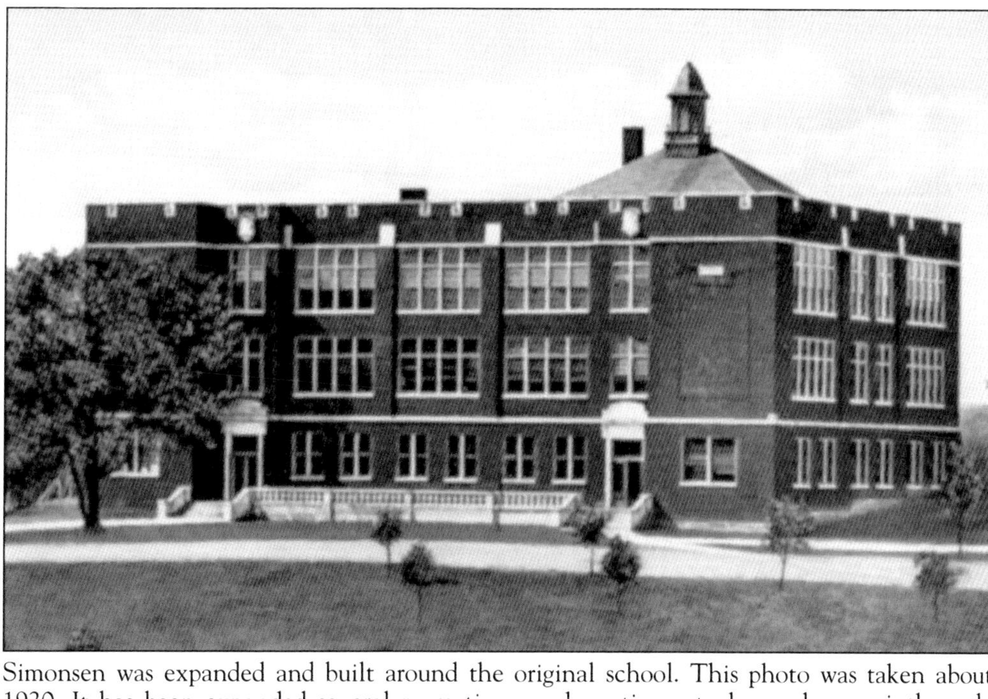

Simonsen was expanded and built around the original school. This photo was taken about 1920. It has been expanded several more times and continues to be used as a ninth-grade building. (Summers Collection; Missouri State Archives.)

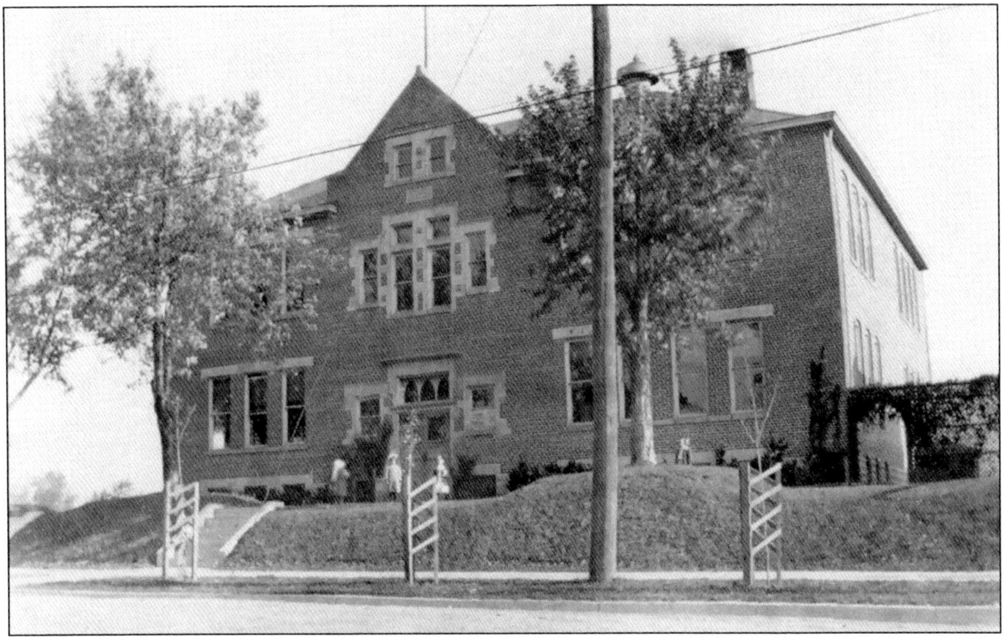

Fairview Elementary School, built in 1904, was on High Street. It was replaced in the late 1930s by East School, and was torn down and replaced by a grocery store—later a car repair shop. (Summers Collection; Missouri State Archives.)

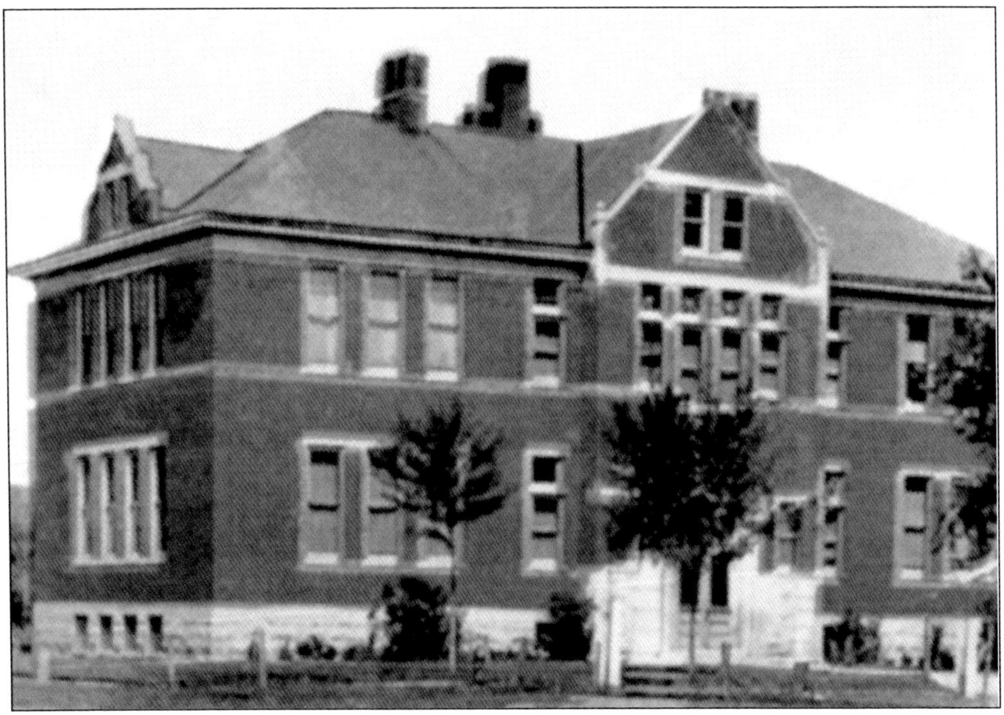

Broadway Elementary School is pictured here on the northeast corner of Broadway and Dunklin Streets, facing south. It was also built in 1904 and is currently used by the Carpenters' Union. (Summers Collection; Missouri State Archives.)

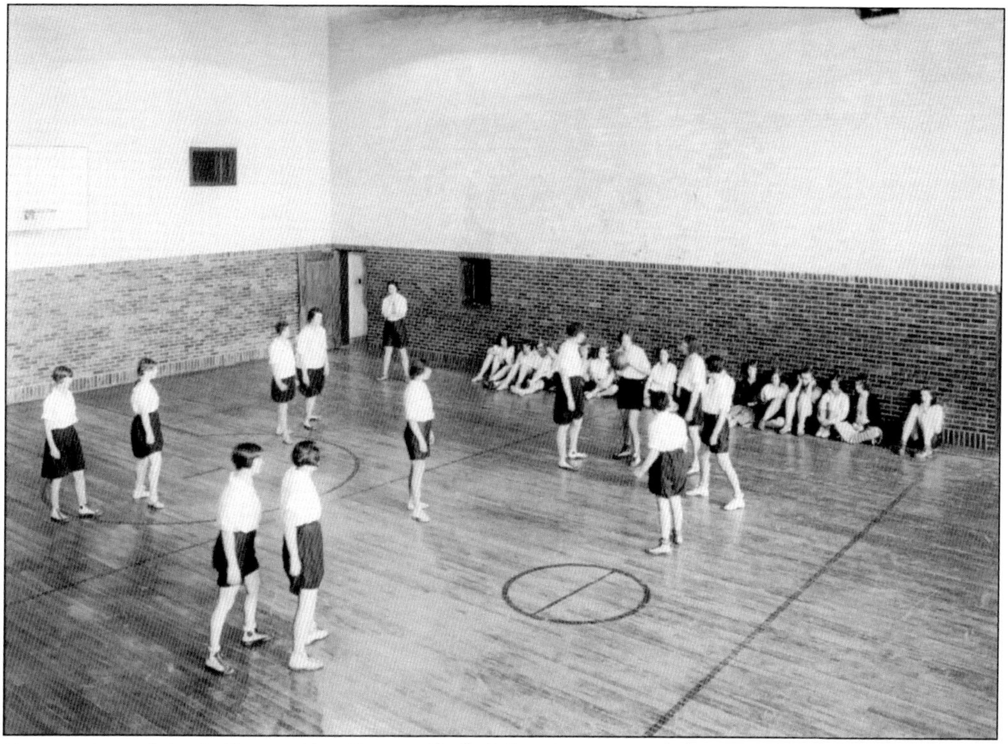

Gymnasium of the Jefferson City Senior High School is pictured during girls' physical education in the early 1930s. (Ehrhardt Collection; Missouri State Archives.)

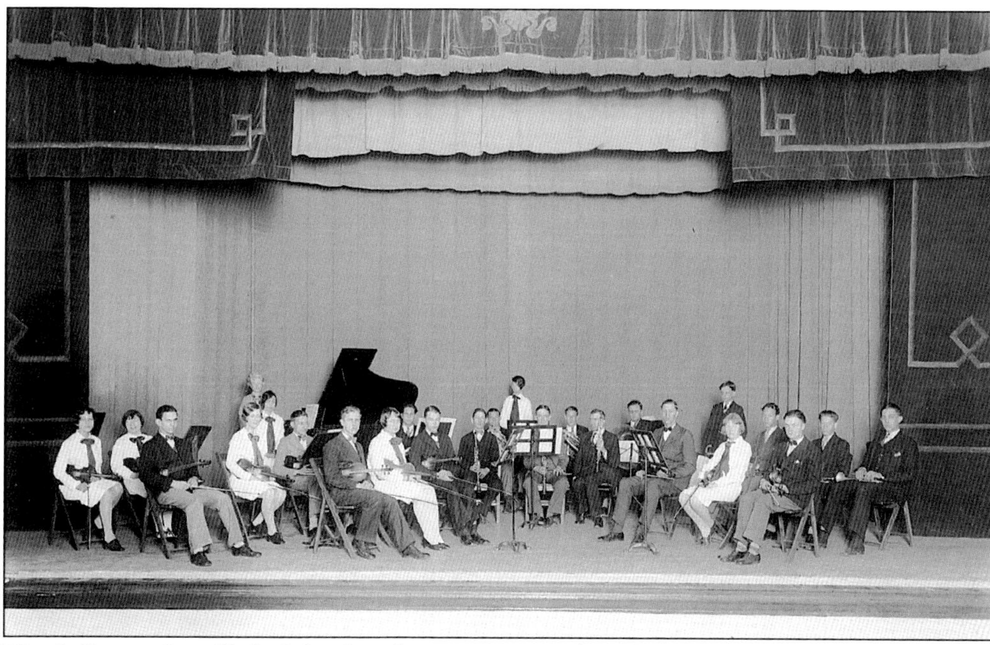

The Jefferson City High School orchestra is pictured performing on stage at Jefferson City Senior High School in the late 1920s. Daisy Siebert conducted the orchestra. (Ehrhardt Collection; Missouri State Archives.)

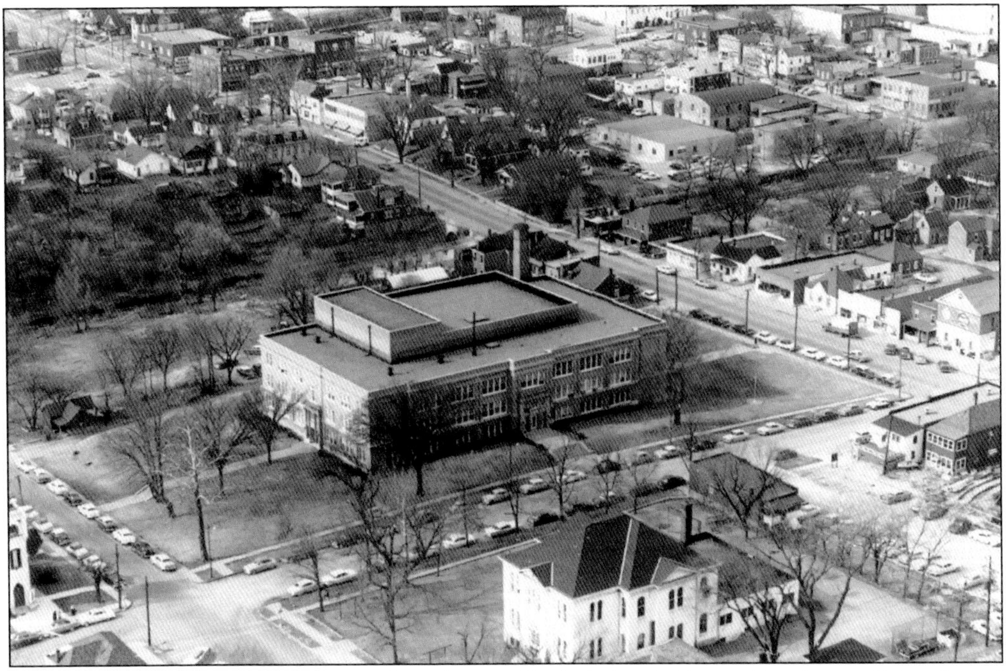

This is an aerial view of Jefferson City Senior High School, Central Lutheran School, and the surrounding neighborhoods before the Rex M. Whitten Expressway was constructed. This photo was taken about 1955. (Summers Collection; Missouri State Archives.)

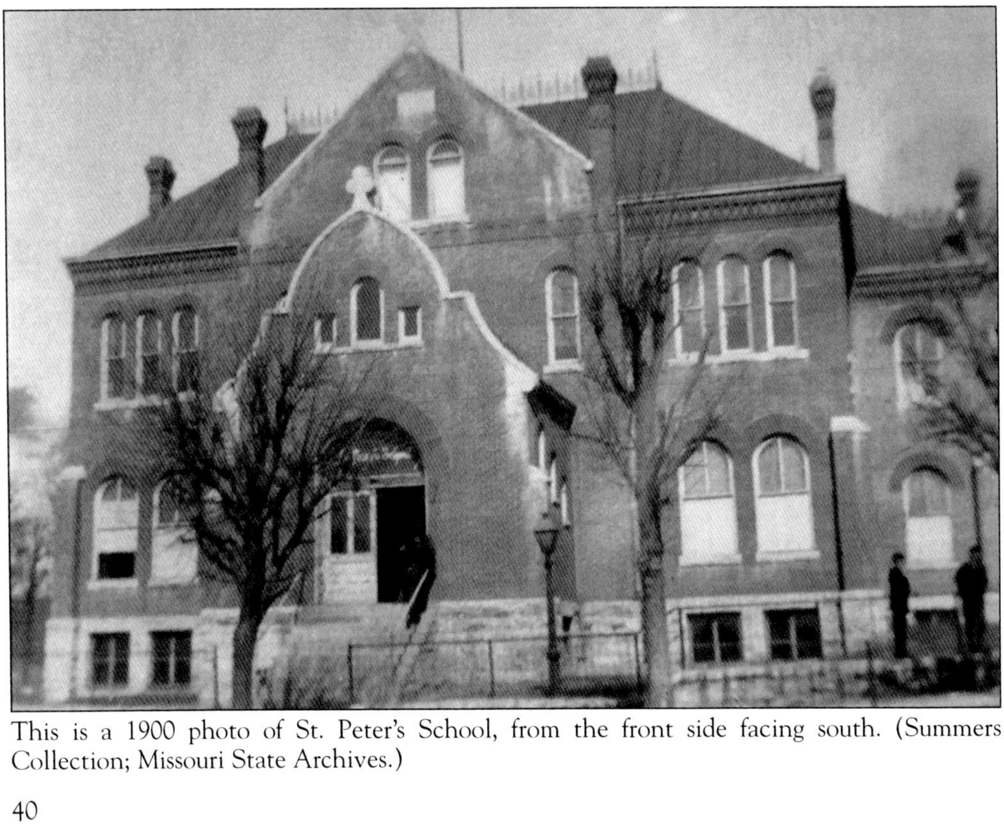

This is a 1900 photo of St. Peter's School, from the front side facing south. (Summers Collection; Missouri State Archives.)

Old Jefferson City Jail on the corner of Monroe and McCarty Streets was a wonderful old rock structure. (J.J. Prost.)

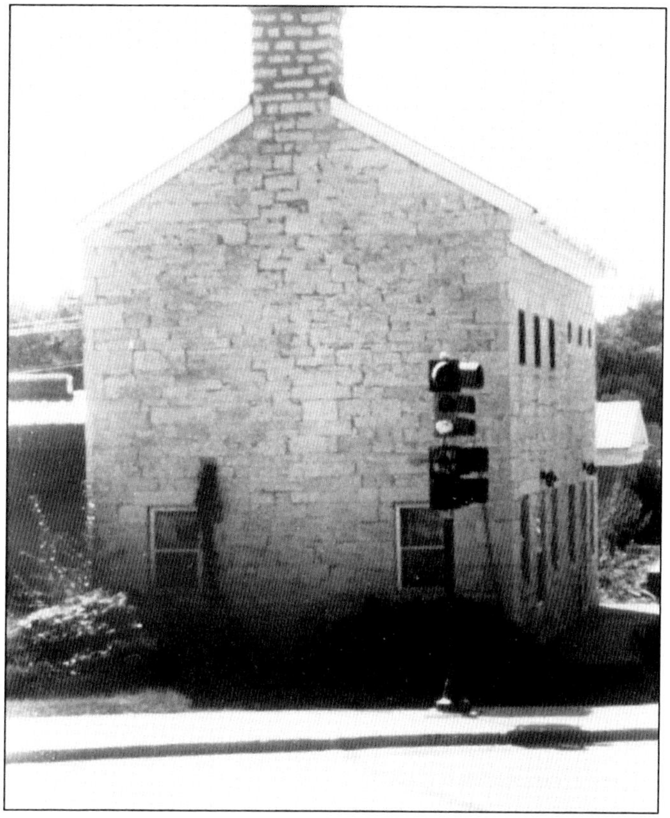

The demise of one of the oldest buildings in town and the birth of the preservation movement in the City of Jefferson are depicted here. (The Historic City of Jefferson Archives; Missouri State Archives.)

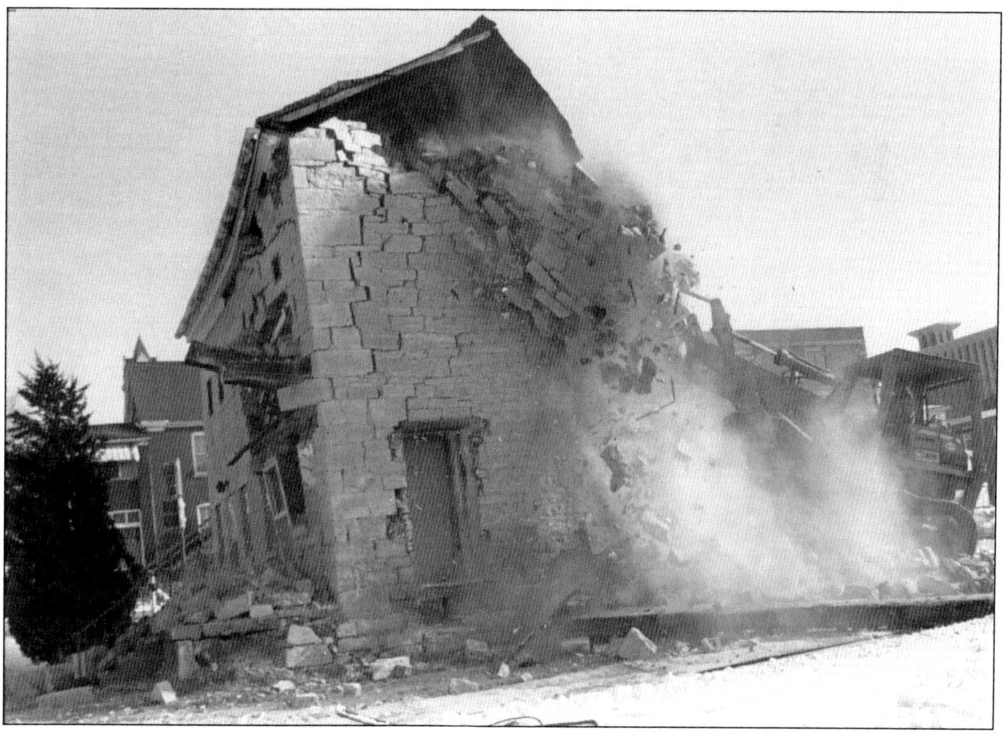

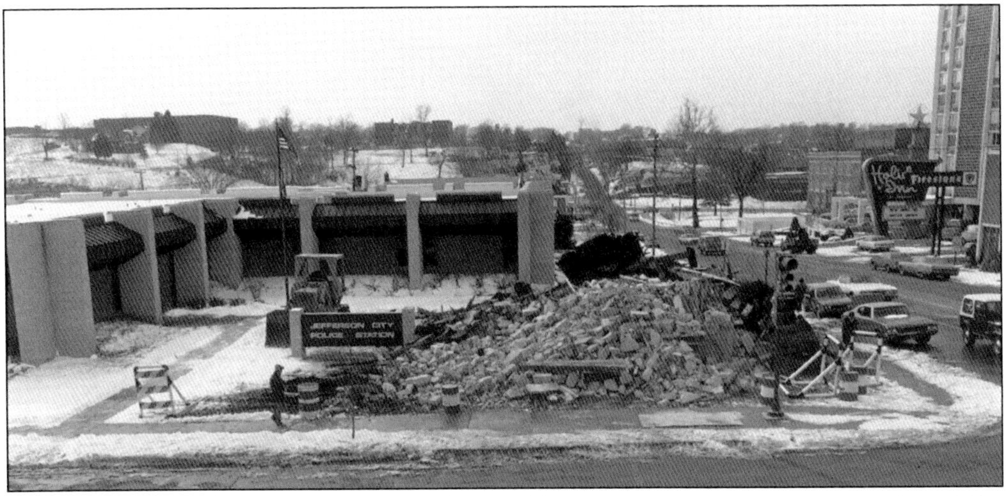

This is the aftermath of the destruction, about 1981—again one of our treasures was lost. (The Historic City of Jefferson Archives; Missouri State Archives.)

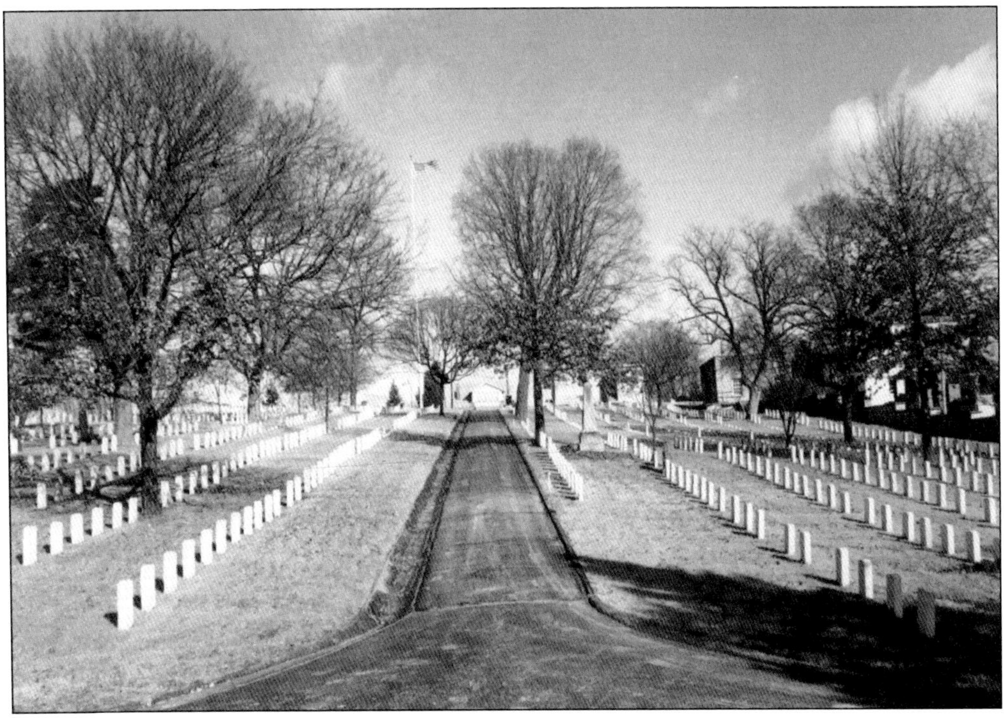

The National Cemetery between Miller and McCarty Streets is pictured here. About halfway up the photo is a monument to the people of the Centralia massacre, when "Bloody Bill" Anderson and his troop of irregular southern sympathizers killed innocent people in Centralia, Missouri. This was taken in the fall of 1986. (Summers Collection; Missouri State Archives.)

Three

THE IMPORTANCE OF TRANSPORTATION

The City of Jefferson was placed and planned because of its location on the Missouri River, the main highway in the 1820s, so that legislators could easily reach the seat of government of the new State of Missouri. By the 1850s, the railroad was another means of travel. The City of Jefferson became a railhead for a few years, with cattle and wood railroad ties being shipped from here. In 1896, the first bridge to cross the Missouri River at the City of Jefferson was built by the Jefferson City Bridge Corporation, members of the Commercial Club. The bridge was made a toll bridge to help offset the cost of construction. In 1911, the first streetcar began operation, allowing a greater freedom to leave the insular neighborhoods. There was so much more automobile and truck traffic after World War II that a modern bridge needed to be built in order to handle it. The traffic problems increased so much, with many commuting in and out of the City of Jefferson to get to their jobs, that a second bridge became necessary. So in 1991, that was done to bring us into the 21st century.

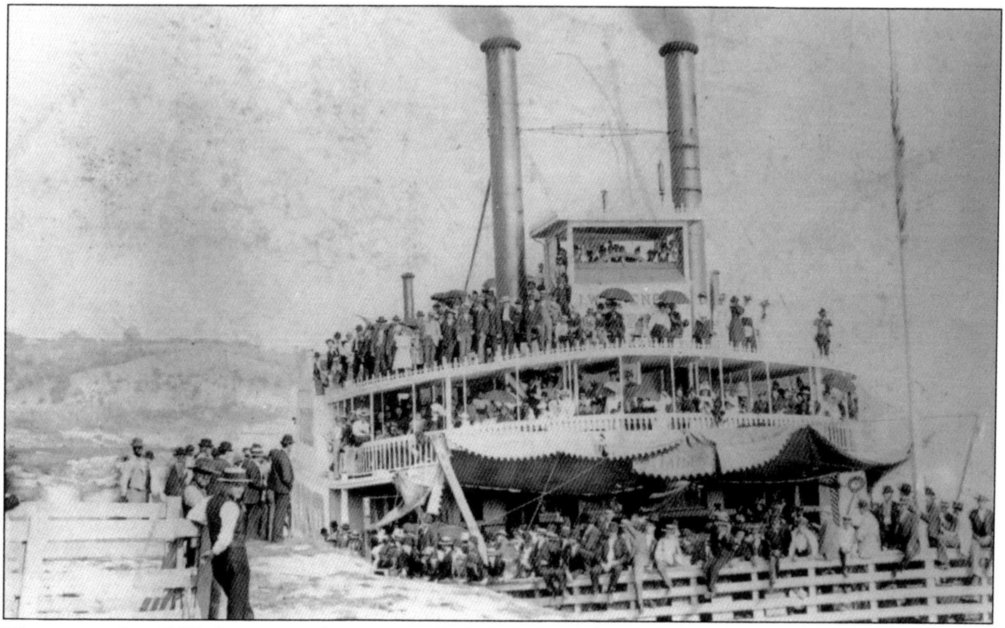

The steamship *J.W. Spencer* is firing up at Lohman's Landing, preparing to move down the river. This photo was taken about 1890. (Summers Collection; Missouri State Archives.)

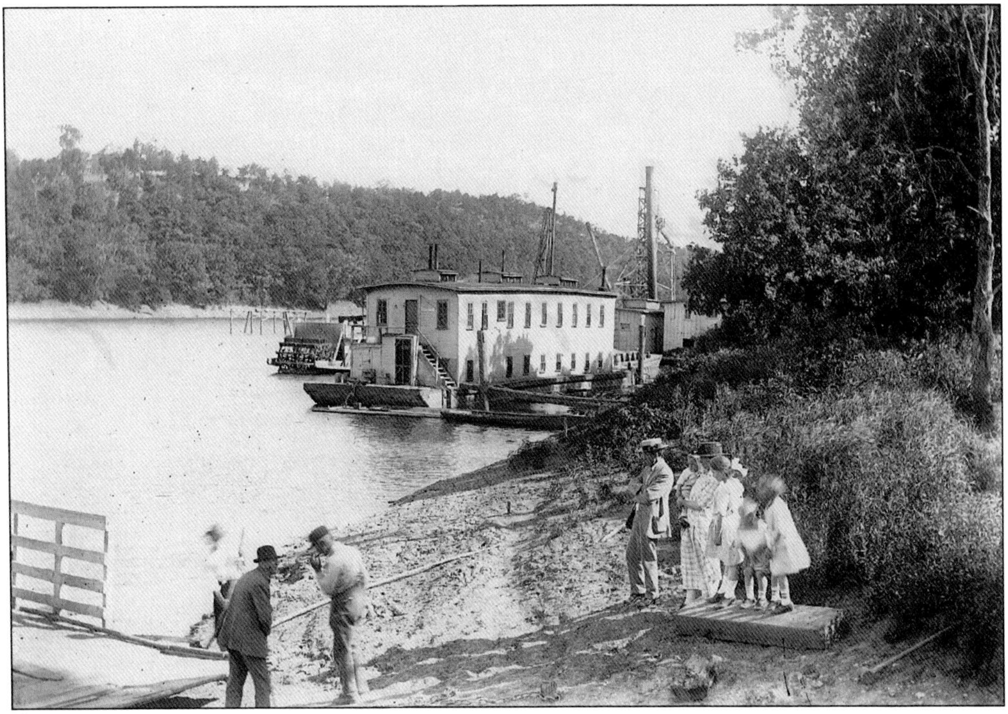

The Huber Ferry crossed the Osage River connecting Osage and Cole Counties 12 miles east of Jefferson City. It was in operation until a bridge was constructed in 1921. (Summers Collection; Missouri State Archives.)

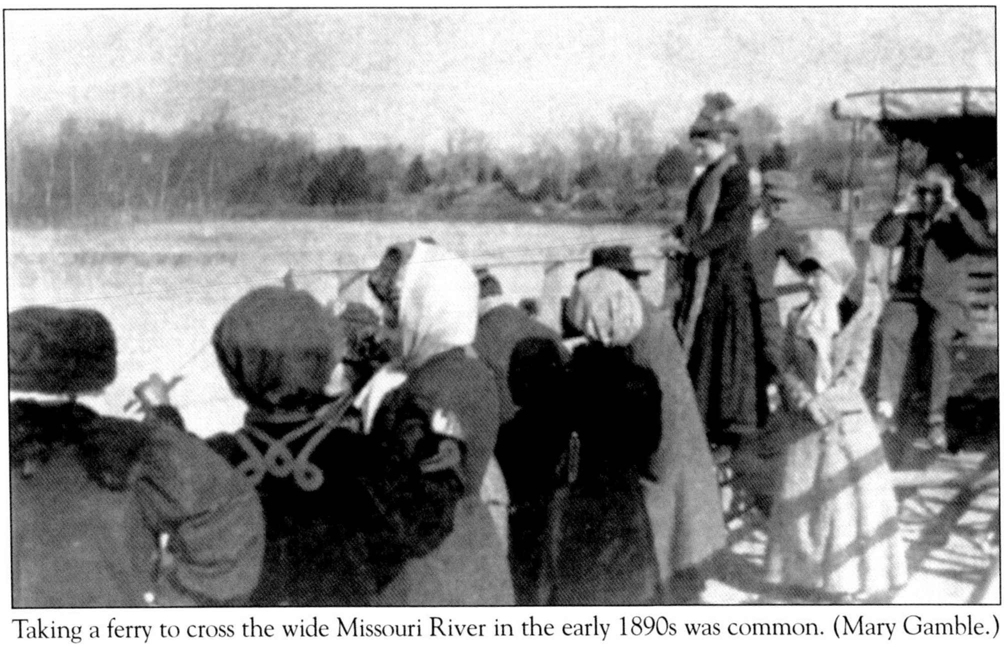

Taking a ferry to cross the wide Missouri River in the early 1890s was common. (Mary Gamble.)

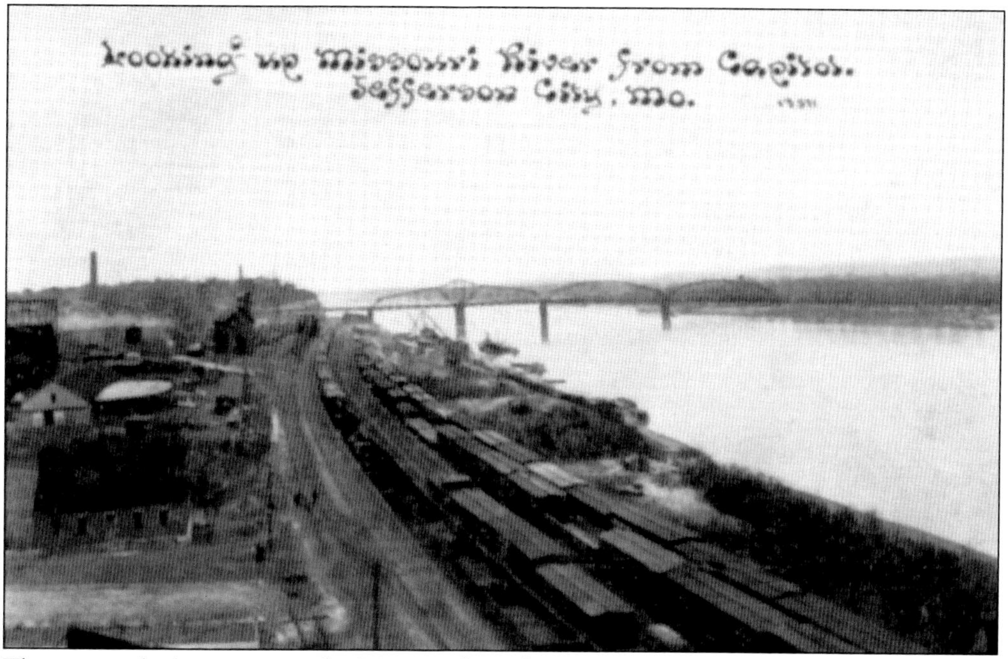

This view is looking west up the Missouri from the Capitol Building, about 1910. Of interest is the first bridge built across the Missouri River at Jefferson City, the railroad yard, the water tower, and the barges in the river. (Summers Collection; Missouri State Archives.)

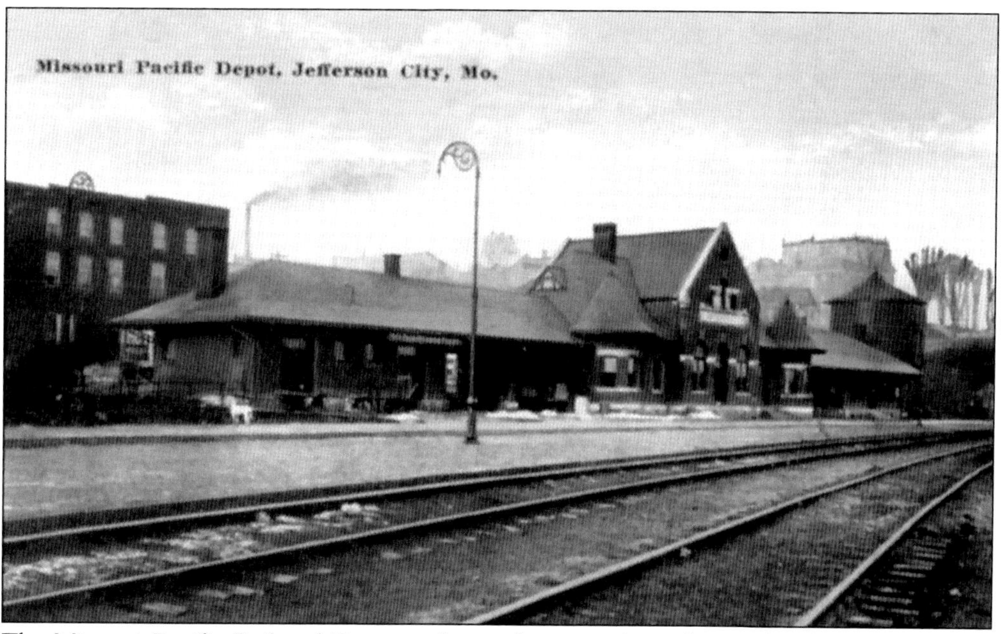

The Missouri Pacific Railroad Depot is depicted as seen from the north side of the railroad tracks. The depot is at the foot of Monroe Street. In the background, to the right on the bluff, is the Governor's Mansion. This photo was taken in the 1920s. (Summers Collection; Missouri State Archives.)

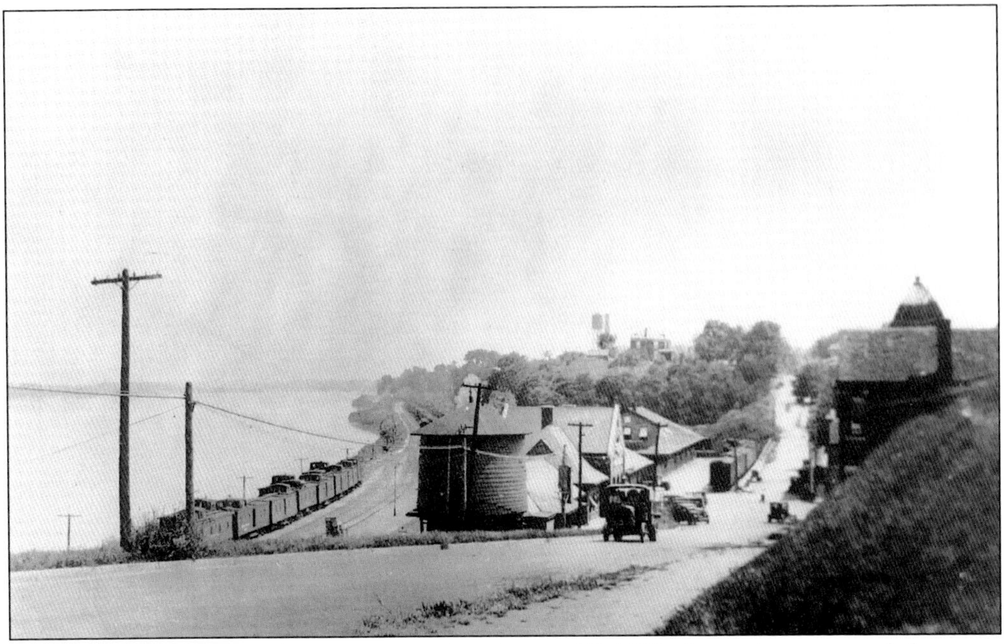

This view of the train tracks going east, taken August 15, 1923, shows the water tank for steam engines, the south side of the depot, the Mansion, and the prison in the background. (Summers Collection; Missouri State Archives.)

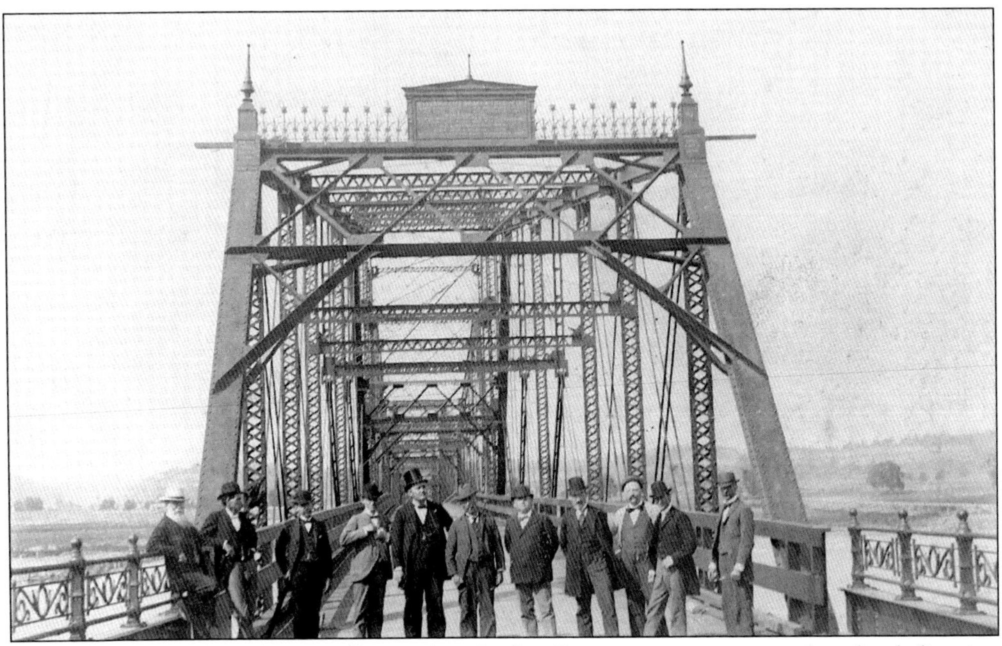

The Board of Directors of the Jefferson City Bridge Corporation are pictured at the dedication of the new bridge in June 1896. Third from the right is Rudolph Dallmeyer. The bridge tolls barely paid the note on the bridge, so the directors eventually sold the bridge to financial interests in the east. (Summers Collection; Missouri State Archives.)

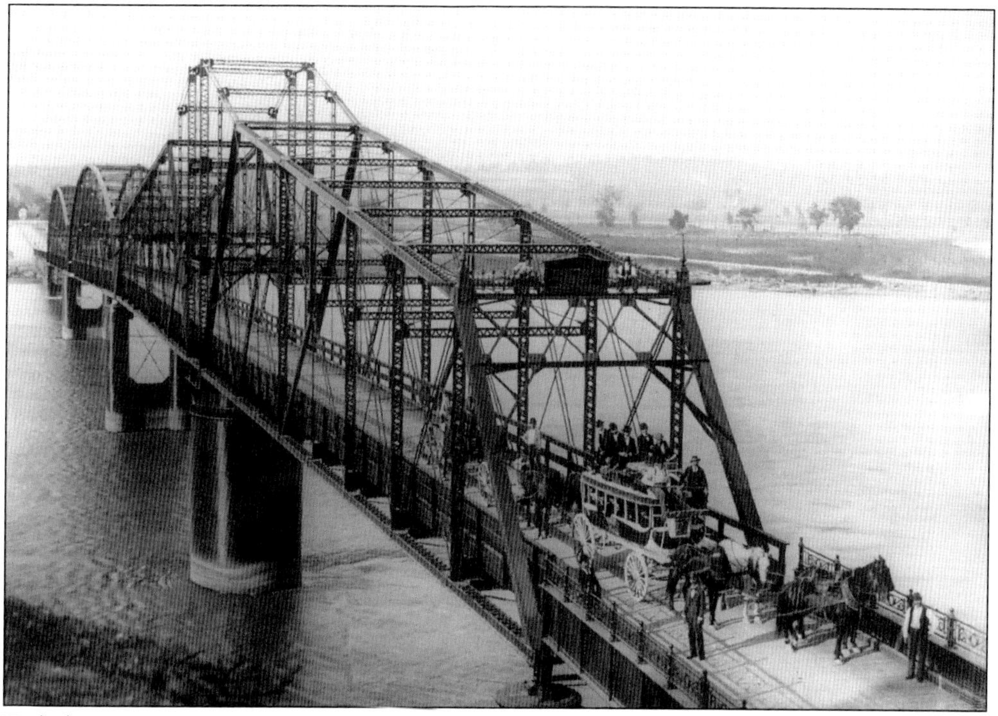

To help transport people across the river from Callaway County and points north to shop in the City of Jefferson, a "bus" service was established to pick up passengers from Cedar City and North Jefferson City. This was replaced with trolley service. This photo of the horse-drawn bus, which was entered from the back, was taken about 1898. (Summers Collection; Missouri State Archives.)

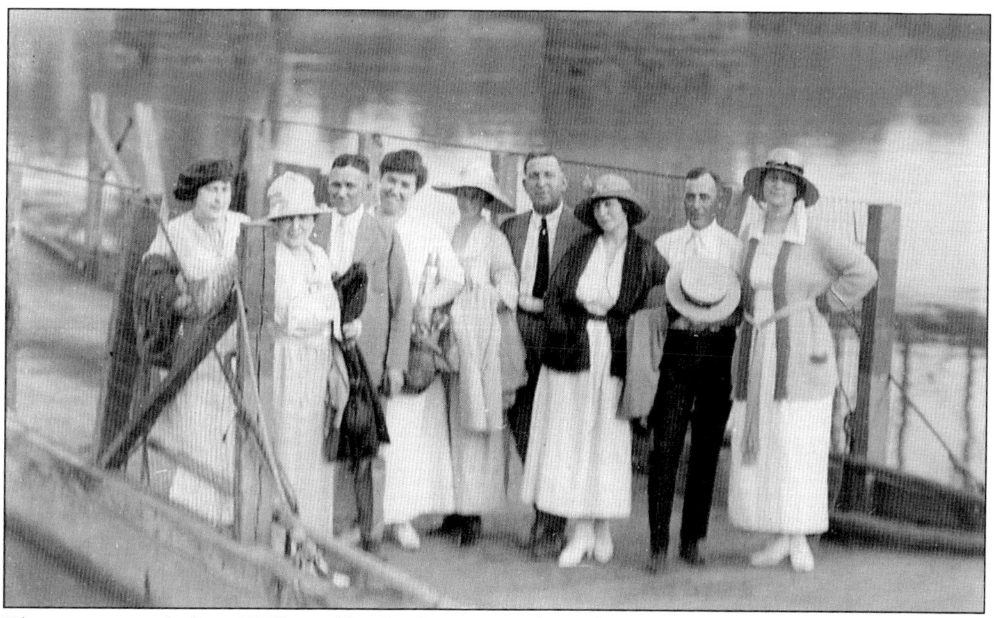

This group, including William Hoefer, Laura Hoefer, John Johnston, and Pauline Dallmeyer Hoefer, was crossing the river by ferry about 1910. (Dottie Dallmeyer.)

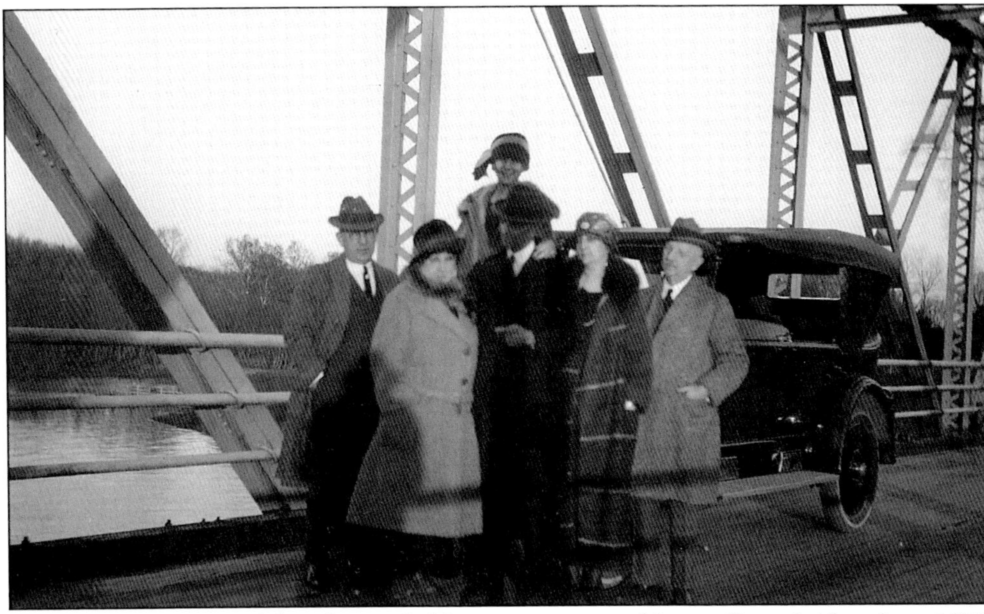

Rudolph Dallmeyer and friends traveled by touring car on Moreau River bridge about 1920. (Dottie Dallmeyer.)

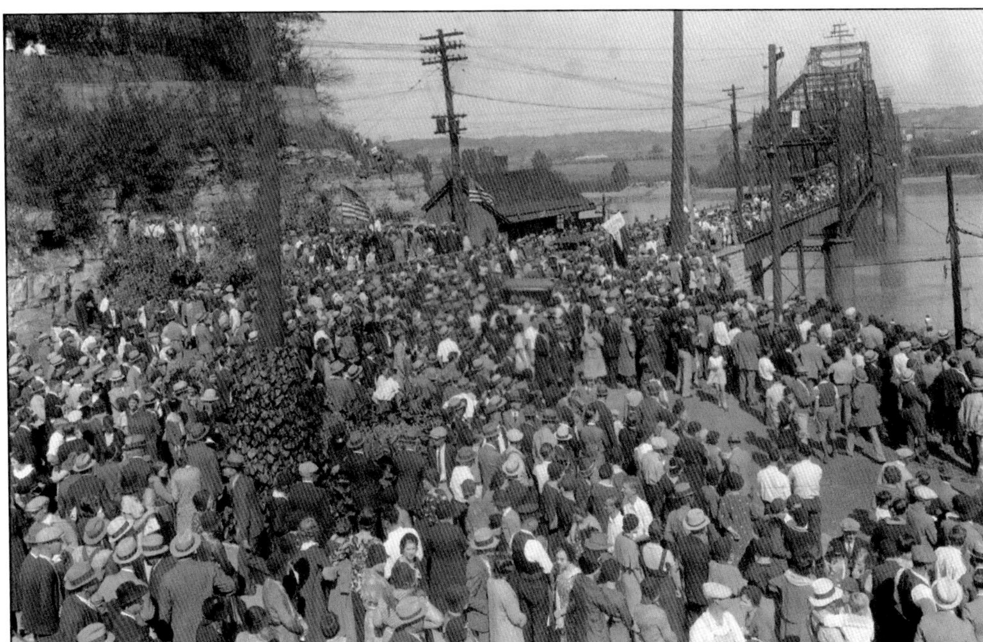

A crowd gathered at the toll booth to celebrate the last toll ride across the Missouri River bridge on October 15, 1932. The citizens of the City of Jefferson felt that the eastern bridge owners were not keeping the bridge well. Instead, they were simply collecting the money from the tolls with little care for the bridge, so Clifford Scruggs led a movement to return most of the stock in the bridge back to the City of Jefferson. When he was successful in this plan, the stockholders gave the bridge to the Missouri State Highway Department, which made it a toll-free bridge. (Cole County Historical Society.)

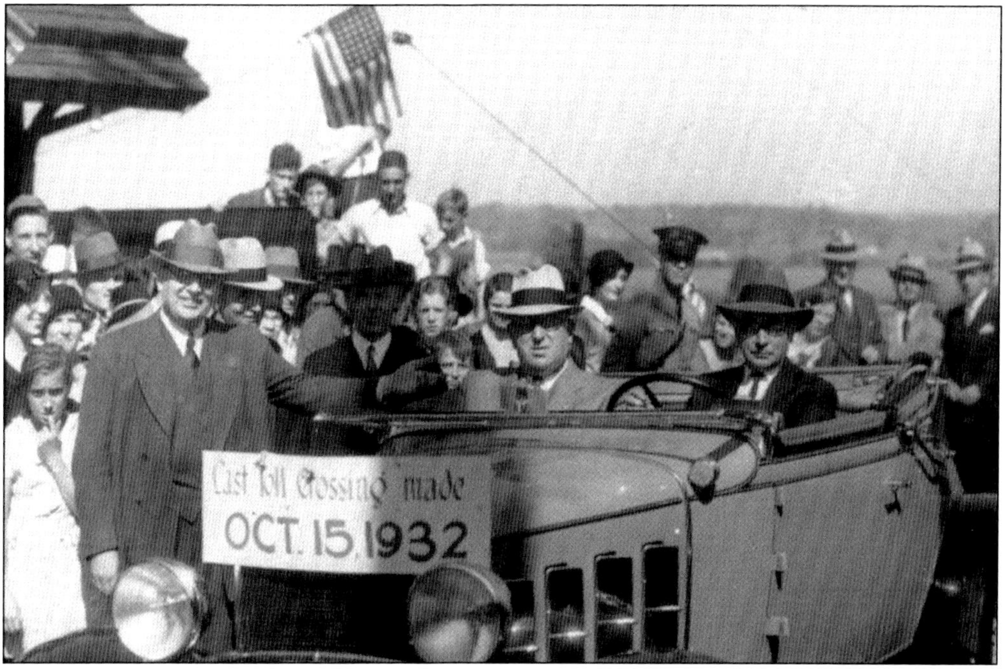

The last toll crossing of the Missouri River bridge on October 15, 1932, was made by Mr. Nolan, who had also made the first toll crossing in June of 1896. Driving the car was Col. Linxweiler, the postmaster, with Mr. Nolan in the passenger seat. Clifford Scruggs and Hugo Holowrath are standing to the left of the car. (Cole County Historical Society.)

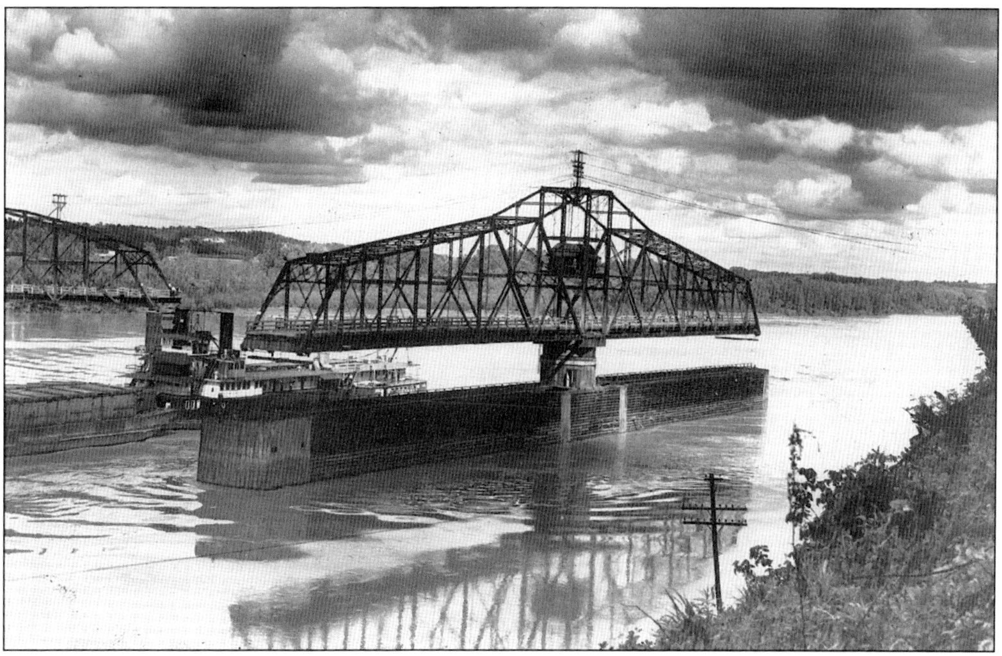

The first Missouri River bridge at the City of Jefferson, in the 1940s, turned to allow river traffic to pass. Note the control house placed above car level and the protective pilings around the turned bridge. (Joe Kroeger.)

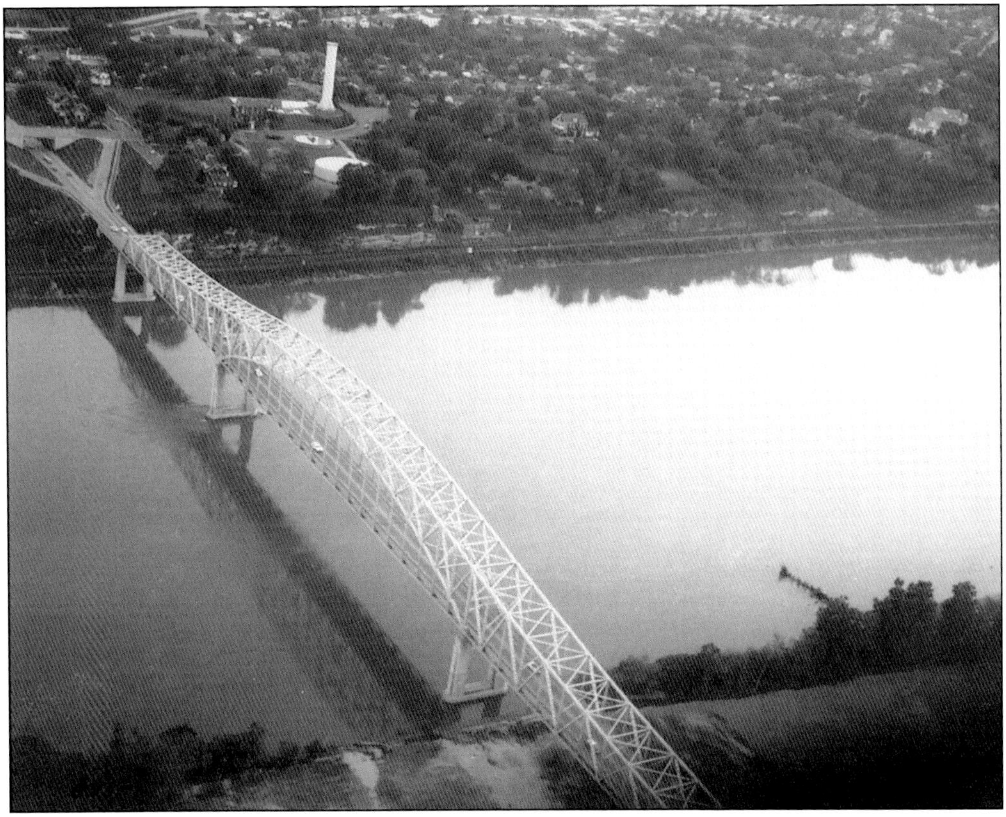

This aerial view of the second bridge built at the City of Jefferson was taken about 1956. Note the water tower and plant in background. (Joe Kroeger)

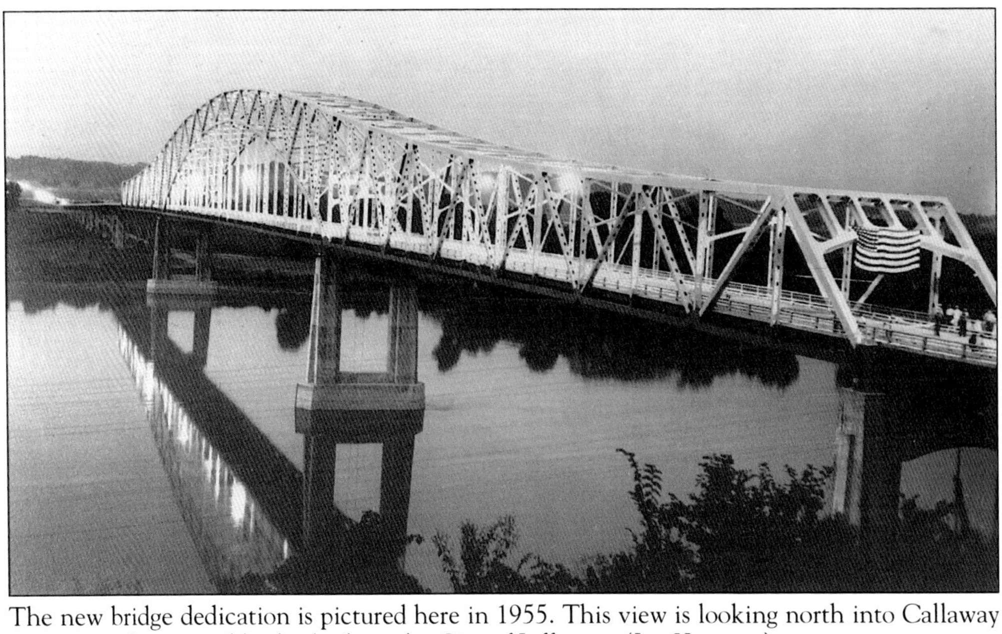

The new bridge dedication is pictured here in 1955. This view is looking north into Callaway County at the second bridge built in the City of Jefferson. (Joe Kroeger.)

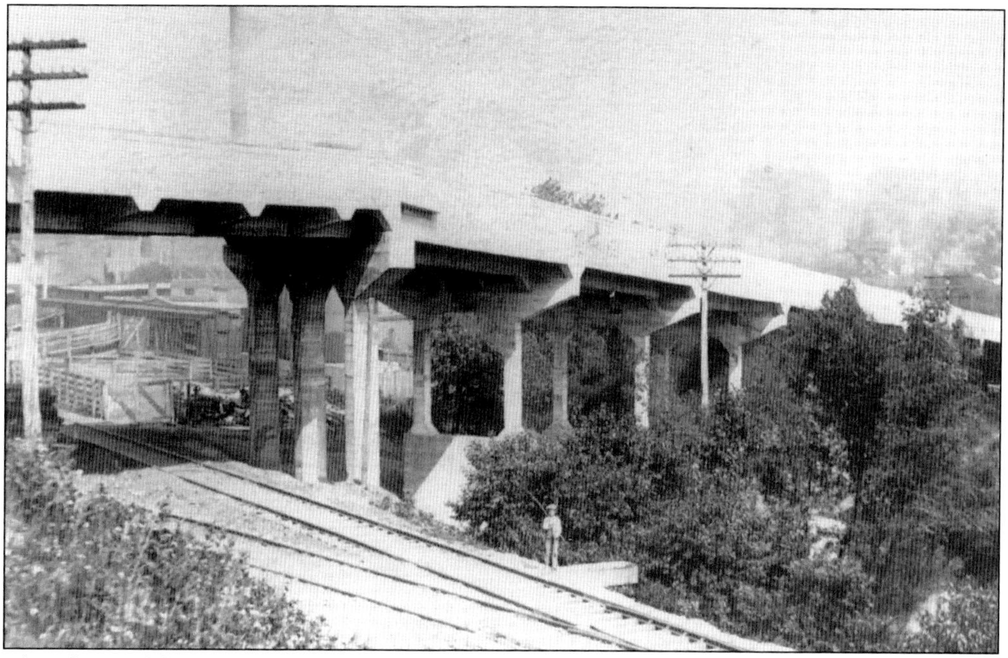

This photo of the first High Street viaduct was taken about 1920, showing cattle yards and the Bagnell Branch Railroad. (Bryan Pope.)

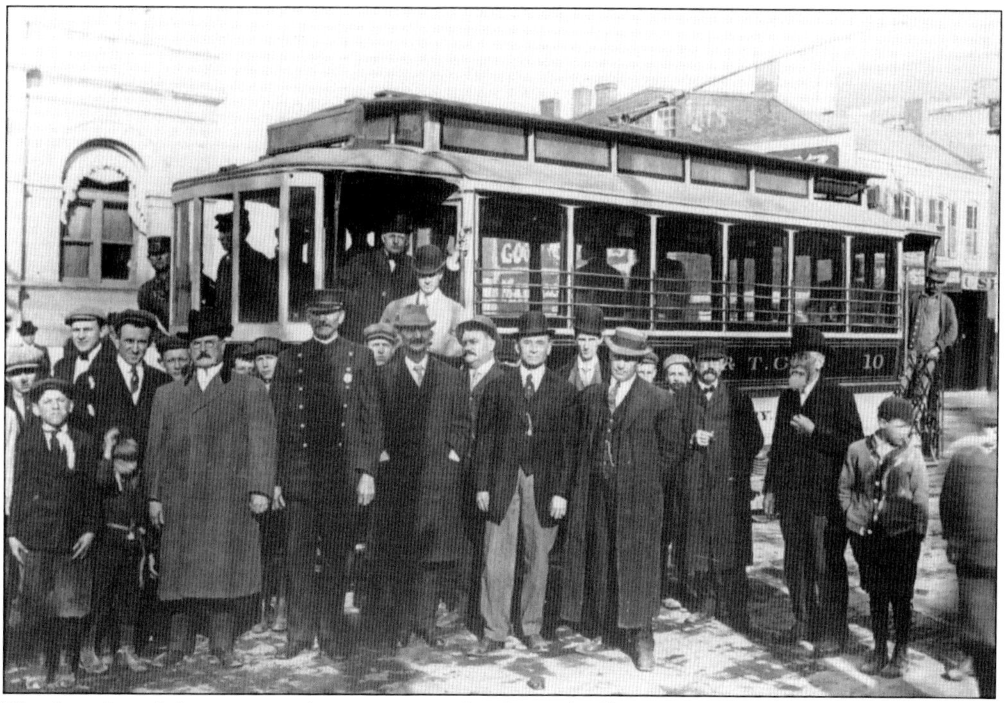

The first day of the streetcars' operation in the City of Jefferson was April 1, 1911. Some of the local citizens gathered here include "King" Heinrich, the "Furniture King" who was the mayor, left of the policeman; to the left of him is Louis Ott, and on the back row, right side in the derby hat is Dr. Joe Summers Sr. (Summers Collection; Missouri State Archives.)

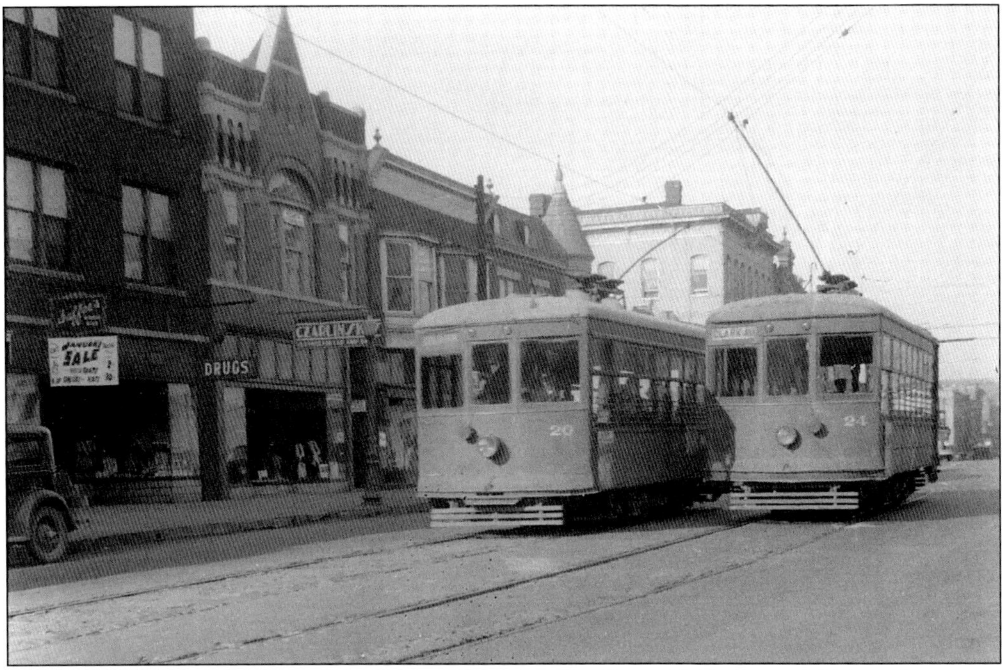

This scene depicts the last day of street car service in the City of Jefferson in 1934, at the corner of High and Monroe Streets. (Summers Collection; Missouri State Archives.)

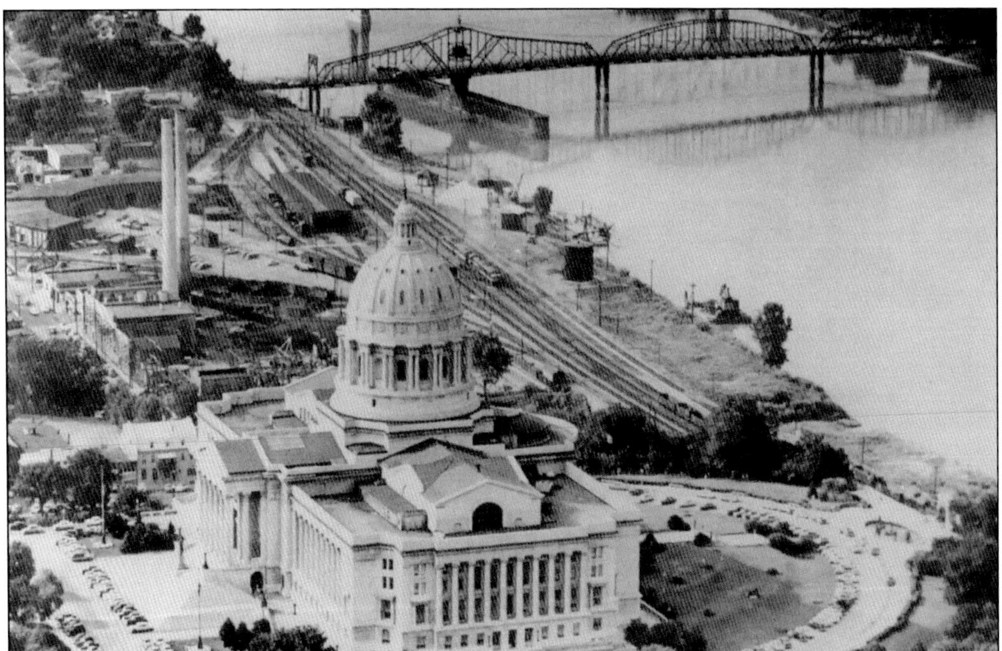

This aerial view of the City of Jefferson shows the main transportation arteries. Note the river with barges, the railroad tracks and round house, and the first and second bridges across the Missouri River. Also note the third Missouri State Capitol and the Missouri Power and Light power plant. (Gerald Massie.)

Four

The Growth of Local Business

The center of business in the City of Jefferson originated on the Missouri riverfront at Lohman's landing. From there it moved up the hill to High Street and west of the capitol in the Millbottom. There were pockets of shops east of town, around the prison, and south of town in the Munichburg area, which were settled mainly by German immigrants. Many of the buildings uptown were built in the 1880s and 1890s.

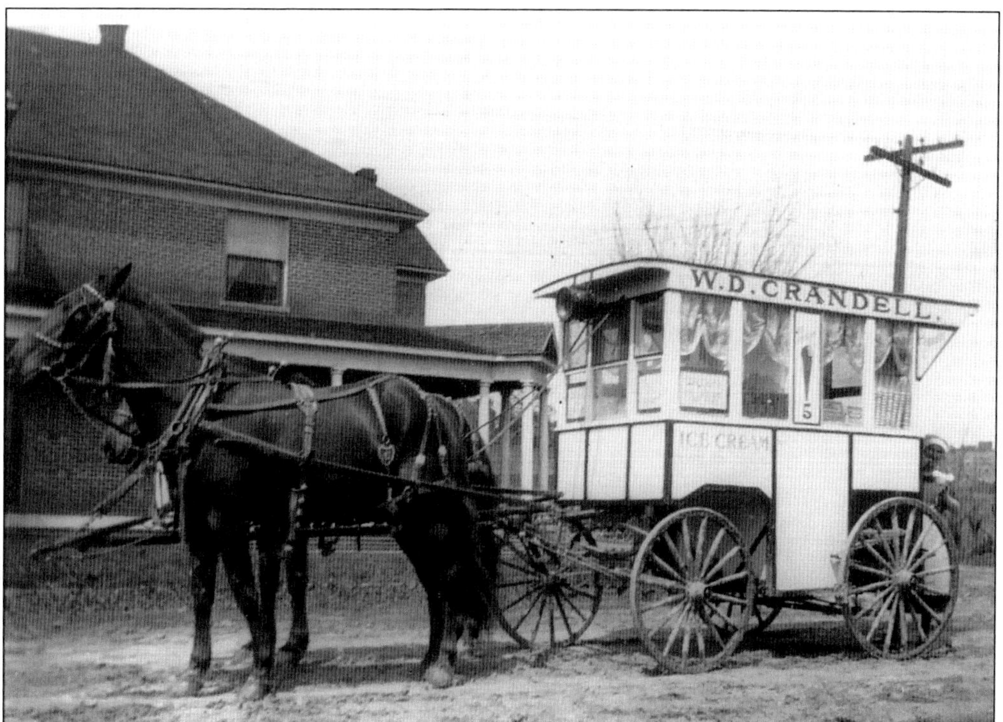

Children just after the turn of the century looked forward to seeing W.D. Crandell's Ice Cream Wagon come down the street. (Summers Collection; Missouri State Archives.)

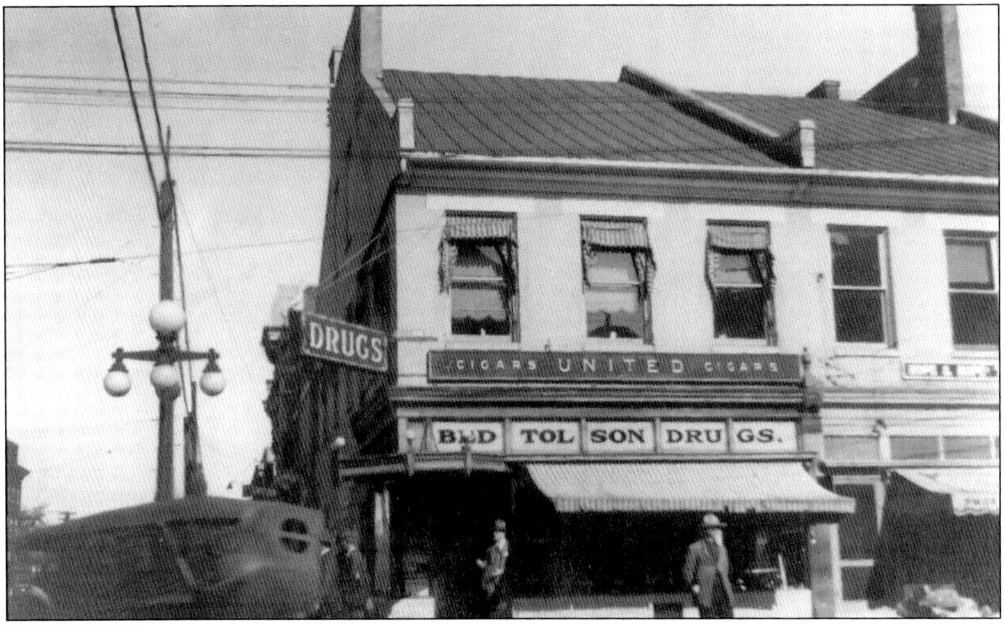

The Hope Building on October 23, 1922, is depicted as the Tolson's Drug Store and Hope Tailor Shop on the corner of High and Madison Streets. (Summers Collection; Missouri State Archives.)

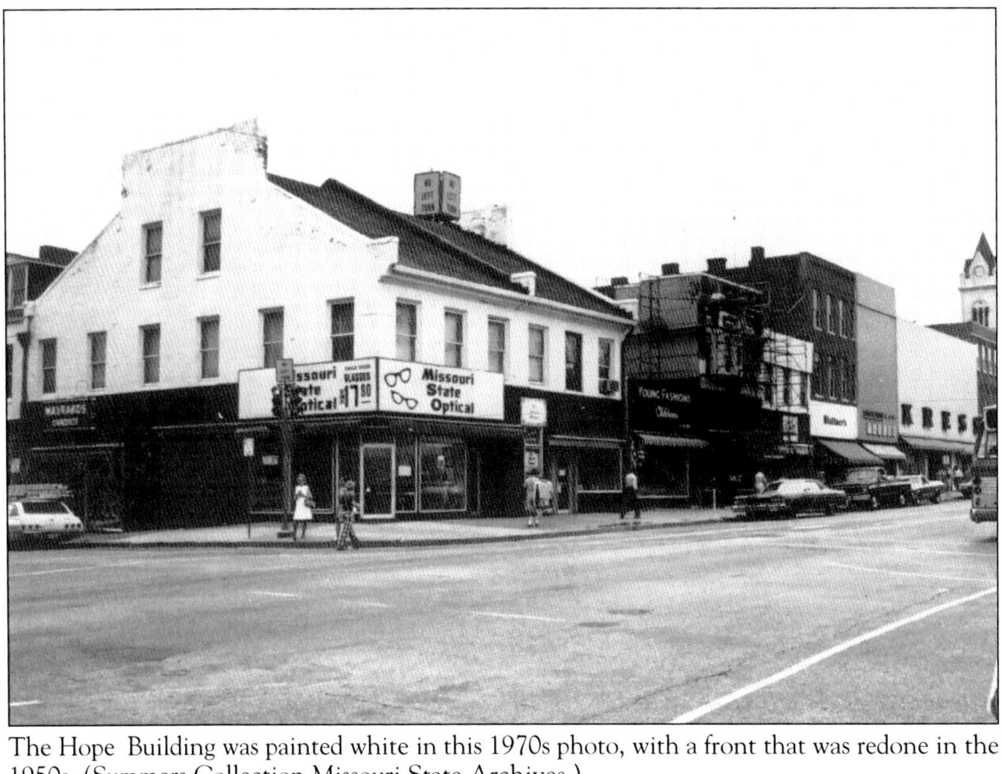

The Hope Building was painted white in this 1970s photo, with a front that was redone in the 1950s. (Summers Collection Missouri State Archives.)

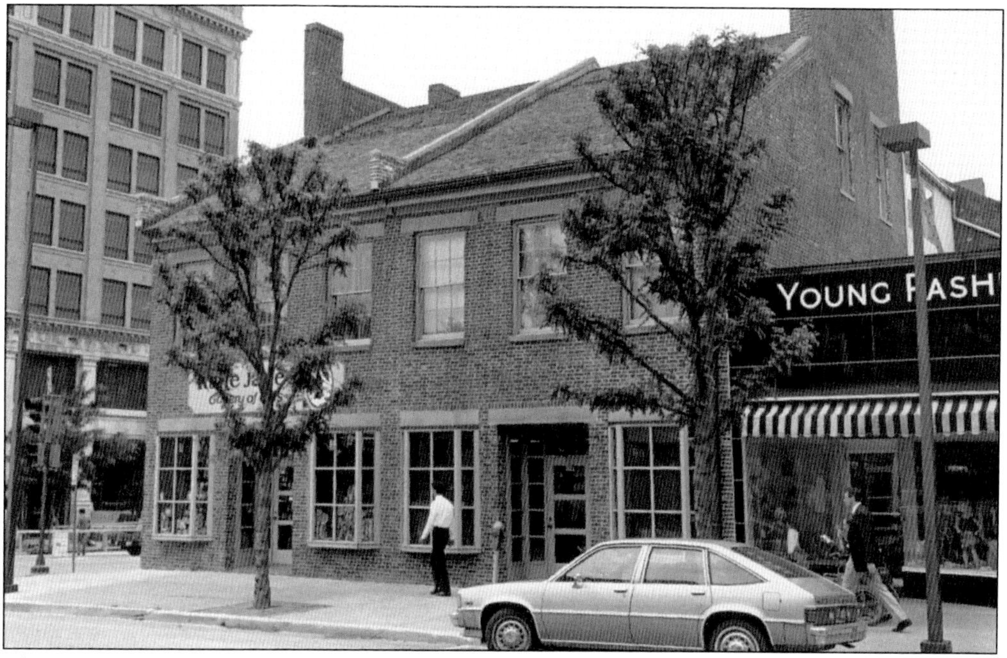

The Hope Building was restored as closely as could be determined to its original appearance. This photo was taken in 1986, when the preservation movement in the community was just beginning. Note the Central Trust Building in back. (*News* and *Tribune* photo.)

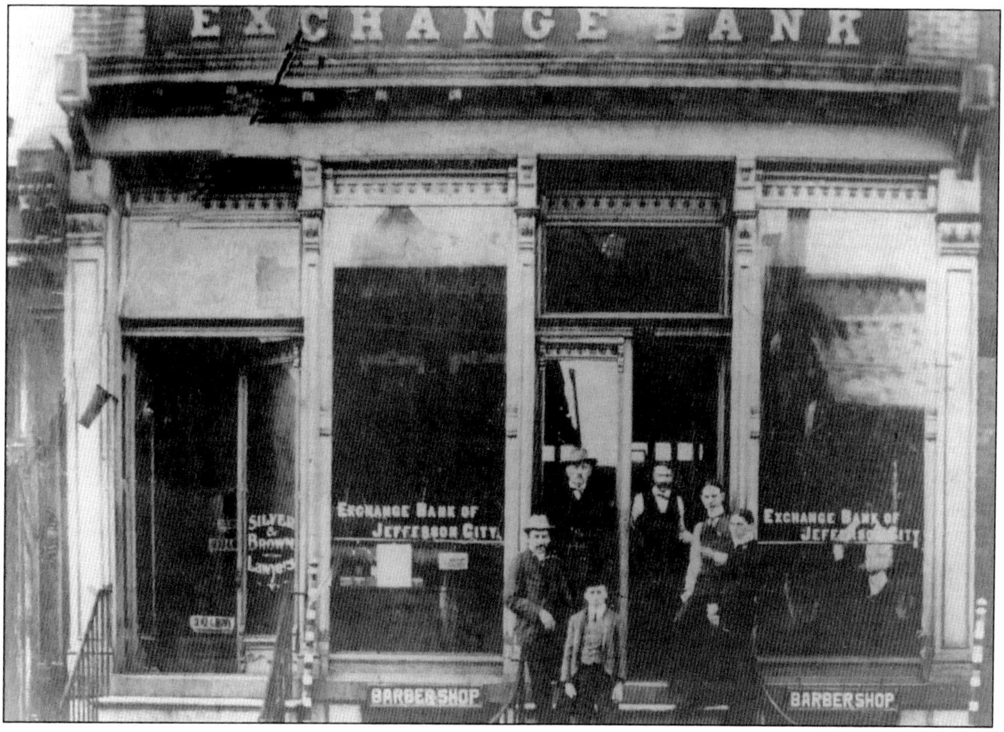

In about 1890, the Exchange Bank shared the building in the 200 block, on the south side of the street, with a barber shop and lawyers' offices. (Summers Collection; Missouri State Archives.)

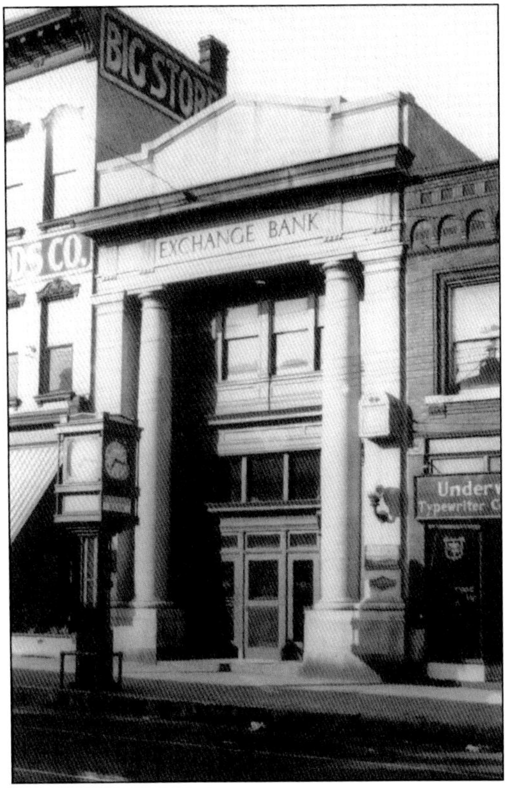

The Exchange Bank is pictured about 1920, with new, grand, brass and stone front with a signature clock by the street. The clock is still situated in front of the now combined Exchange and National Banks. Note Dallmeyer's Dry Goods "Big Store" to the left and the Underwood Typewriter Store on the right. (Summers Collection; Missouri State Archives.)

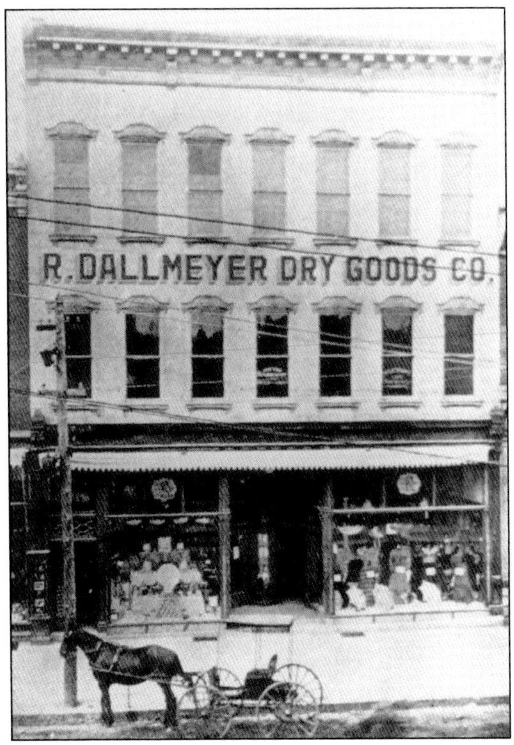

In 1900, R. Dallmeyer Dry Goods Company, on the south side of the 200 block of East High Street, was advertised as the "Big Store" because of combining, remodeling, and adding onto the original building. The second floor contained photographer's studios, doctor and dentist offices, and the third floor was a meeting room for a fraternal order. (Summers Collection; Missouri State Archives.)

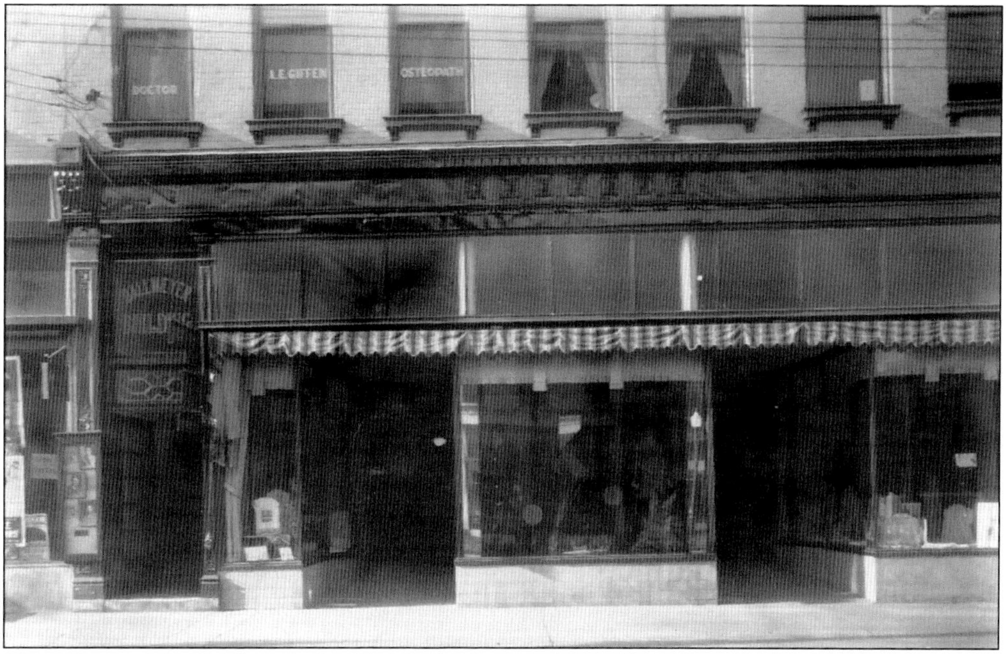

This photo of the Dallmeyer Building, after renovations of the storefront in the 1920s, shows some of the second-floor office occupants. (Photo by Carl Deeg; Ehrhardt Collection; Missouri State Archives.)

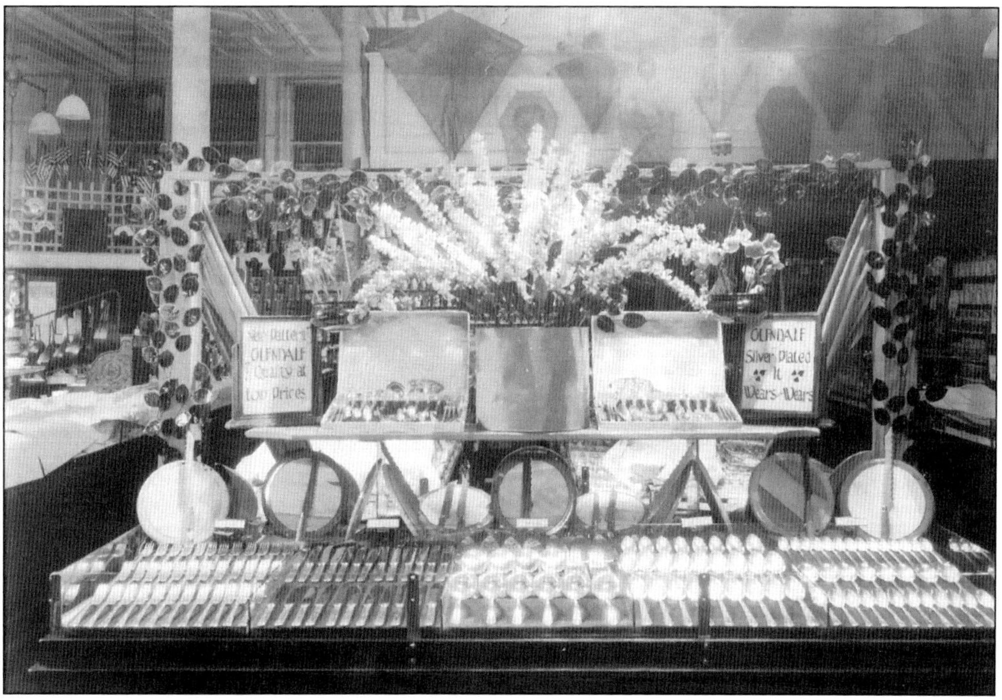

This photo of the interior of R. Dallmeyer Dry Goods Company showing store displays and the upper balcony was taken in the 1920s. (Photo by Carl Deeg; Ehrhardt Collection; Missouri State Archives.)

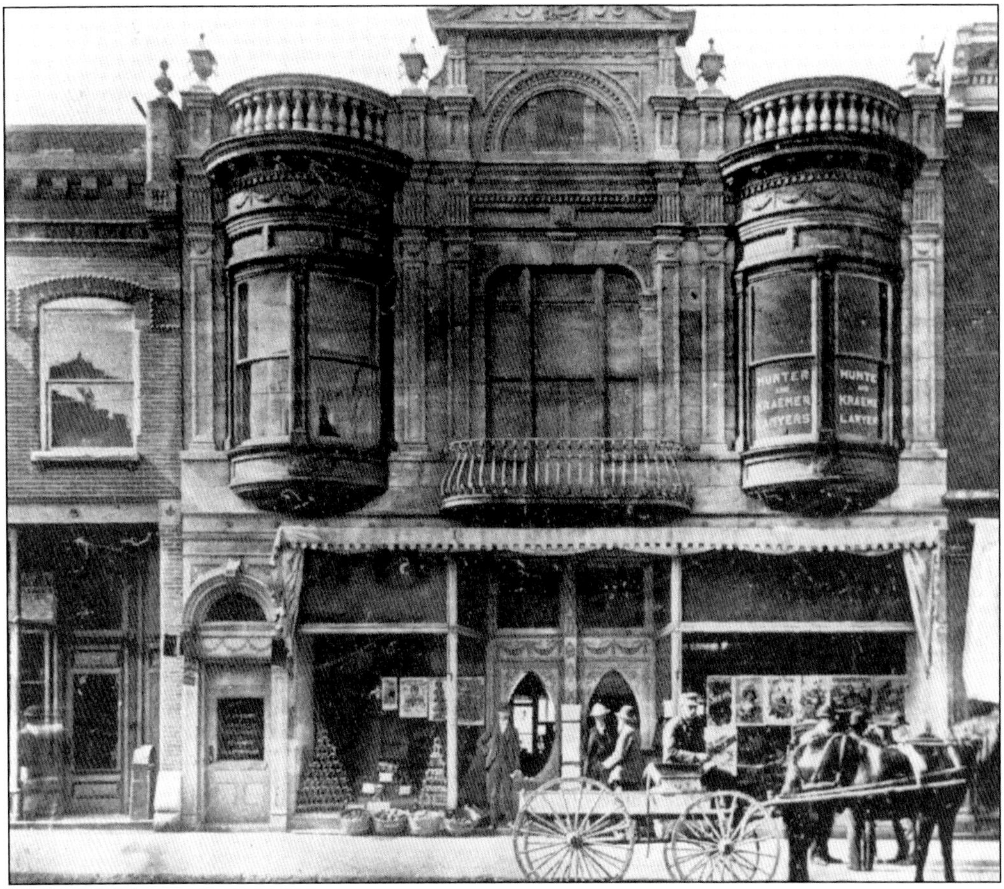

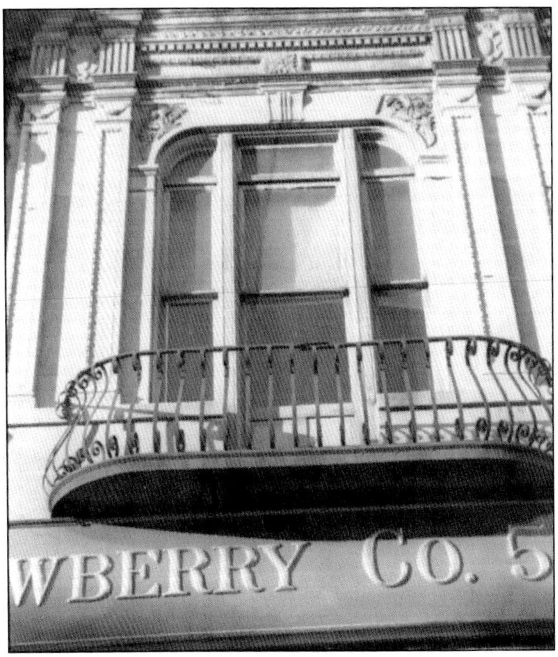

The Binder Building was built in 1898 by Frederick C. Binder, a local architect and builder. This structure was located on the south side of High Street in the 200 block. The front of extruded brass with ornamental ironwork on the balcony was unique, but commonly found in this community of buildings constructed by, or for, German immigrants. At the time of the photo in 1900, a grocery store occupied part of the first floor, and lawyers' offices were on the second. (Summers Collection; Missouri State Archives.)

This close-up of the ironwork and window detail on the Binder Building was taken in the early 1950s, when J.J. Newberry Company 5-10-25¢ Store occupied the first floor of the building. (Summers Collection; Missouri State Archives.)

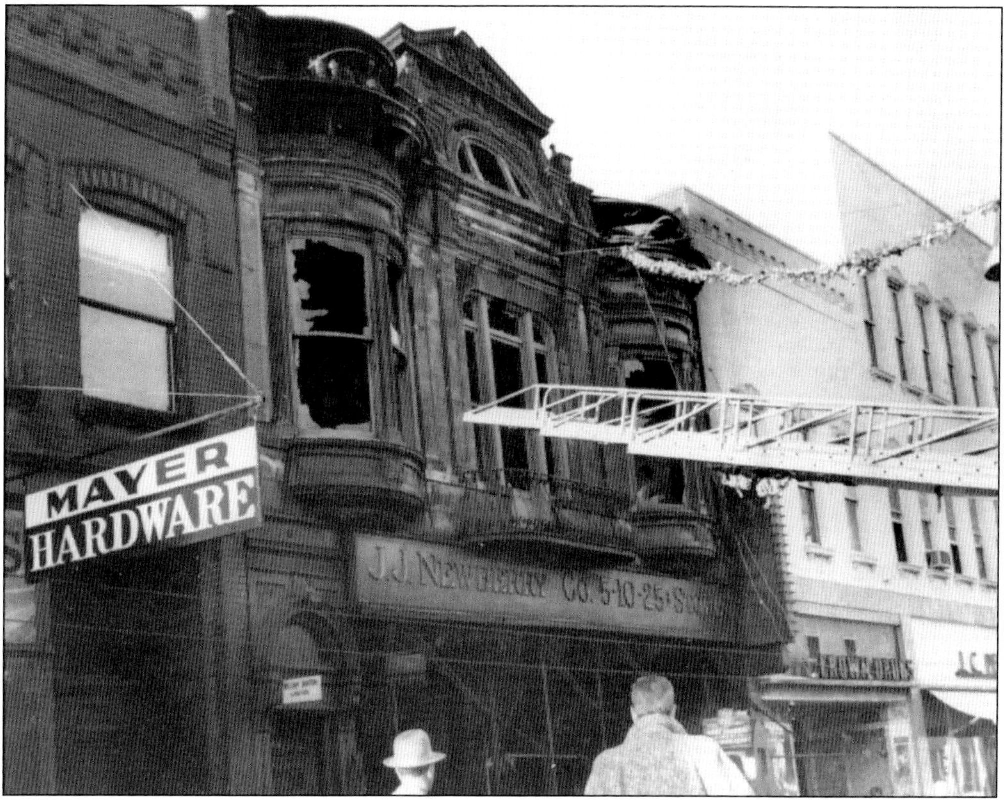

The Binder Building after the fire that destroyed it in 1957. Note Mayer Hardware Store on the left and the Dallmeyer building on right, now with brick exterior painted white and occupied by Crown Drug store and J.C. Penney's. (Joe Kroeger.)

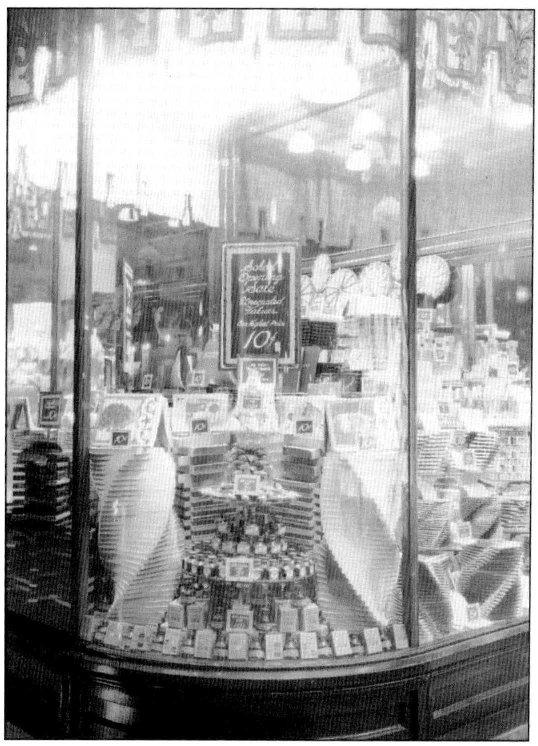

Front window display from Kress 5-10¢ Store in the 1920s. The store was on the north side of High Street, in the middle of the east 200 block. (Ehrhardt Collection; Missouri State Archives.)

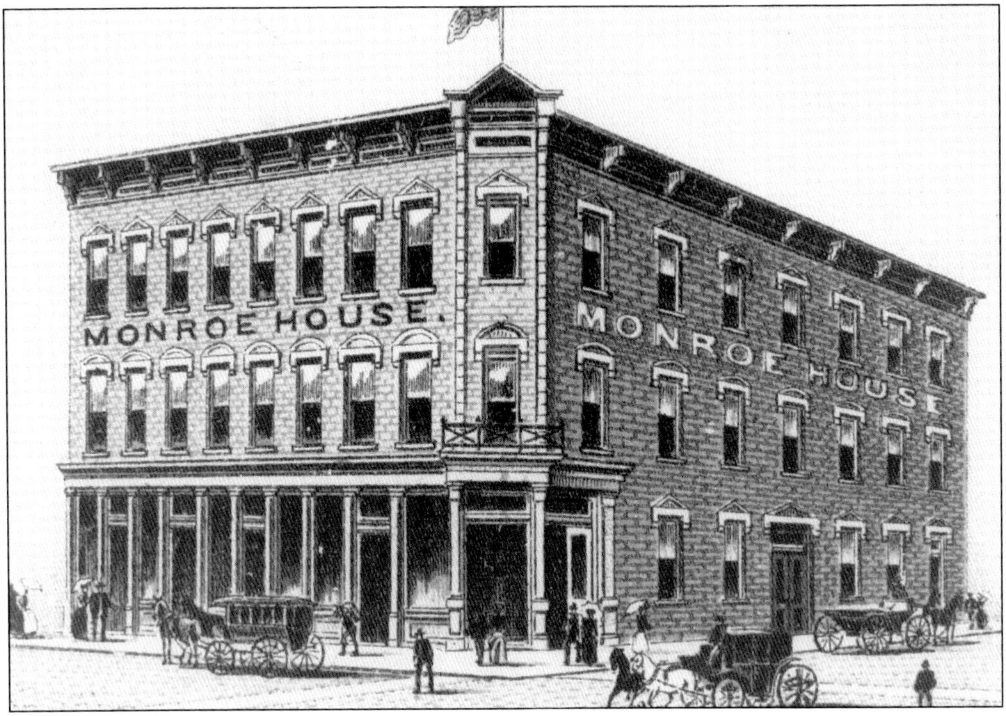

The Monroe House Hotel sketched here as it was planned in 1884. When built, the building, on the corner of High Street and Monroe, was not complete as drawn. The entire building as planned took 100 years to complete, finishing in 1984. In June 2000 the first floor storefront was changed to look like this drawing. (Summers Collection; Missouri State Archives.)

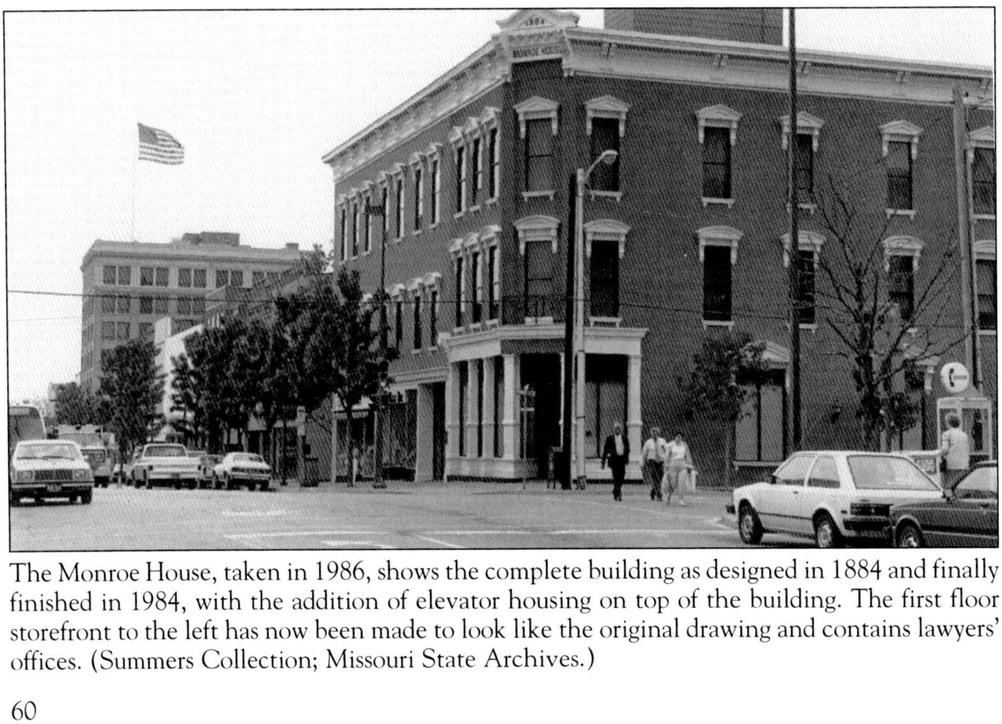

The Monroe House, taken in 1986, shows the complete building as designed in 1884 and finally finished in 1984, with the addition of elevator housing on top of the building. The first floor storefront to the left has now been made to look like the original drawing and contains lawyers' offices. (Summers Collection; Missouri State Archives.)

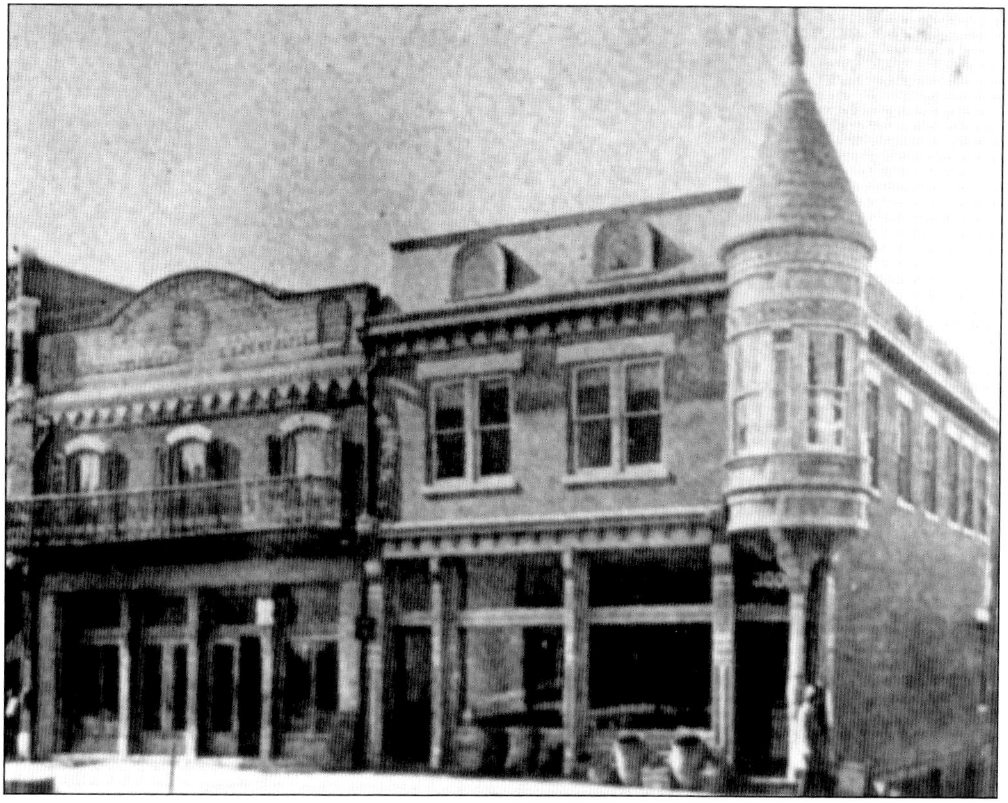

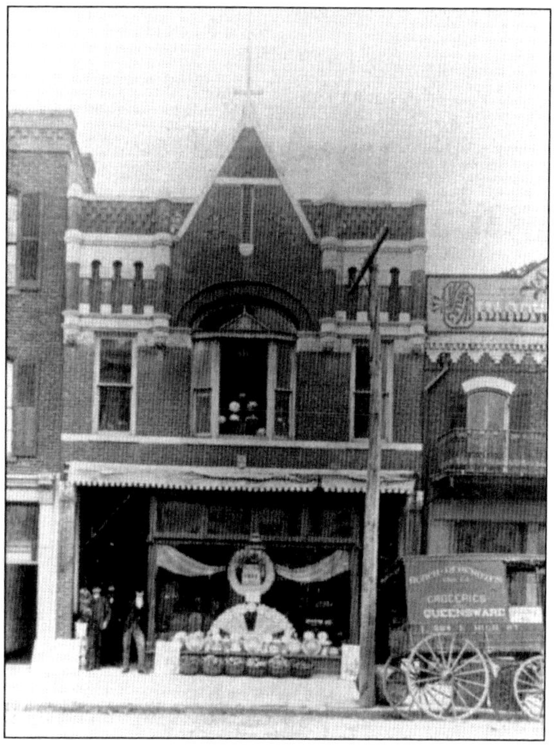

The Democrat Building, at 300 East High, was built in 1873 by the Honorable Joseph R. Edwards to house his newspaper, the *Cole County Democrat*. The building has also been Delmonico's Grocery Store and Jack and Jill's Children's Store on the first floor. The second floor turret with windows was a dentist office, chosen for maximum light for the dentist to work. The building next to it was Bartlett's Book Store, until it burned down, and is now an empty lot. (Summers Collection; Missouri State Archives.)

The Burch-Berendzen Grocer Company was designed by Frank Miller and constructed in 1895. It is an exuberantly detailed Romanesque-Revival building. The building, now occupied with lawyers' offices, has much of its original integrity. (Summers Collection; Missouri State Archives.)

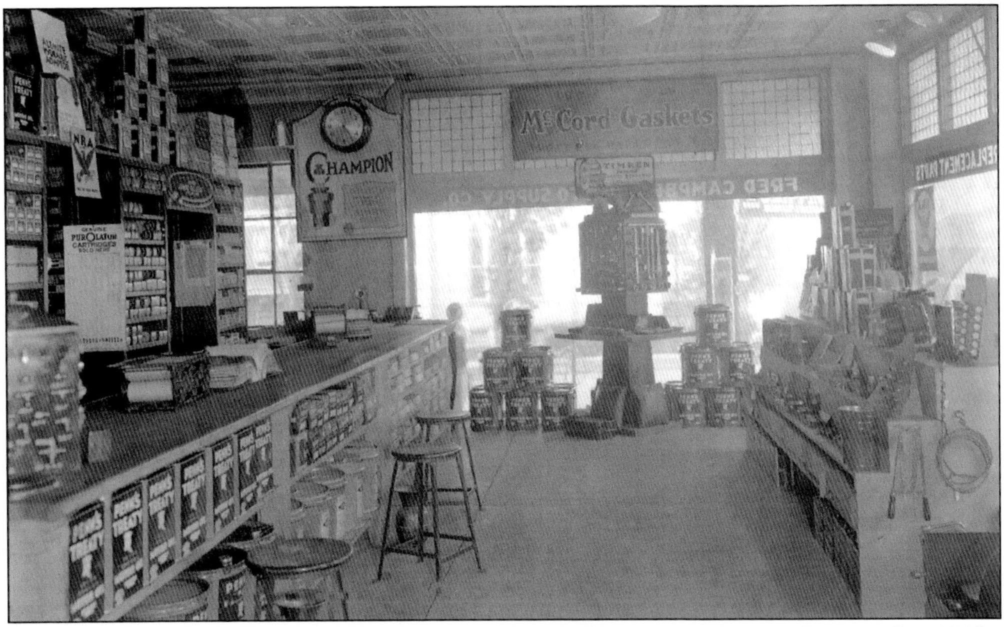

This interior view of the Fred Campbell Auto Supply Company was taken in the 1920s. (Ehrhardt Collection; Missouri State Archives.)

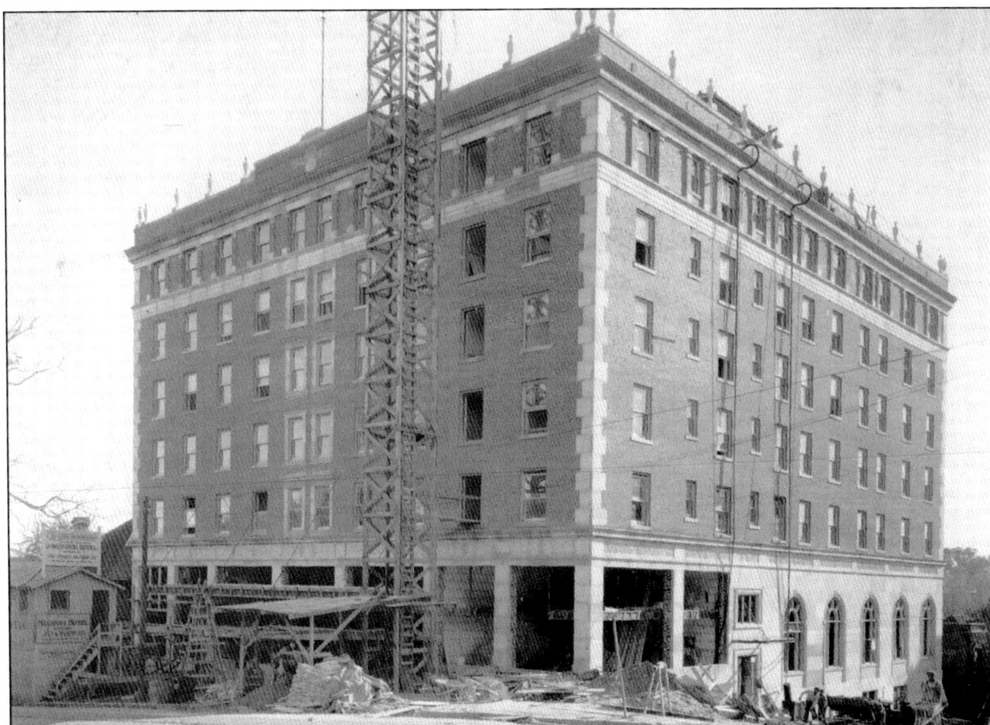

The Missouri Hotel was built in 1927 on the corner of East High and Adams Street. This Carl Deeg photo shows it under construction. The first indoor swimming pool in the City of Jefferson was built in the Missouri Hotel. (Ehrhardt Collection; Missouri State Archives.)

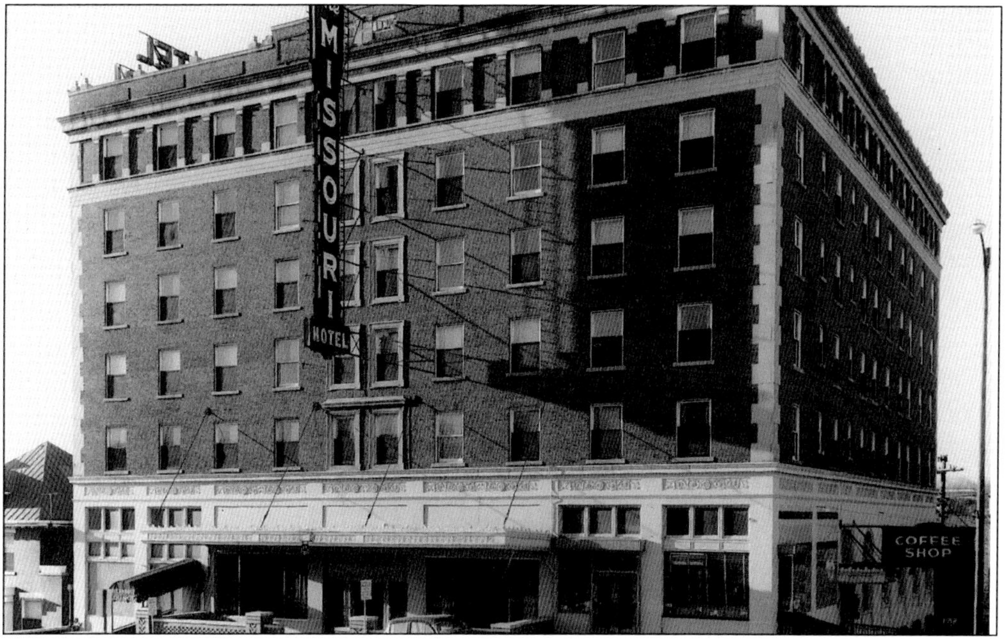

The completed Missouri Hotel, taken in the 1950s, had a coffee shop, banquet rooms, and on the first floor, to the left, was the Steamboat Lounge, entrance under the canopy. The next building to the left is the Bill Irwin house, now torn down to make a parking lot. This building has been extensively remodeled, is almost unrecognizable, and is used now for the Baptist Church state headquarters. (Summers Collection; Missouri State Archives.)

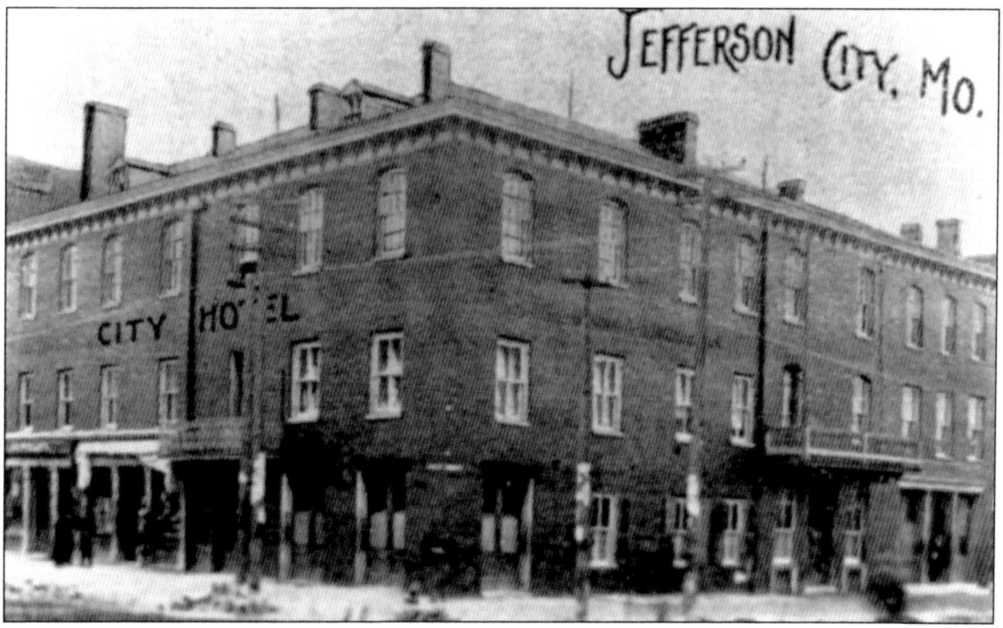

The City Hotel, on the corner of High Street and Madison, contained the Central Trust Bank in the lobby when this photo was taken in 1890. In the early 1900s this building was torn down and the present Central Trust Company building was built. (Summers Collection; Missouri State Archives.)

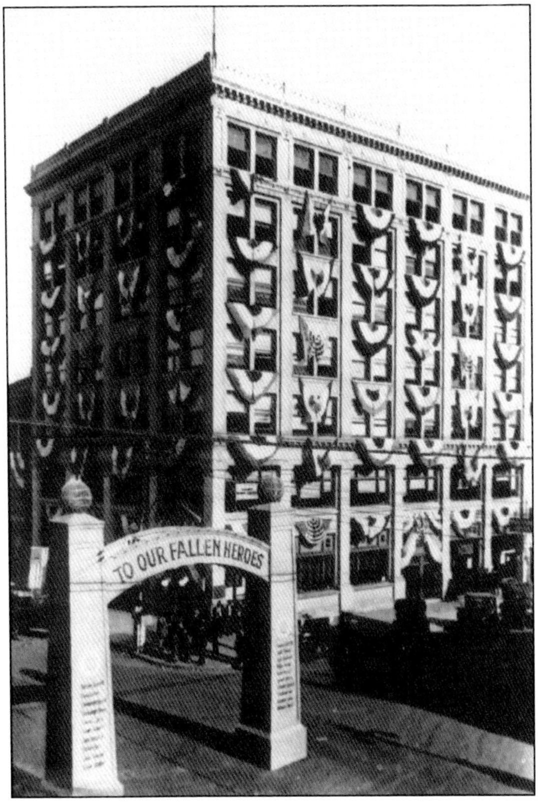

A parade honoring soldiers from World War I, both those who returned and those who did not, passes by the Central Trust Building in 1919. The City of Jefferson has a tradition of crowd-pleasing parades. Here we see bunting hung from buildings and across the streets, and a memorial arch placed over the trolley wires in city's center. The Central Trust Building was home to the Central Trust Bank and several businesses on the first floor, as well as professional offices for doctors, dentists, and lawyers on the upper floors. (Summers Collection; Missouri State Archives.)

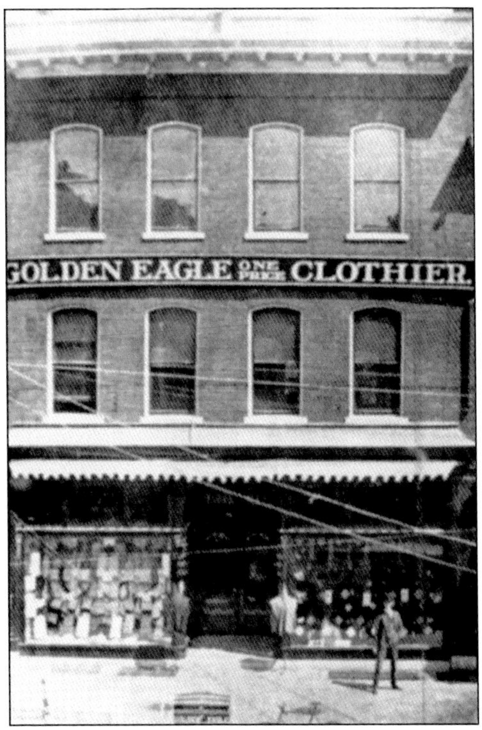

The Golden Eagle Clothing Store, located in the middle of the 200 block of High on the north side, was typical of an uptown merchant in the City of Jefferson. This photo was taken in 1900. (Summers Collection; Missouri State Archives.)

Hoerschen's Bar, as seen in the 1890s, was on the north side of High Street in the 100 block east. Max Meyerhardt's clothing store was just east. Today there is still a bar in the general area of Hoerschen's. (Summers Collection; Missouri State Archives.)

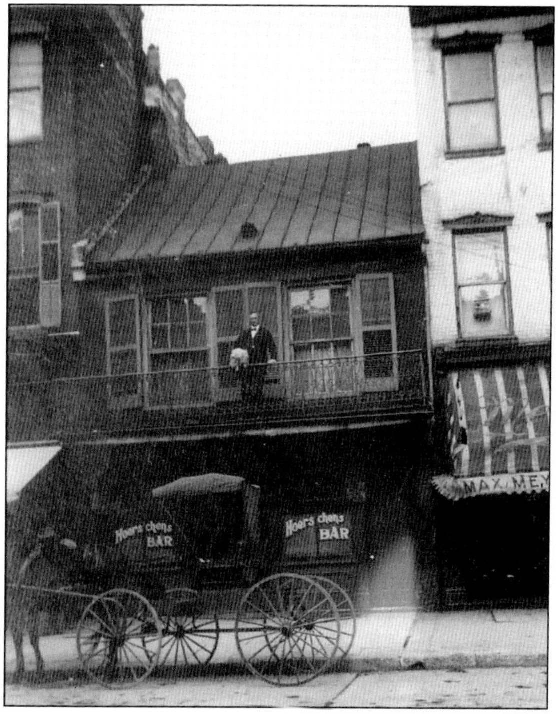

George Porth's Jewelry Store on the south side of the 100 block of East High Street was a beautiful three-bay building, as we see in this photo from 1900. (Summers Collection; Missouri State Archives.)

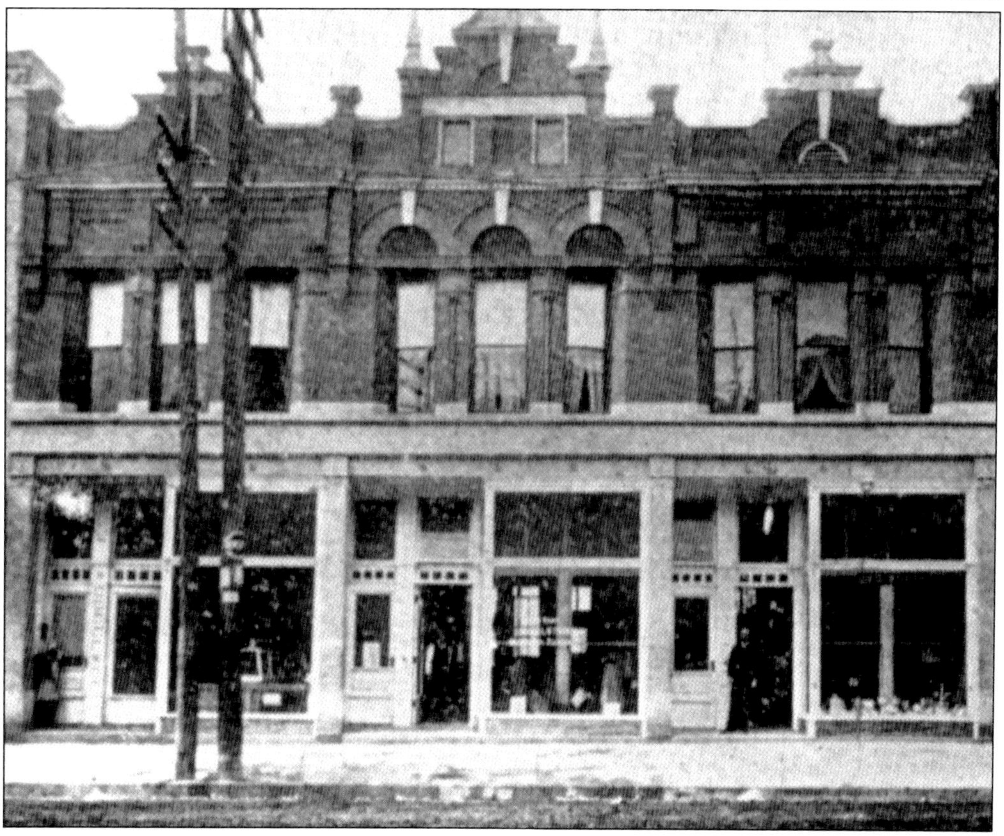

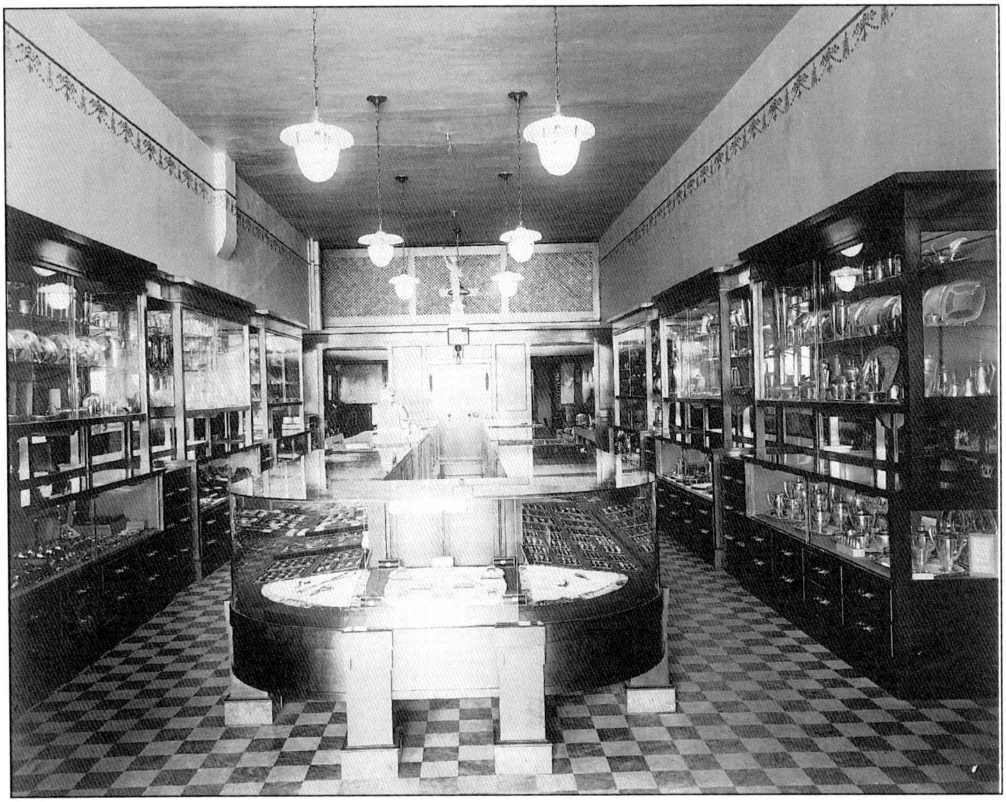

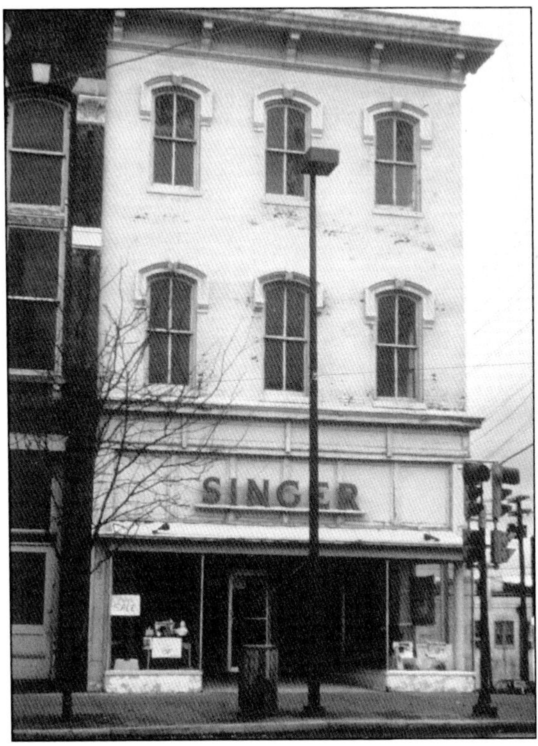

Pictured is the interior of Porth's Jewelry Store after it was remodeled in the 1920s. Many of the same cabinets and showcases are currently being used in this shop today, although it is no longer a jewelry store. (Summers Collection; Missouri State Archives.)

The L.C. Lohman Store was built the early 1880s. L.C., who was in business with his father, Charles F., at Lohman's Landing, bought his father out and established this store up the hill from the original store on the Missouri River. This photo, taken in the 1970s, shows the building painted white.(Summers Collection; Missouri State Archives.)

The L.C. Lohman Store after it was beautifully restored in the mid-1980s. (Summers Collection; Missouri State Archives.)

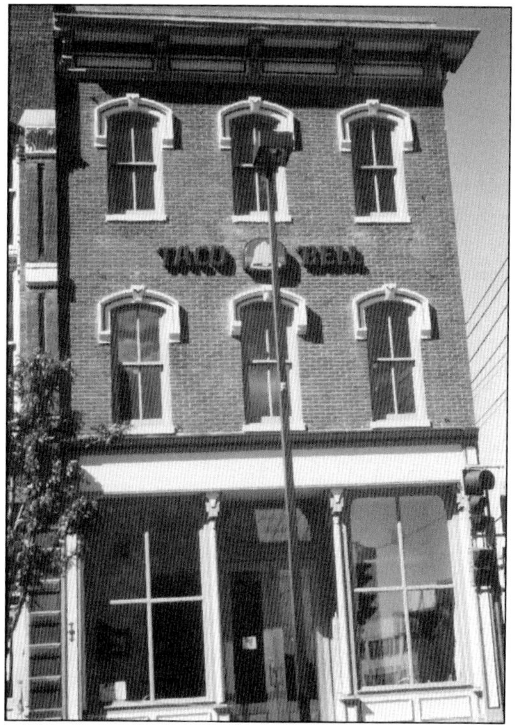

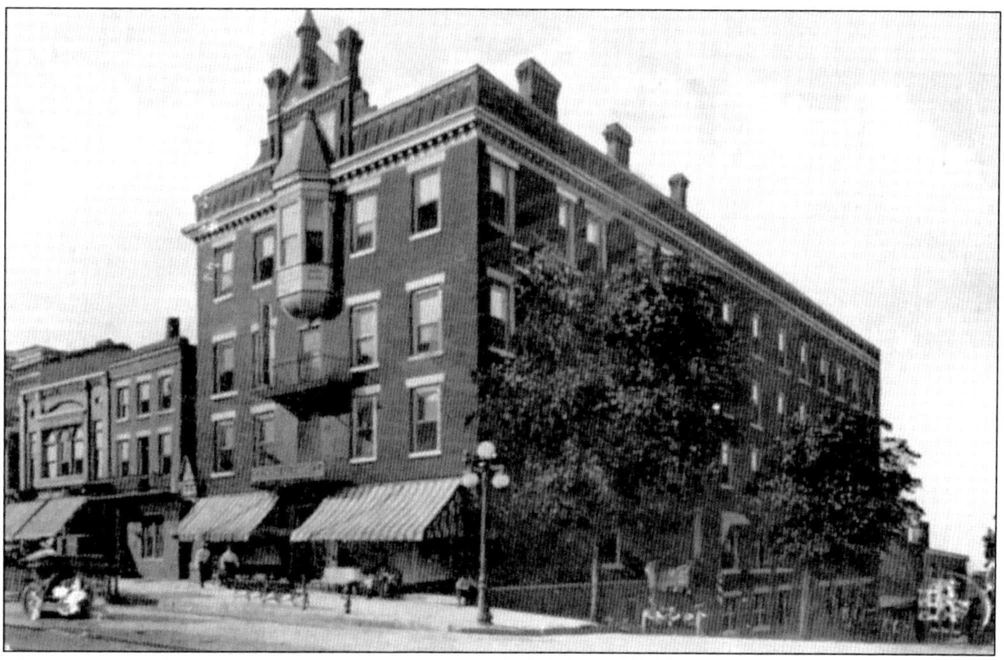

The Central Hotel on the northwest corner of High Street and Jefferson Street about 1900, after being remodeled in 1899. This building was torn down in the 1970s to offer a better view of the Capitol. (Summers Collection; Missouri State Archives.)

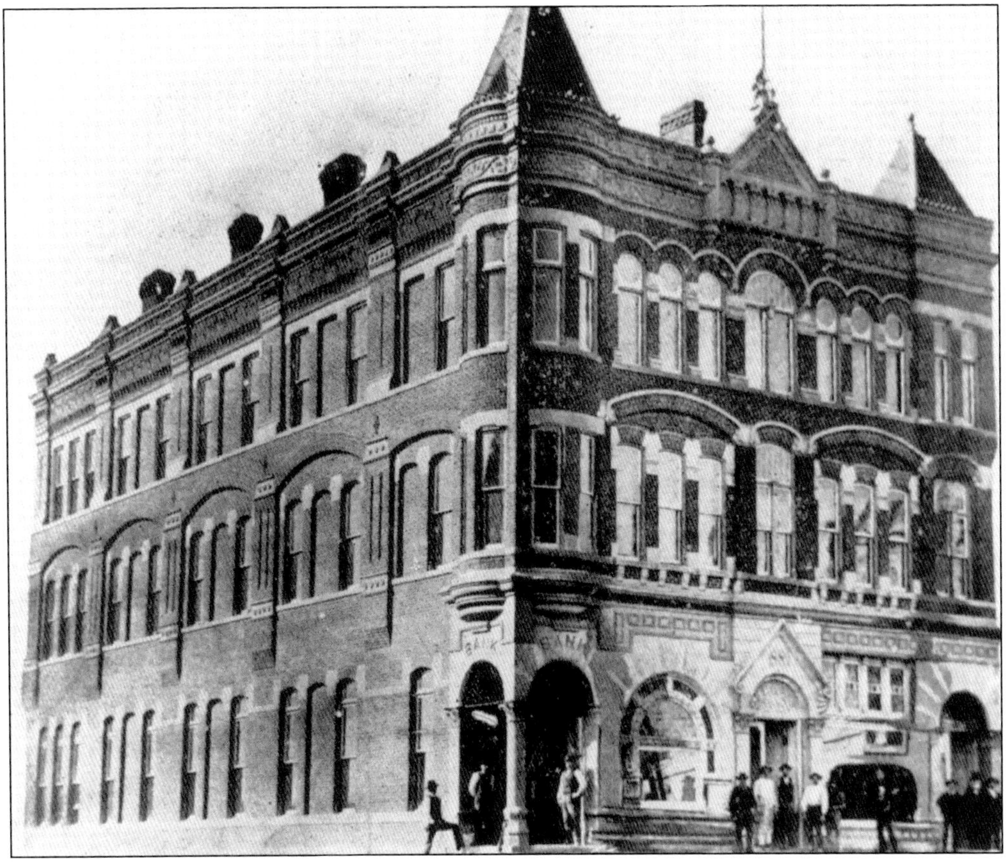

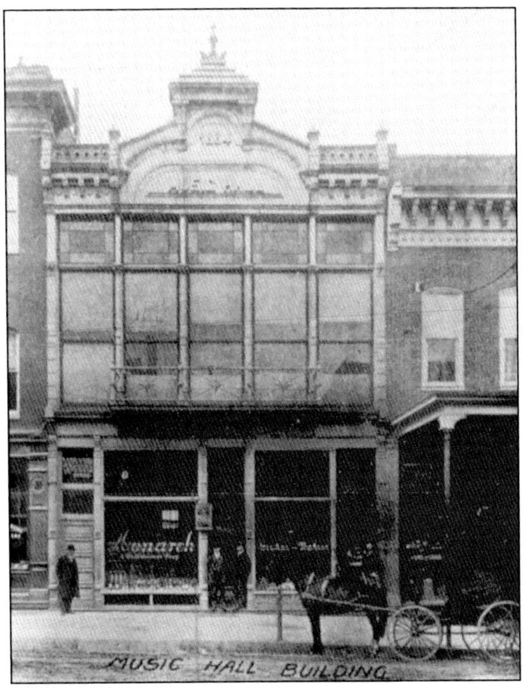

The Merchant's Bank was built under the leadership of L.C. Lohman. The bank occupied half of the first floor, and a shop occupied the other half. The east side of the second floor was occupied by six offices, which included over the years a newspaper bureau, a dentist, and several lawyers. On the west side of the second floor were the rooms of the Commercial Club. The fraternization of competitors developed as the forerunner for the Chamber of Commerce. The Masonic Lodge occupied the third floor. This photo was taken in 1900. (Summers Collection; Missouri State Archives.)

The Music Hall Building was built in 1884, with large windows to allow for maximum lighting. (Summers Collection; Missouri State Archives.)

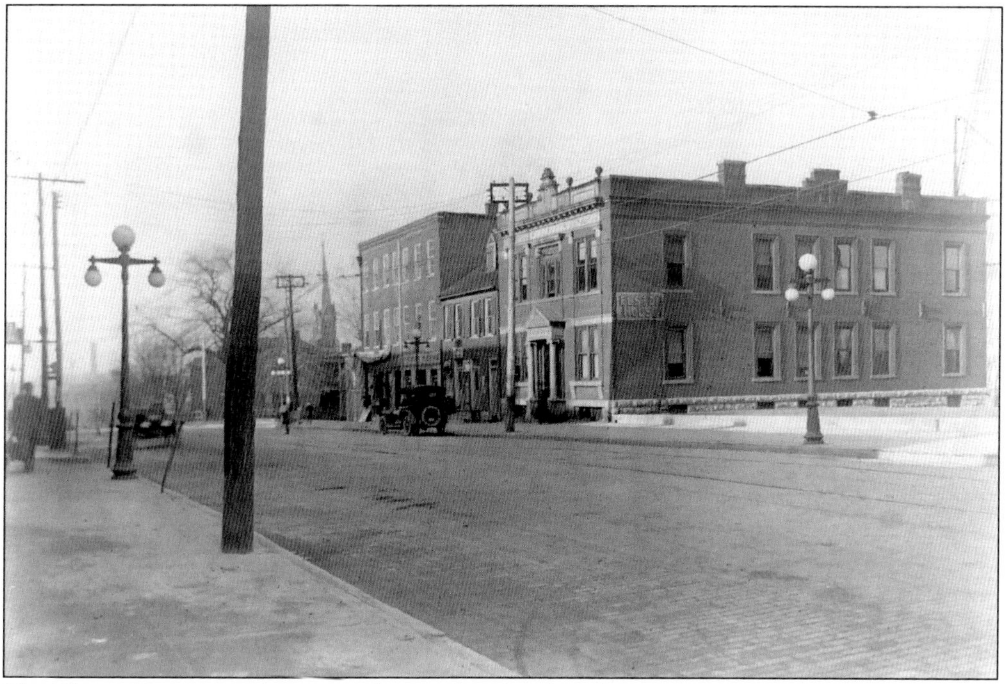

The Elston House Hotel was on the north side of High Street in the 200 block west, near Washington Street. Note St. Peter's Church in the background. (Summers Collection; Missouri State Archives.)

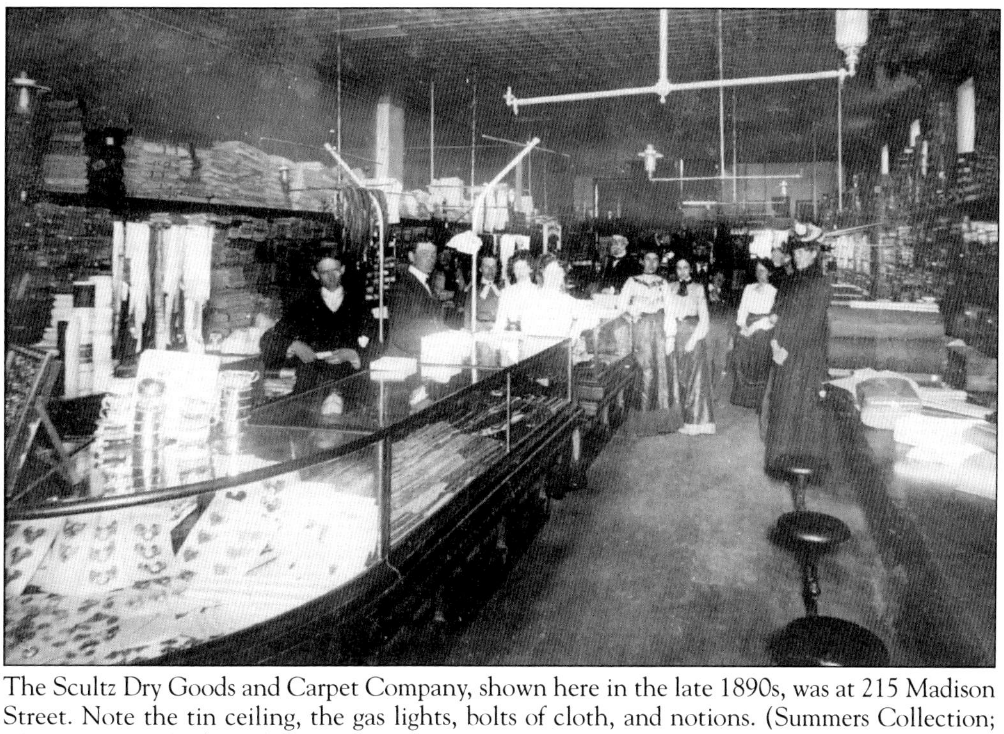

The Scultz Dry Goods and Carpet Company, shown here in the late 1890s, was at 215 Madison Street. Note the tin ceiling, the gas lights, bolts of cloth, and notions. (Summers Collection; Missouri State Archives.)

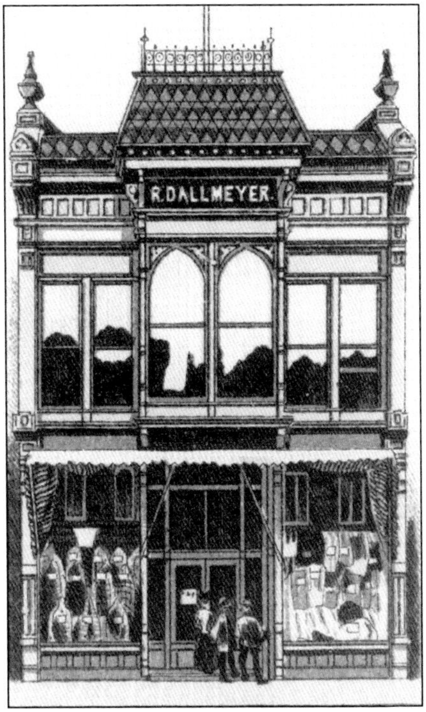

Rudolph Dallmeyer started his Dry Goods Store on Madison Street in 1881. The store eventually moved to High Street in 1898 into a building his father-in-law, Frank Schmidt, built. (Summers Collection; Missouri State Archives.)

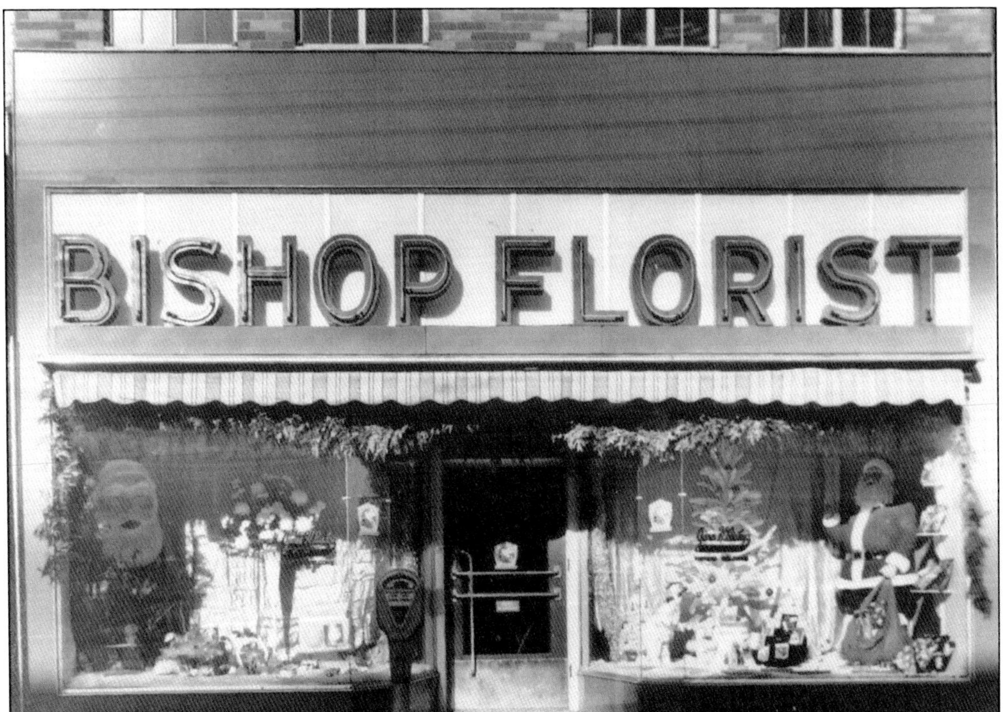

Pictured here in the 1950s, Bishop Florist was on the west side of Madison. Mr. Bishop, who owned the florist, was the organist at Grace Episcopal Church. Today, in the same building, is River City Florist.(Zeal Wright.)

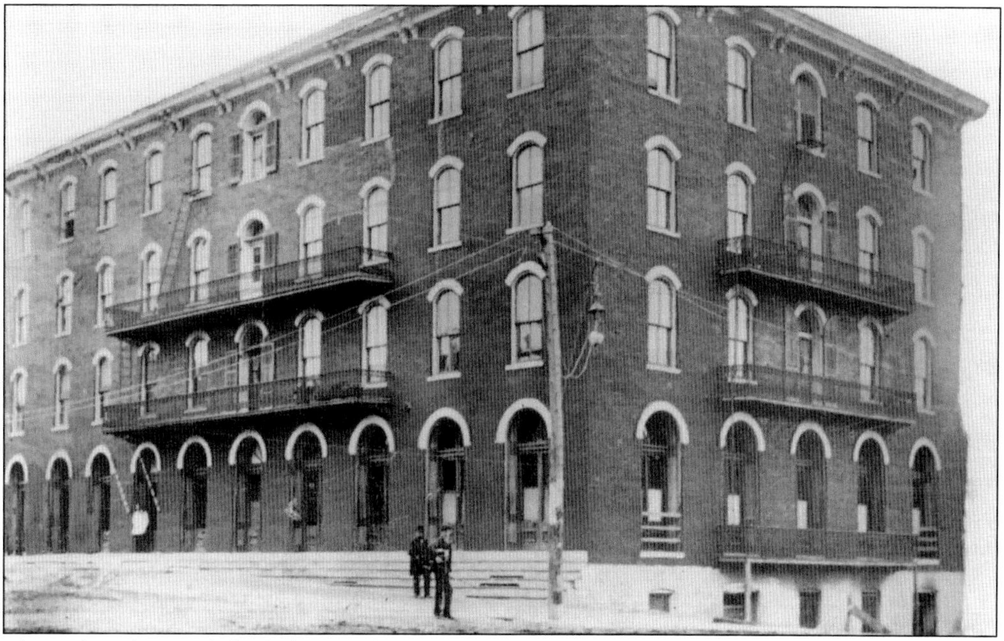

The Schmidt Hotel, built by Frank Schmidt, on the corner of Madison and what was then East Main Street. The hotel burned down and was replaced with the Madison using the same foundation. When the first hotel caught fire, the Schmidt family and some of the guests salvaged what they could of the furnishings by throwing feather beds off the balconies and throwing breakables on top of them. Today a mirror that was saved that way is in a descendant's home. This photo is from the 1880s. (Summers Collection; Missouri State Archives.)

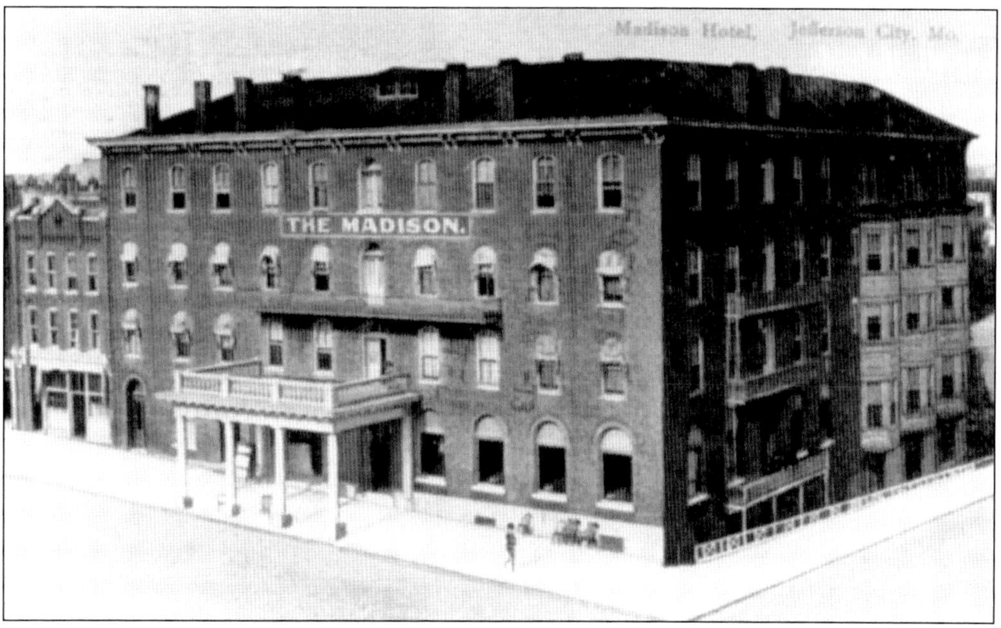

The Madison Hotel replaced the Schmidt Hotel using some of the same foundation, and is located on the same corner of Madison and East Main Streets. This picture is dated *c.* 1900. (Mary Gamble.)

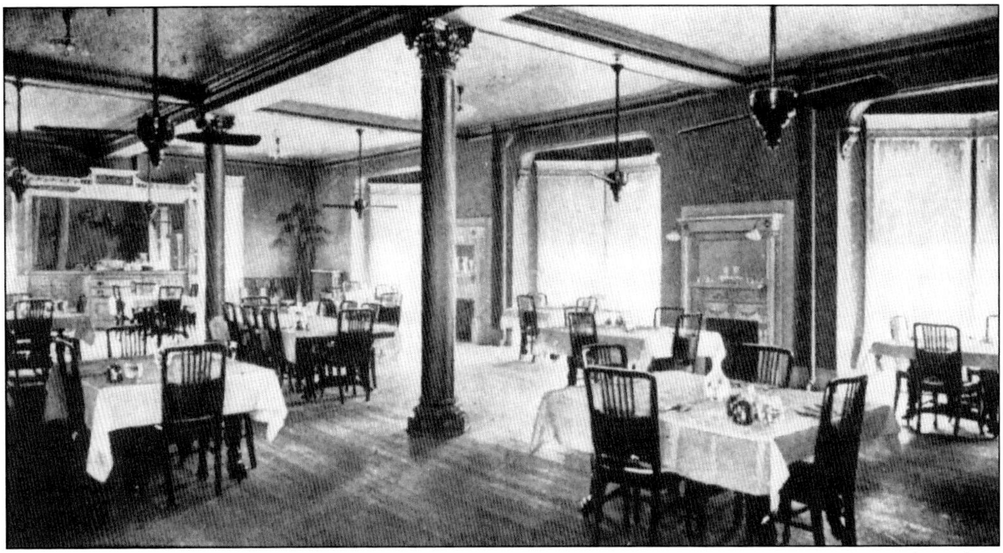

The main dining room of the Madison Hotel is pictured here about 1900. Note the ceiling fans and elegant fireplaces. (Homer Ferguson.)

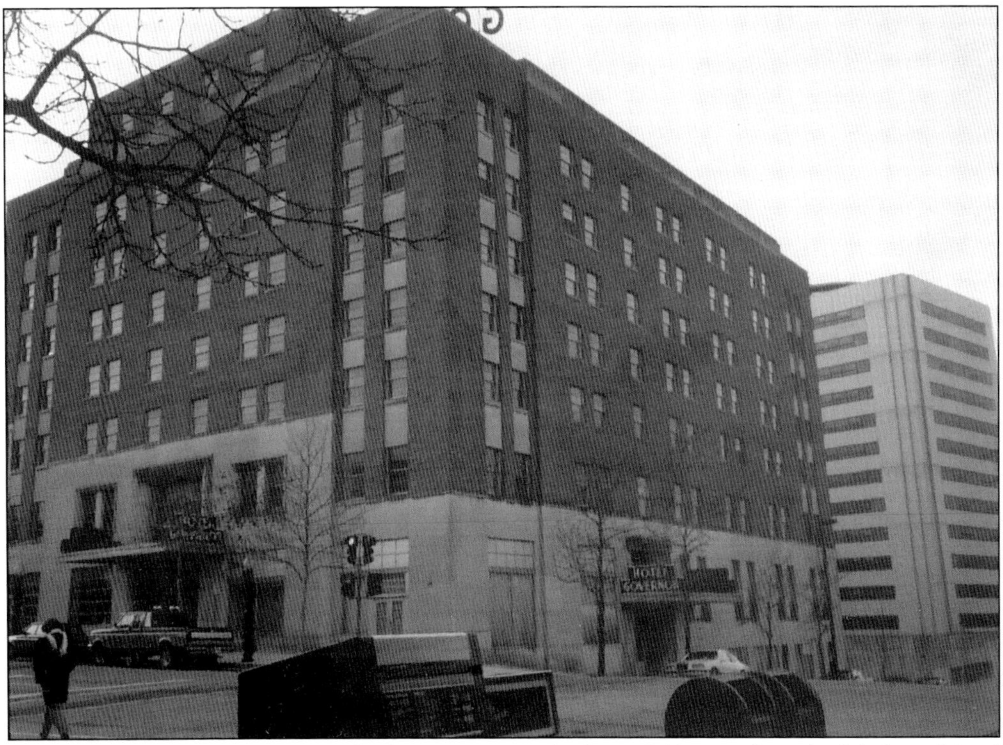

The Hotel Governor, as seen in the late 1980s, was built *c.* 1940 to replace the Madison Hotel that burned in the late 1930s. Since this photo, the hotel went out of business, sat empty for several years, and now, after extensive remodeling, is opening with a bank, shops, a restaurant on the main floor, state and private offices, and a meeting room. (Historic City of Jefferson Archives; Missouri State Archives.)

A building that was on the west side of the 300 block of Madison that sold office supplies is pictured here. This photo was taken in the early 1950s and shows the wrought iron balcony that was typical of many buildings in the City of Jefferson built in the 1880s and 1890s. This building has been torn down for yet another parking lot. (Summers Collection; Missouri State Archives.)

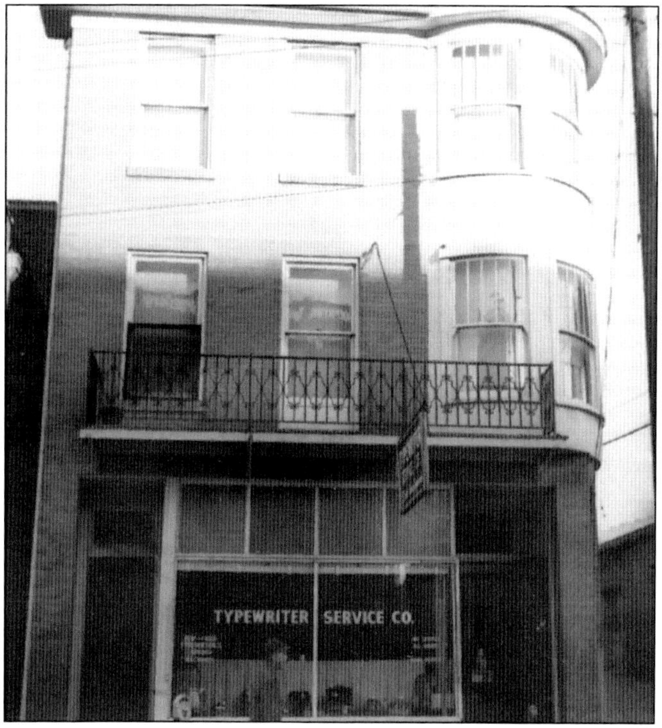

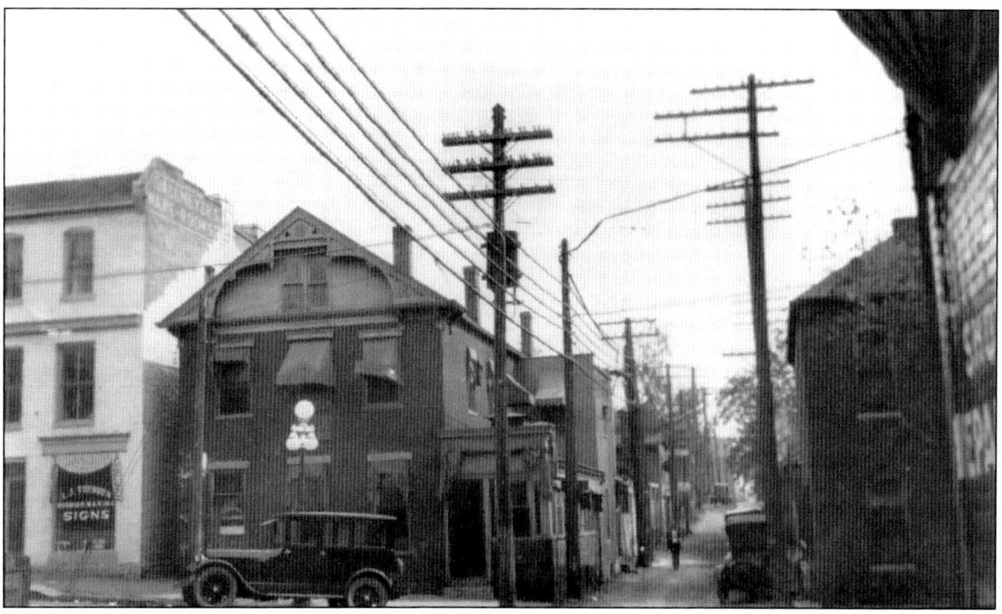

The Capitol Telephone Company, October 13, 1924, on the east side of the 300 block of Madison Street on the alley now known as Wall Street. This building too was torn down for more surface parking and the building of a telephone tower in the 1960s, which since has been removed. (Summers Collection; Missouri State Archives.)

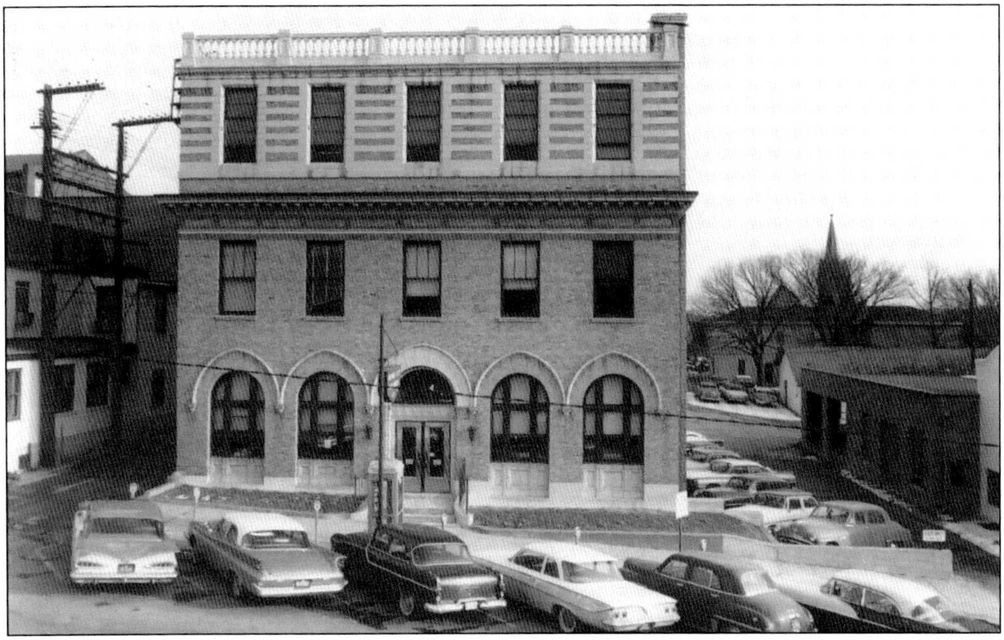

The new telephone company building appears here as it looked in 1957. The building is in the 300 block on the east side of the street, just across the alley from the original building. It has had several additions built on and an aluminum false front attached. (Summers Collection; Missouri State Archives.)

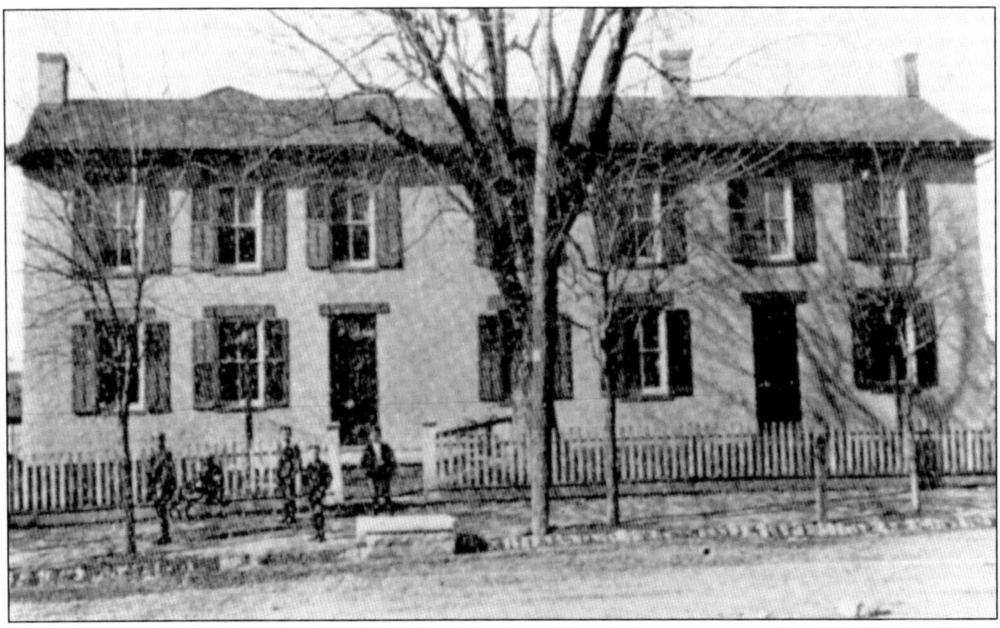

The McCarty House Hotel, owned and run by Burr H. McCarty, was in the 100 block of East McCarty Street. This was a very popular hotel in the mid-19th century because of its good food, hospitality, and the character of its owner. Later the hotel was turned into "flats," in one of those apartments the senior author of this book was born. It has been torn down to make a parking lot. (Summers Collection; Missouri State Archives.)

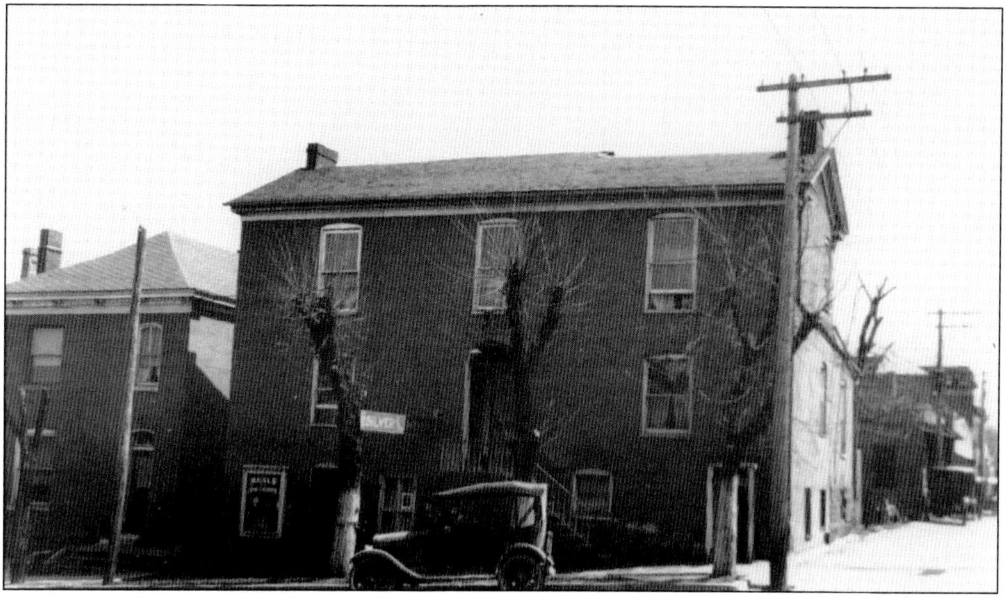

The Silver Moon Hotel and Cafe, a hotel for African Americans, was located on the 200 block of Monroe Street. The all-white Cole County Medical Society met in their private dining room. In the background down the alley is the Menteer Bottling Company. This photo was taken April 15, 1924. This building, too, was torn down for parking. (Summers Collection; Missouri State Archives.)

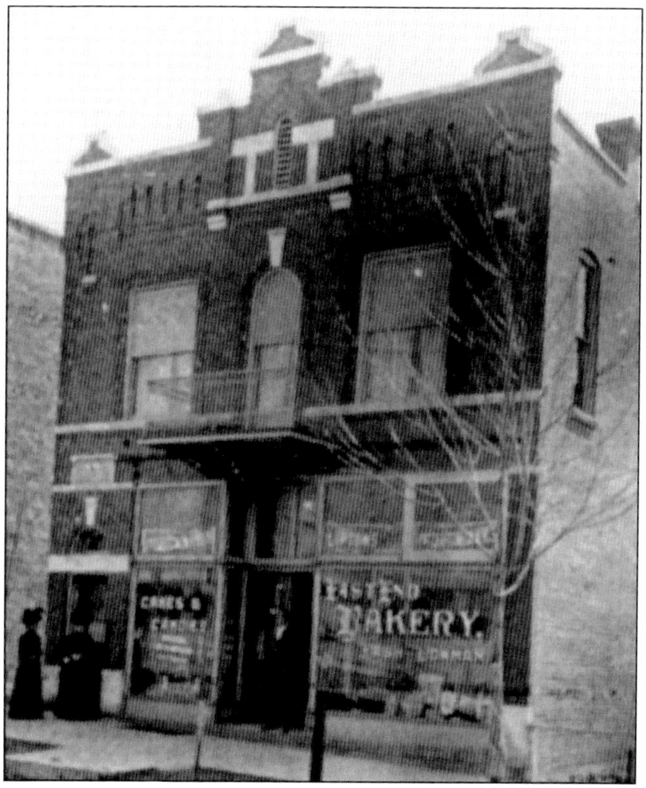

East End Bakery was part of a cluster of shops and businesses on East High Street, several blocks from the main uptown area. Fortunately, most of the buildings are still in this neighborhood, with much of the original architectural integrity intact, but housing different shops. (Summers Collection; Missouri State Archives.)

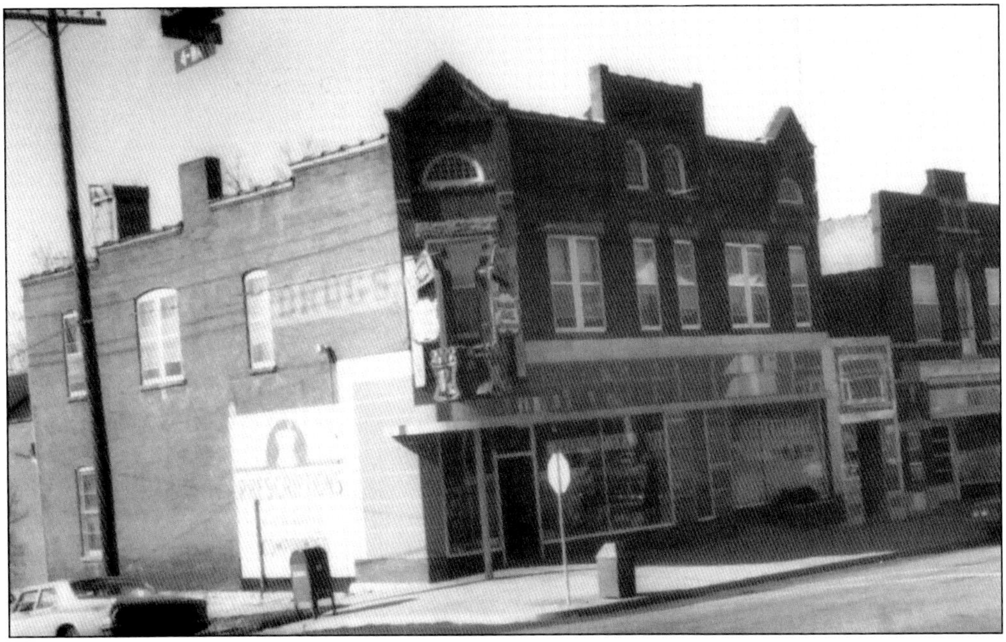

Whaley's East End Drug Store, at 630 East High Street, is also in the cluster of shops on East High Street. Other shops, such as Midstate Vacuum Company and Bertha's Sewing Shop, are seen in the reflection of the windows. Whaley's was built in 1896 and has been a drug store since 1906. (George Grazier Collection; Missouri State Archives.)

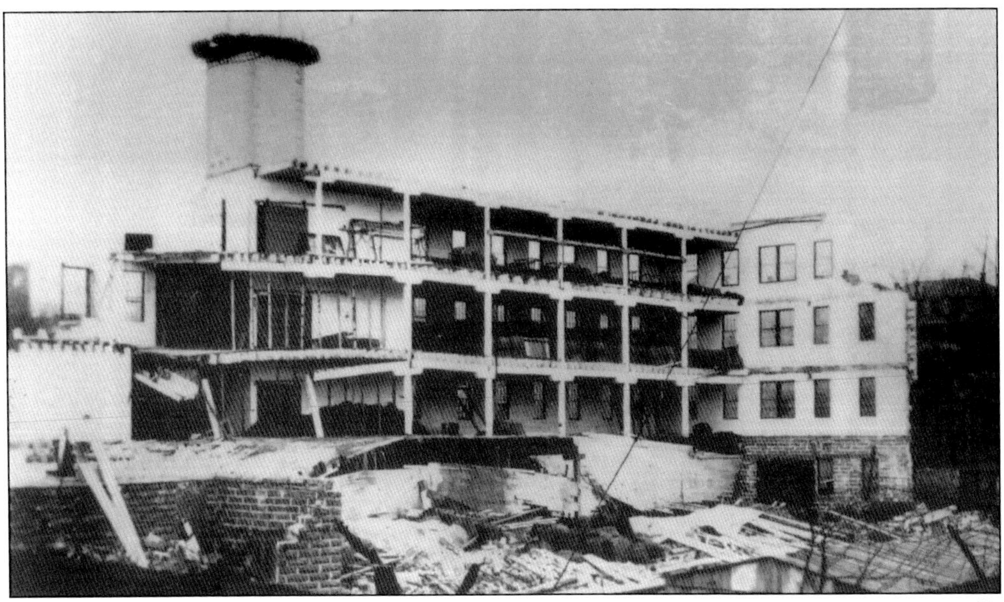

Carson Broom Factory was destroyed as a result of a union struggle in about 1920. Originally located in the prison, this building was built to remove the factory from the compound. Union laborers, unhappy with the use of cheap prison labor, destroyed the factory with a bomb just before it was to be occupied. It was rebuilt with only the first floor of the original building. It is now occupied by Shryack and Hirst Wholesale Grocery Company. (Summers Collection; Missouri State Archives.)

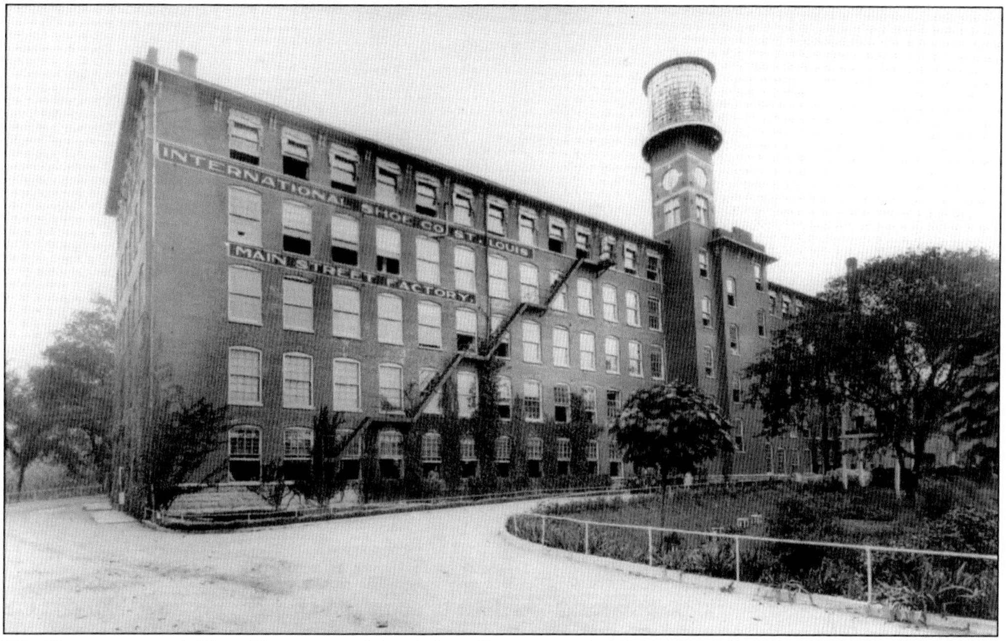

The International Shoe Factory, on East Main Street, was built on land bought by the Commercial Club. The land was given to the owner of the shoe factory—another factory located within the prison—in an effort to entice him to keep his business in the city after it was removed from the prison compound. It remained a shoe factory until the late 1950s, when it closed. The building is now mainly used for warehouse space. (Summers Collection; Missouri State Archives.)

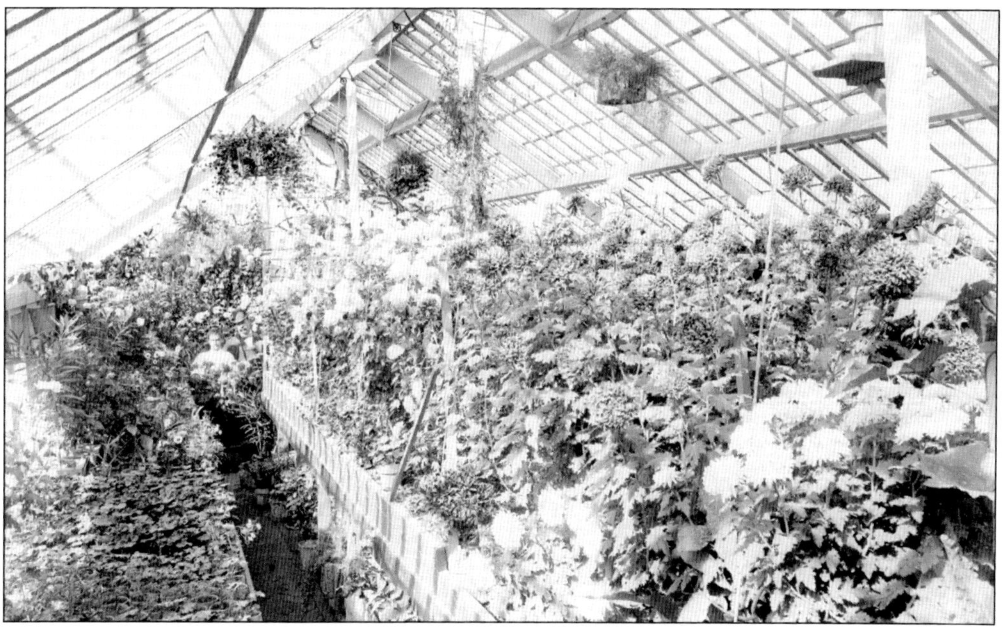

Interior of Busch's Florist pictured here about 1900. Hugo Busch bought out Nagel's Florist in 1890. The florist is on the south side of the City of Jefferson, at the corner of Madison and Dunklin Streets. Busch's Florist was in the Busch family until just a few years ago. It is still in business at the same location. (Ehrhardt Collection; Missouri State Archives.)

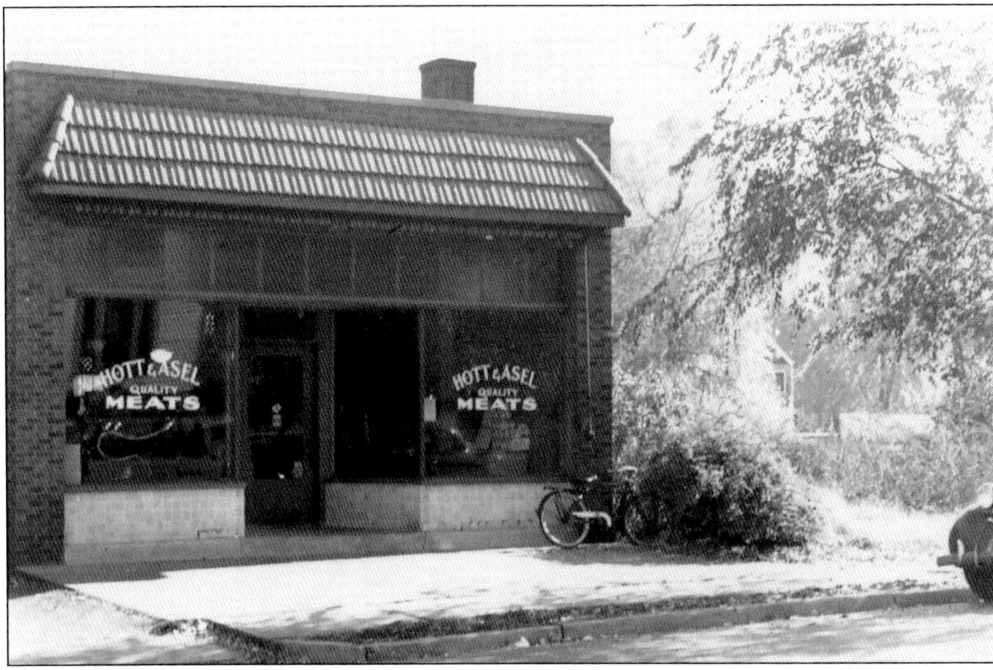

Hott and Asel Meat Market was on the south side in an area known as Munichburg, so named for the multitude of German immigrants who settled in the area. This shop, on Madison Street, was known for its excellent sausage. This photo was taken in the late 1930s. (Mary Gamble.)

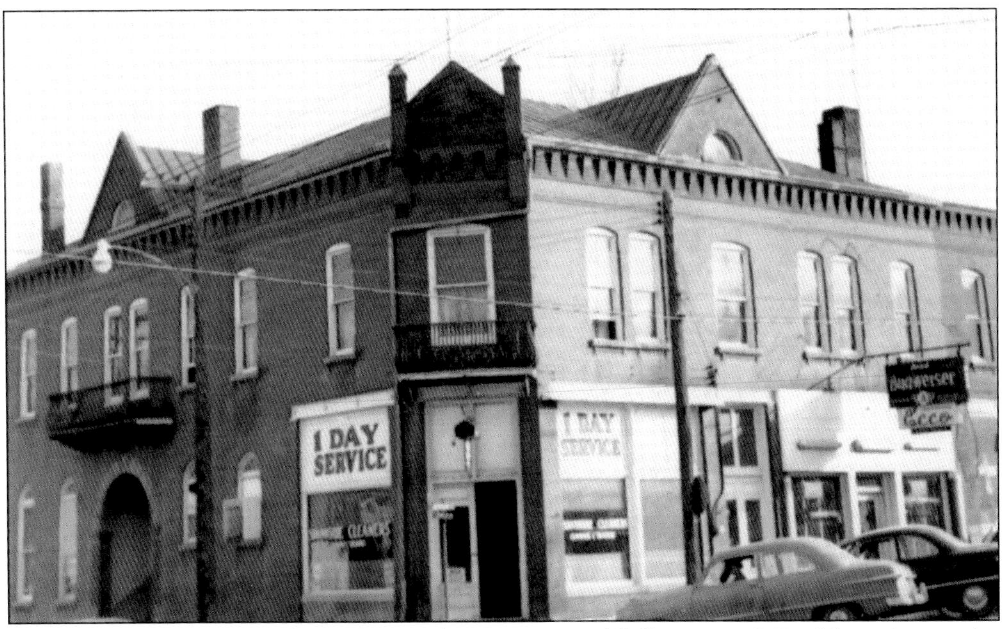

The Farmer's Home Hotel, on the southeast corner of Jefferson and Dunklin, also in the Munichburg area, was said to be a place where farmers would stay when they came to town to sell their produce. The Ecco, a restaurant and bar, has been in this location since the early 1940s. Note the ornamental ironwork on balconies and the brick work in the surrounding buildings. This photo was taken about 1954. (Summers Collection; Missouri State Archives.)

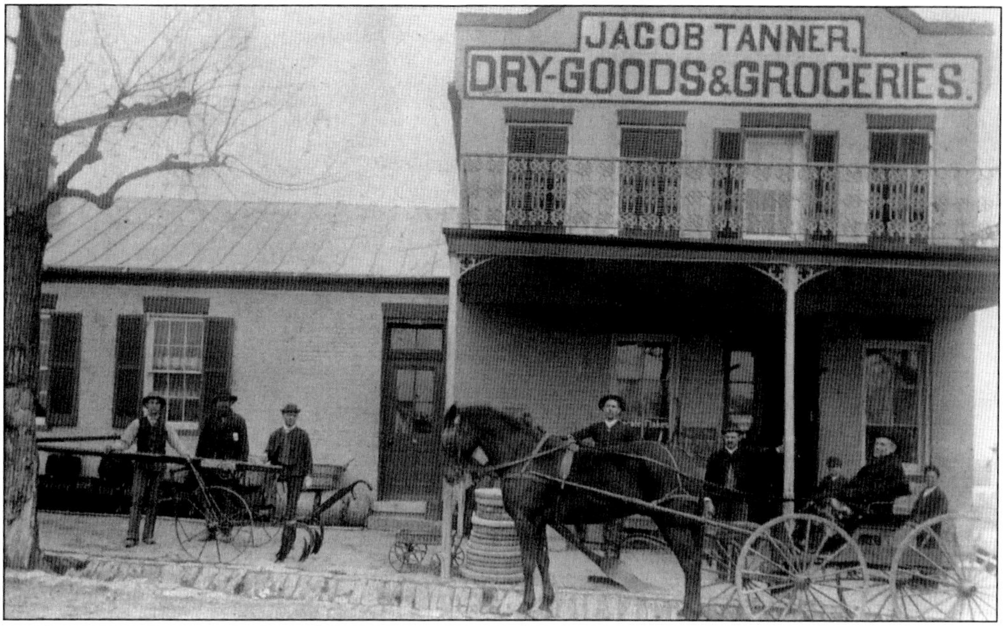

Jacob Tanner's Dry-Goods and Groceries was on the southwest corner of Jefferson and Dunklin, pictured here about 1890. This was also in the Munichburg area and had unique ironwork. Later, the family went into the funeral business at the same location. (Summers Collection; Missouri State Archives.)

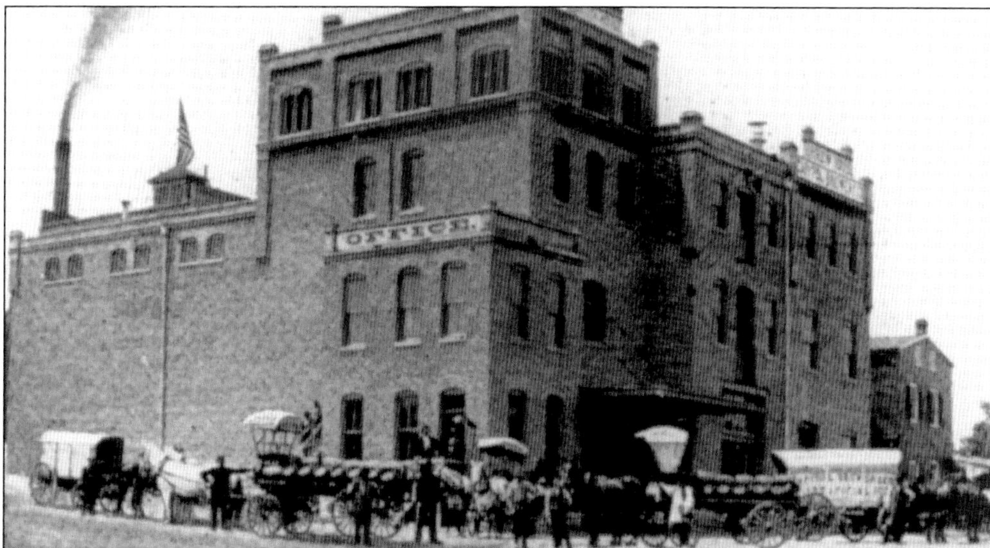

The Capitol Brewery Company was owned by the Moerschel brothers. The brewery, under several owners, had a 100-year history, from 1849–1949, and was located in the Munichburg area on Dunklin Street. During prohibition it bottled soft drinks. After World War II, when Anheuser-Busch transported their bottled beer all over the United States, the competition proved to be too much for this local brewery. The family who owned it still has a soft drink bottling plant close to the brewery location. This photo is from the 1890s. (Summers Collection; Missouri State Archives.)

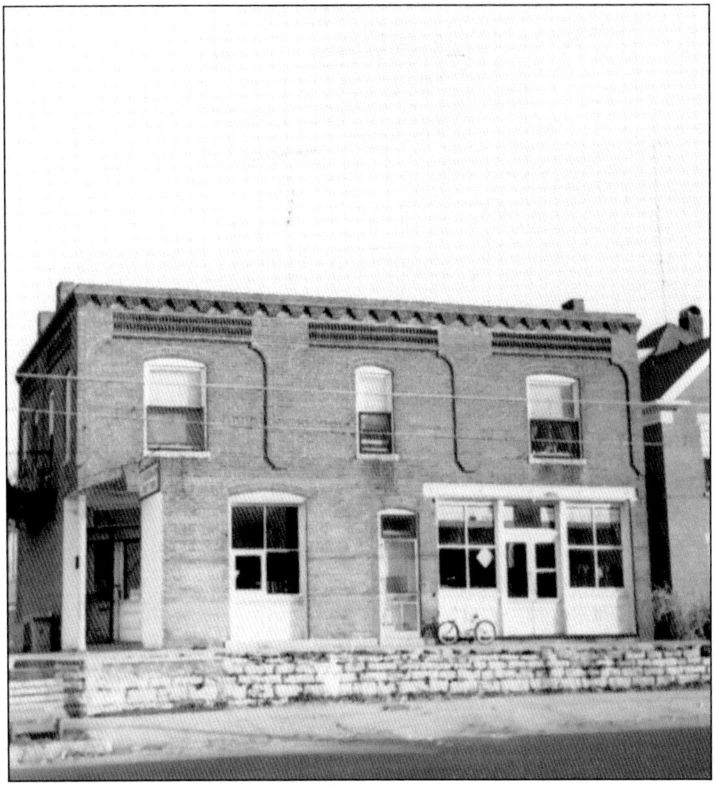

A neighborhood grocery on the southeast corner of Jefferson and Atchison also in Munichburg. Note the brick and ironwork. This photo was taken about 1954. (Summers Collection; Missouri State Archives.)

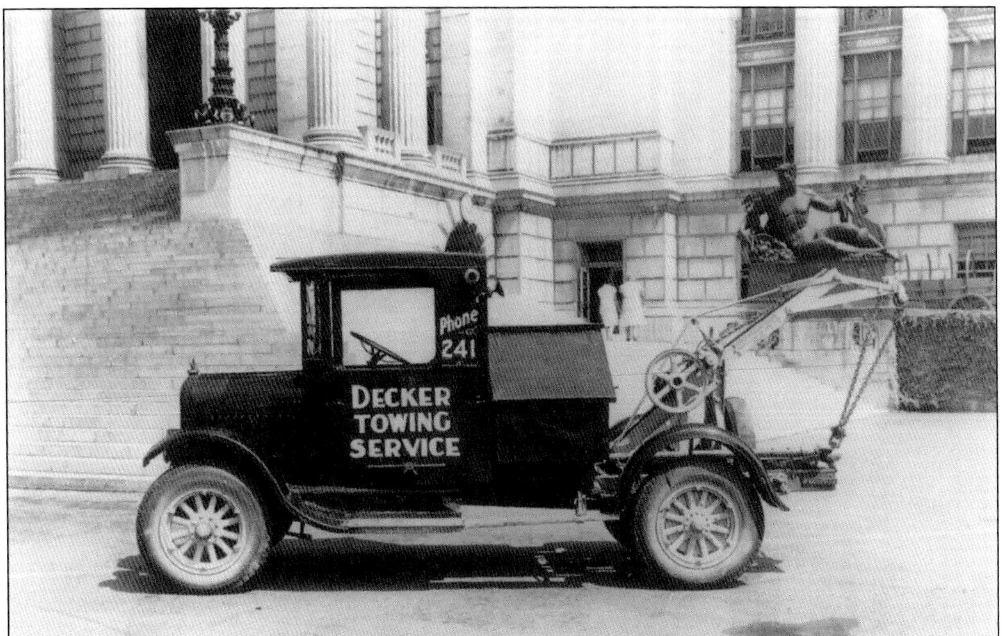

The first tow truck in the City of Jefferson was built by William Decker III, and is proudly displayed in front of the Capitol about 1925. Mr. Decker had a Dodge dealership and car repair shops located on High Street and Jefferson at different times. (Bill Decker.)

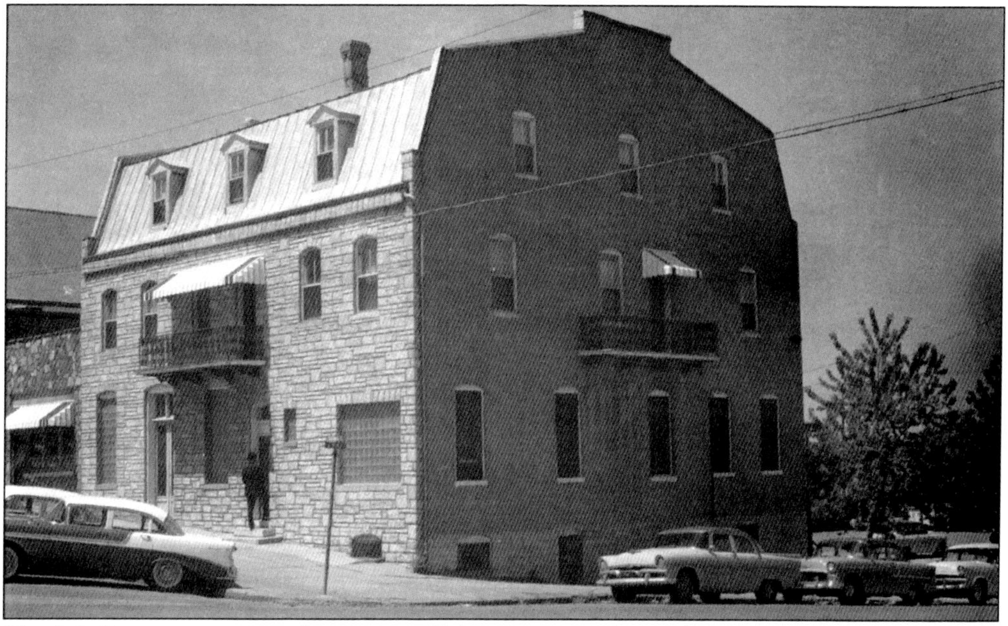

The J.C. Bruns grocery on the corner of Main Street and Broadway can be seen in this 1958 photo. Note the stone and ironwork. The building was eventually torn down for parking. (Joe Kroeger.)

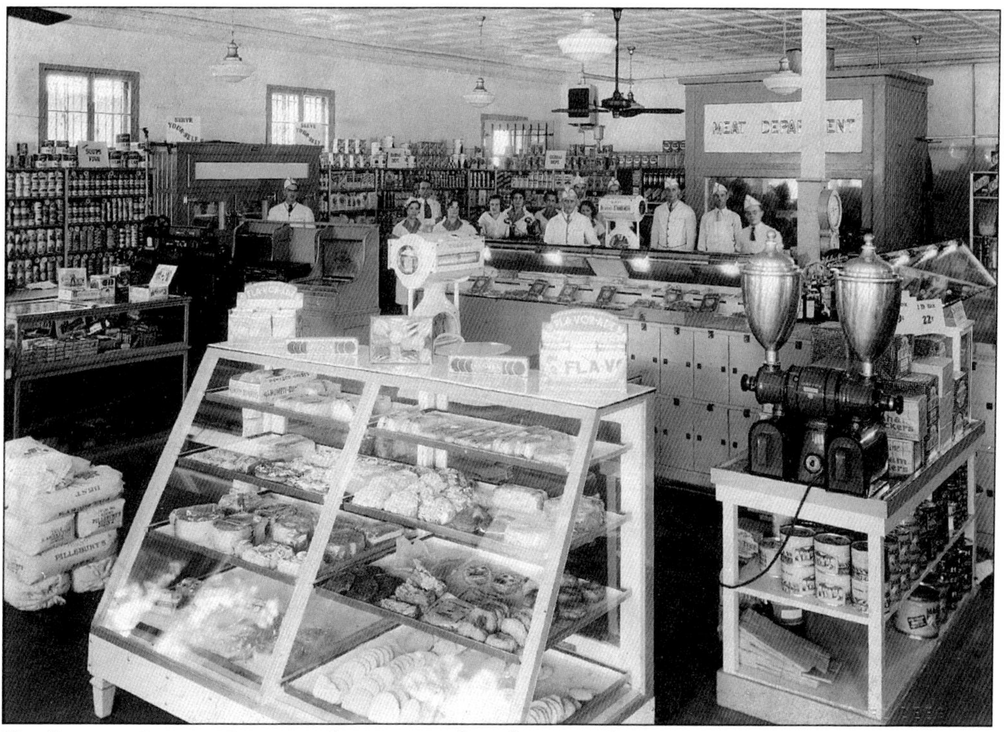

Knollmeyer Grocery Store on the corner of Mulberry and West McCarty later became Kroger Grocery Store. This 1920s photo was taken by Carl Deeg. (Ehrhardt Collection; Missouri State Archives.)

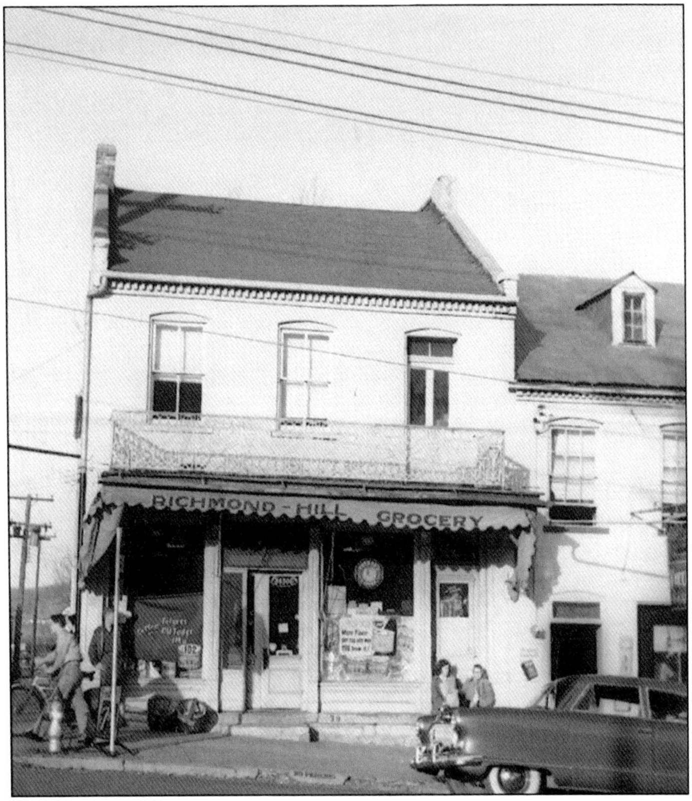

Richmond Hill Grocery Store at 630 West Main Street was built about 1870. It is on the northeast corner of Boliver and West Main Street, a block from what was the tollbooth for the old bridge. Richmond Hill is an extended part of the Millbottom area of the City of Jefferson. This photo was taken about 1954. Again, note the beautiful ironwork. (Summers Collection; Missouri State Archives.)

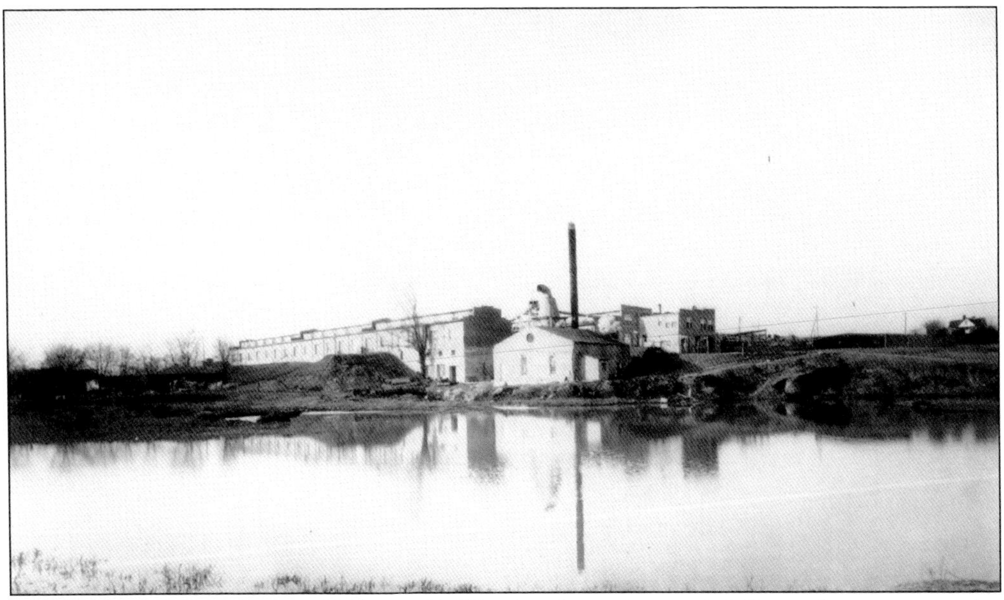

This manufacturing plant on Highway 50 West has housed several different factories over the years. They included Hayes Hickory Hitters, a wooden car bumper manufacturer; The Egg Crate and Filler Company; a duck decoy company; and the Oberman Men's Pants Manufacturing Company. Currently the building is being used as the Elks Club. This photo was made about 1920. (Jim Twyman.)

Five

Millbottom and Floods

The area just west of the Capitol was known as Goose Bottom, originally because of geese being raised in the bottom and swimming on Wears Creek. Along Wears Creek, two flour mills were built and a busy community of mainly German Catholics developed. Many in the area worked at the mills, on the river, and for the railroads and other businesses that developed in the neighborhood. Most of the residents attended church at St. Peter's Catholic Church. The neighborhood came to be called Millbottom.

Since the area was around Wears Creek, it was often subject to flooding. Being a tributary of the Missouri River, the creek often flooded with spring thaws or an excess of rain. People were accustomed to moving their belongings to the second floor when floods came, which they did on a regular basis. Over the years, there have been many major floods. The "Five Hundred Year" flood swept through in 1993, so named because it was thought the area had not seen the likes of a flood so destructive for half a millennium.

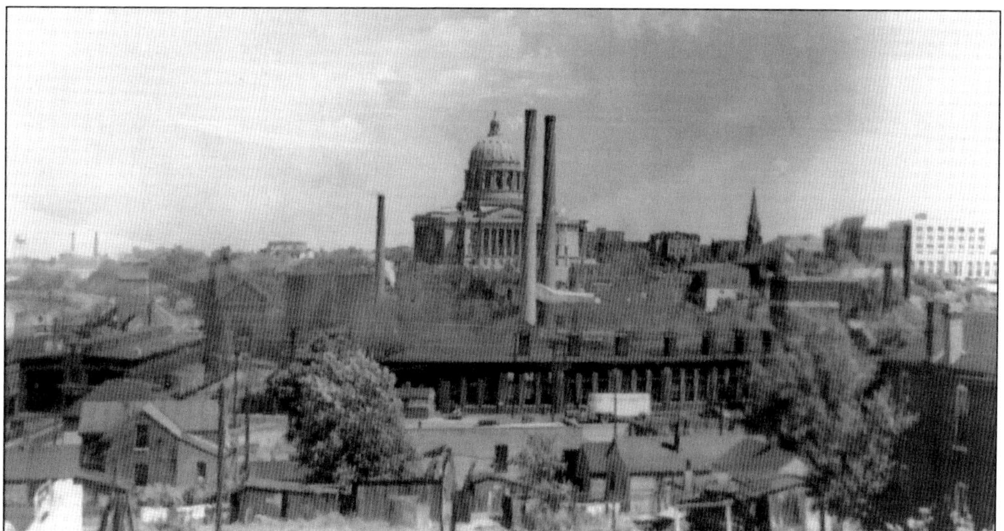

Pictured is Millbottom, looking east in 1939. Some of the notable points are the houses, railroad tracks, and round house. At the bend in the river is the prison, the white painted Governor's Mansion, the present capitol, the United States Post Office and Courts, St. Peter's Church, the Supreme Court, and the new Broadway State Office Building. (Joe Kroeger.)

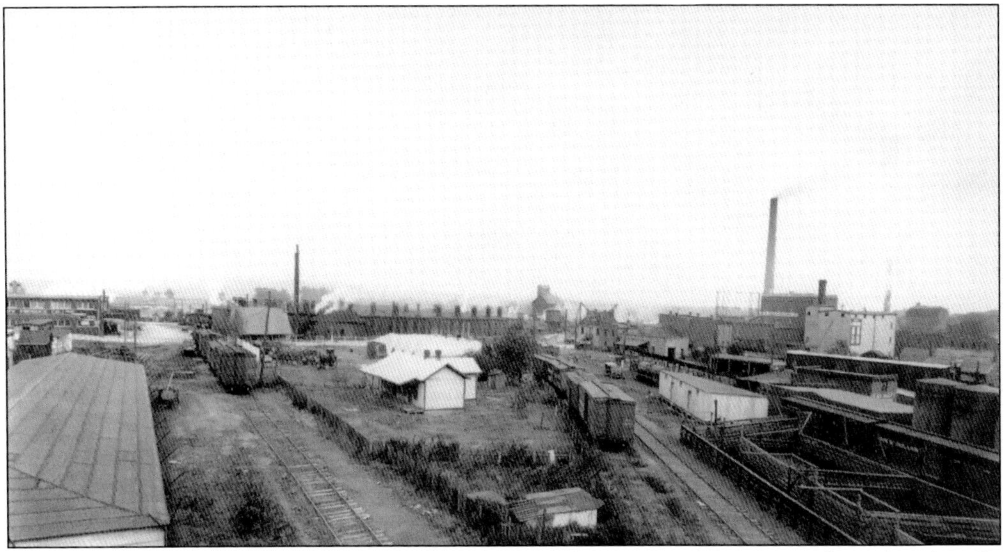

The neighborhood of Millbottom, looking north towards the river about 1910. The railroad tracks branched off the main east-west line, to deal with industry in Millbottom. In the center of the photo on the horizon, note the cattle pens, the Jefferson City produce, the feed store, Dulle Mills, the power plant, and the railroad round house with housing mixed in. (Jim Twyman)

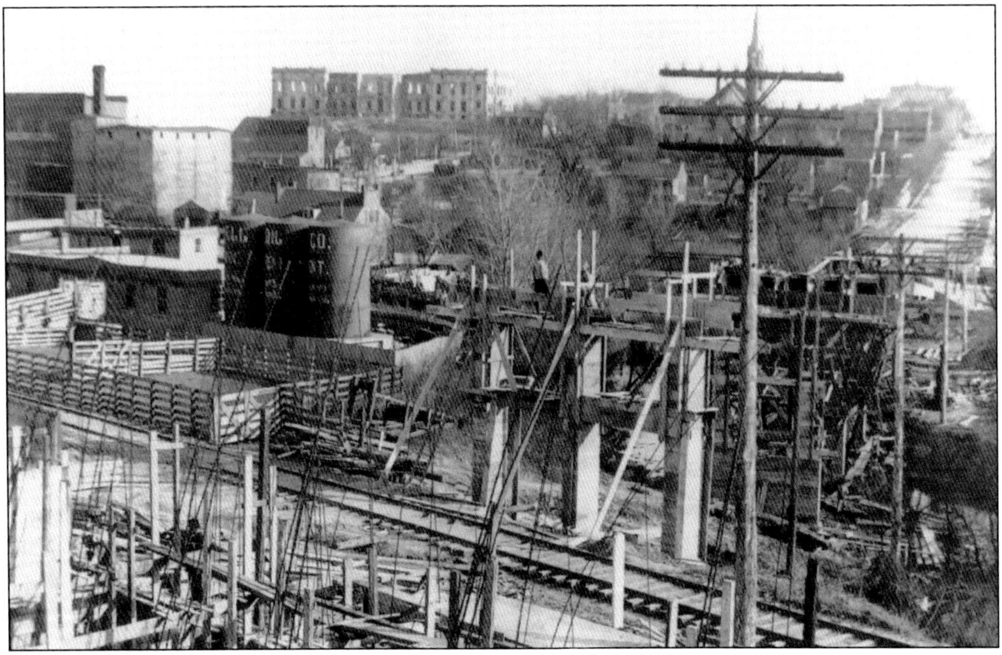

The first High Street Viaduct under construction, with forms in place to pour concrete for foundation. The scene is taken from the bluff above, in 1911, looking from west to east of Millbottom. Note cattle pens, oil storage tanks, Dulle Mills, St. Peter's Church, the burned-out shell of the Capitol and at the top of High Street, in the top right of the photo, the United States Post Office and Courts Building. (Bryan Pope)

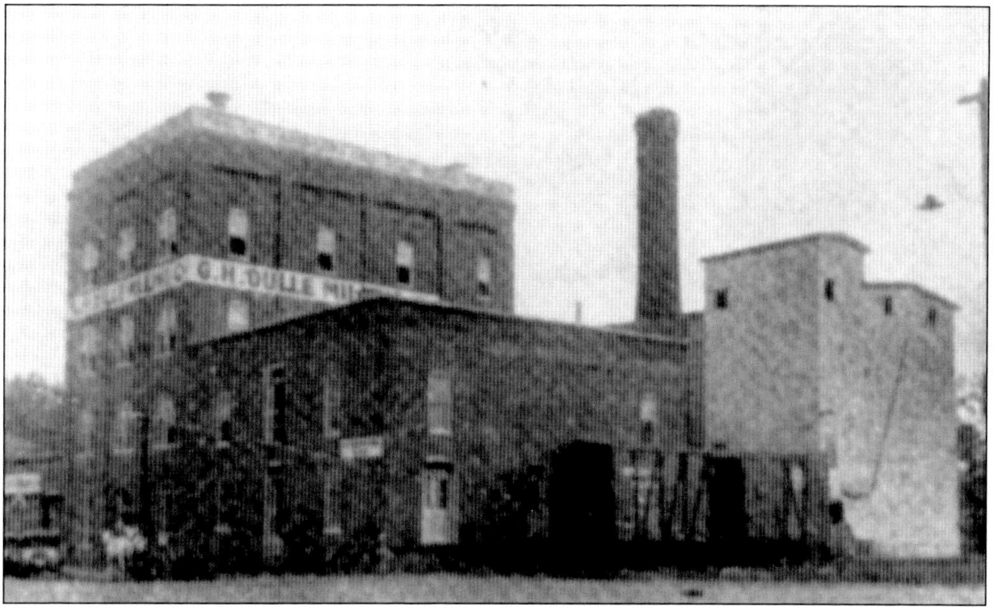

The G.H. Dulle Mill, about 1931, shows a boxcar near. Dulle flour was shipped by train all over the nation and even internationally. St Peter's Church is in the background. (Summers Collection; Missouri State Archives.)

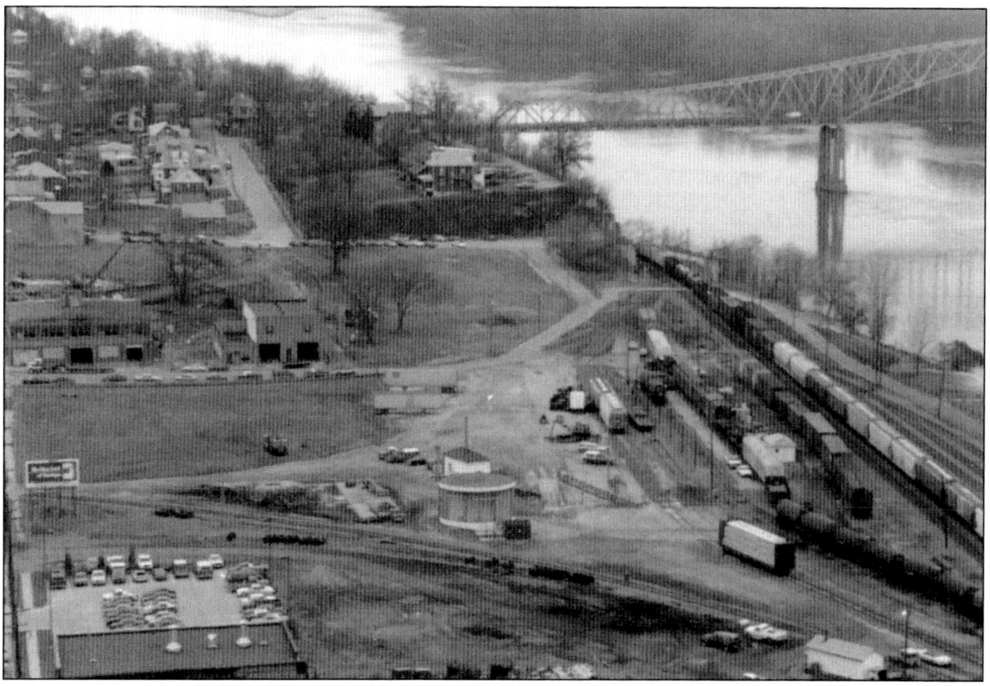

Millbottom viewed from the top of the Capitol in January 1987, with most of the original buildings removed during the "urban renewal" days of the 1970s. Note the railroad is still in place east-west, although there are not as many spurs off to the south. The power plant is still in place and we see the second Missouri River bridge up river. (Summers Collection; Missouri State Archives.)

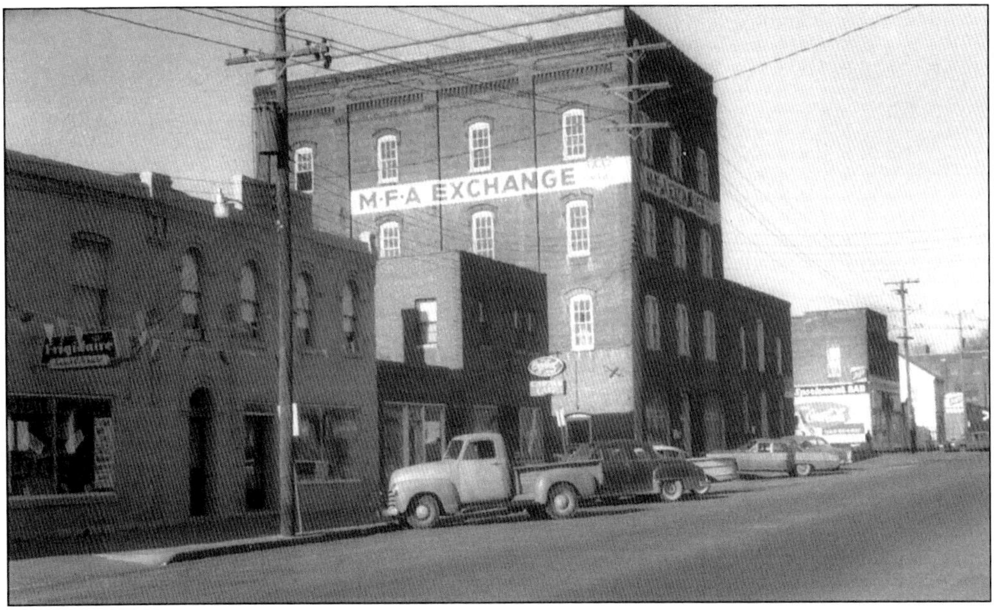

View of businesses in Millbottom, in 1940s, on West Main Street looking west. (George Grazier Collection; Missouri State Archives.)

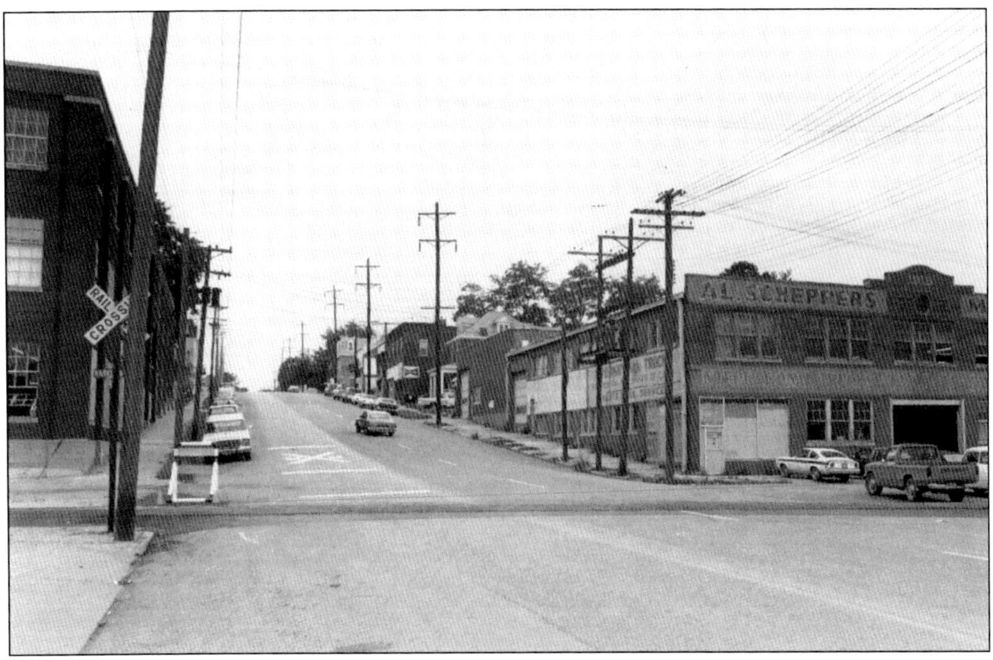

This photo of Millbottom at the corner of West Main Street and Harrison Street was taken in the early 1970s showing the Missouri Department of Transportation Building, which remains today, on the left. On the right was Al Scheppers' truck dealership, with houses and businesses behind. At the top of the hill is Richmond Hill Grocery. All of these buildings have been torn down to build the James C. Kirkpatrick State Information Center, except the Richmond Hill Grocery Store, which has been turned into a daycare center particularly for state workers. (Historic City of Jefferson Archives; Missouri State Archives.)

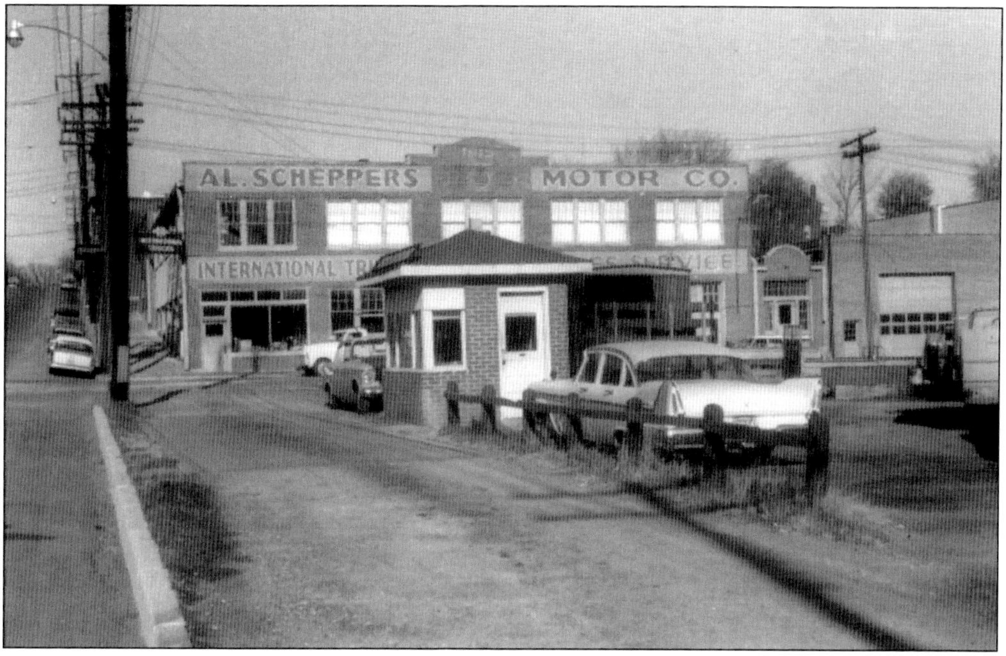

More businesses in Millbottom, north of West Main Street, on Harrison Street, were Al Scheppers' Motor Co. and the City Scales in the foreground. This is now a parking lot and the James C. Kirkpatrick State Information Center. The buildings shown here are all torn down.(George Grazier Collection; Missouri State Archives.)

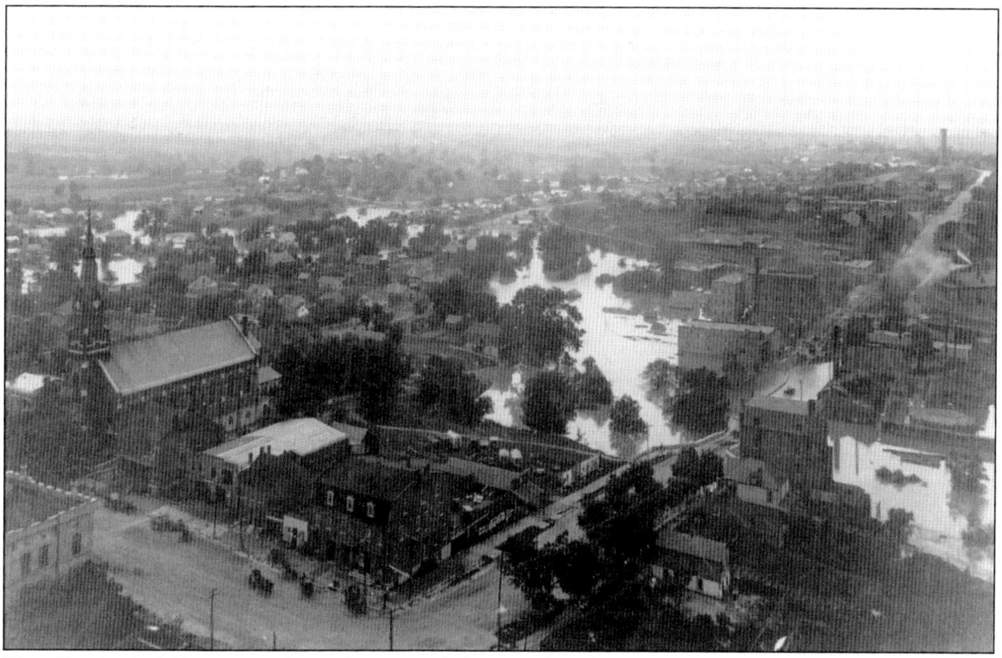

The flood of 1903 as seen from the capitol dome. This shows water from Wears Creek backing up over West Main Street and low-lying areas. St. Peter's Church and the State Armory are seen in the lower left corner. (Joe Kroeger.)

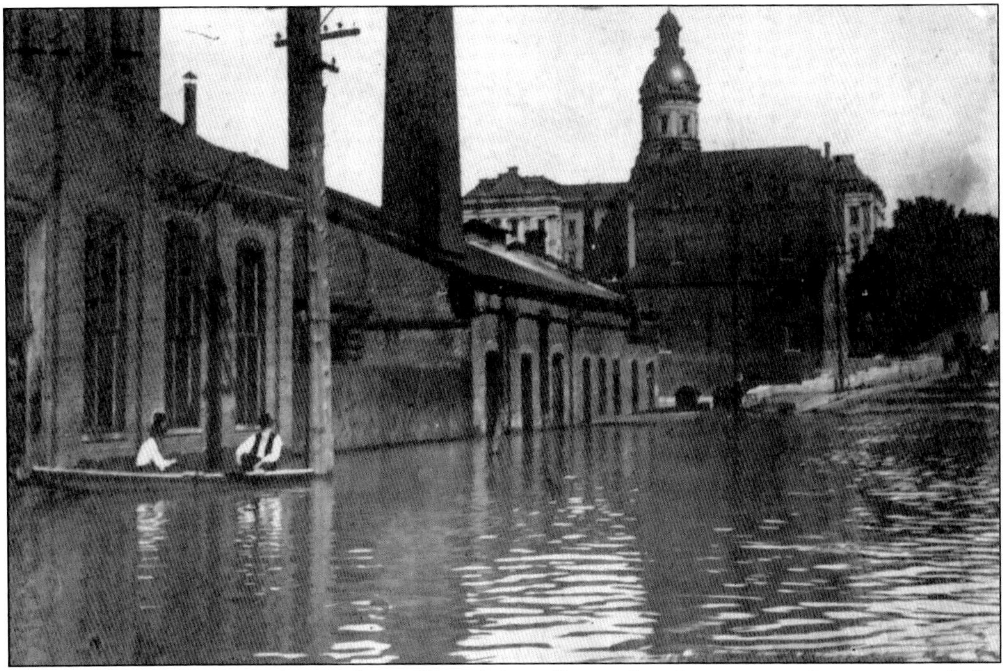

Two men floating in a boat along West Main Street by the power plant, west of the Capitol, during the flood of 1903. The second capitol, with renovations from 1888, is in the background.(Joe Kleene Collection; Missouri State Archives.)

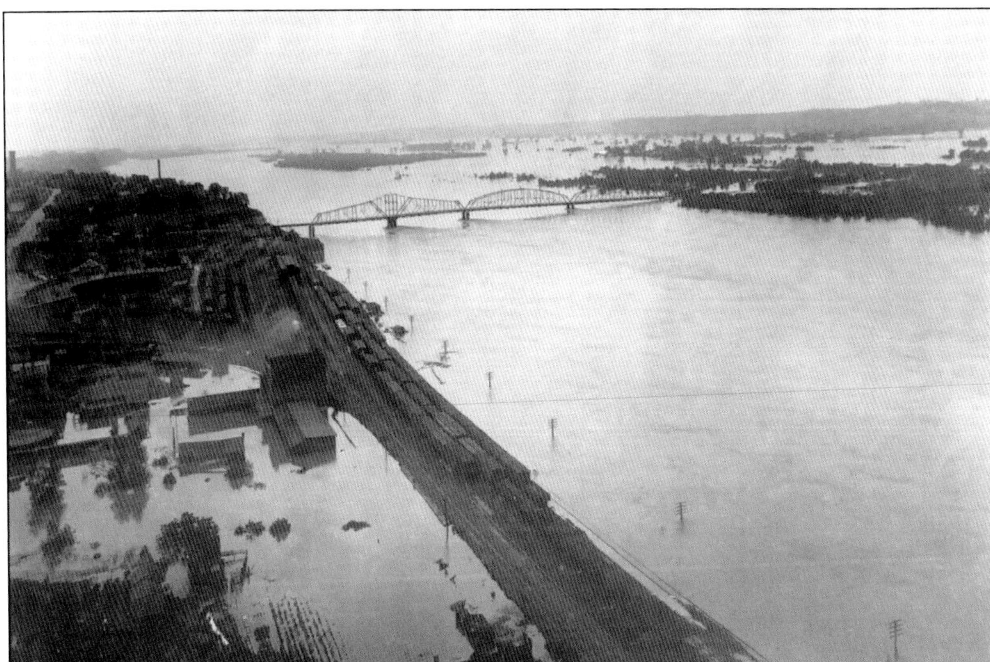

Another view of the flood of 1903 from the capitol dome, glancing northwest into Callaway County as well as Wears Creek overflowing. Note the round house, the 1896 bridge, and the water tower in the background. (Joe Kroeger.)

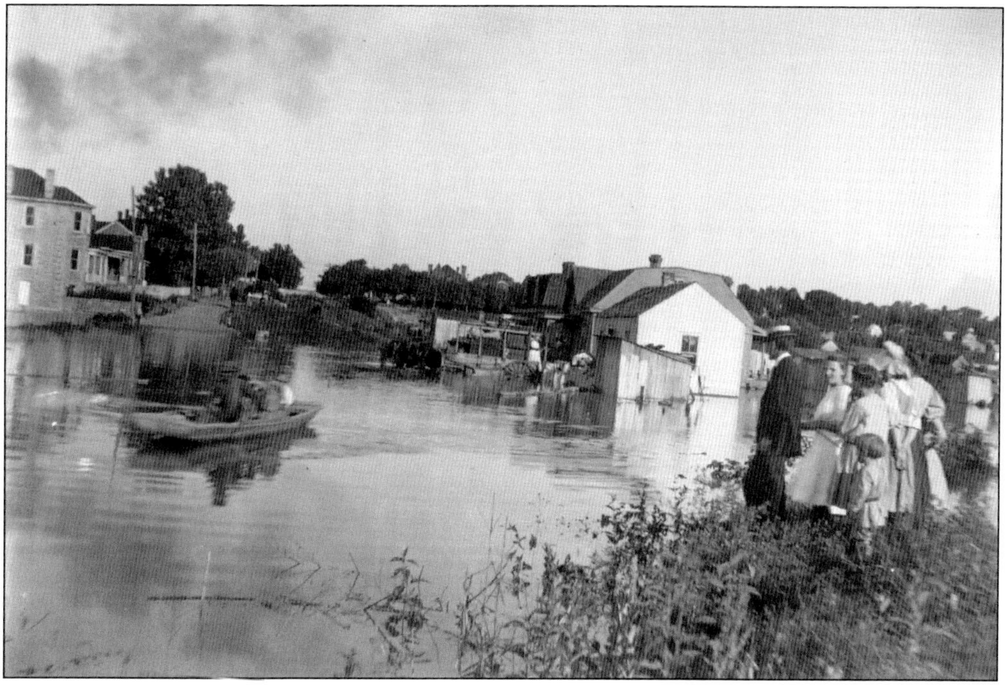

The flood of 1906 just south of Millbottom on Mulberry Street. A family looks on while a boat travels down the street. (Joe Kroeger.)

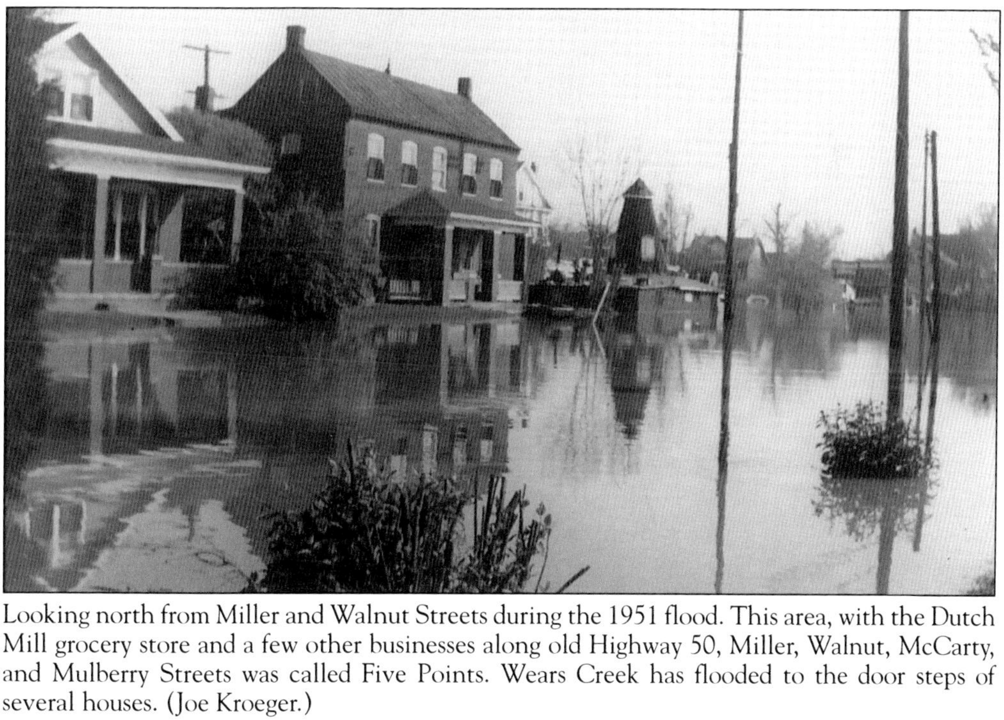

Looking north from Miller and Walnut Streets during the 1951 flood. This area, with the Dutch Mill grocery store and a few other businesses along old Highway 50, Miller, Walnut, McCarty, and Mulberry Streets was called Five Points. Wears Creek has flooded to the door steps of several houses. (Joe Kroeger.)

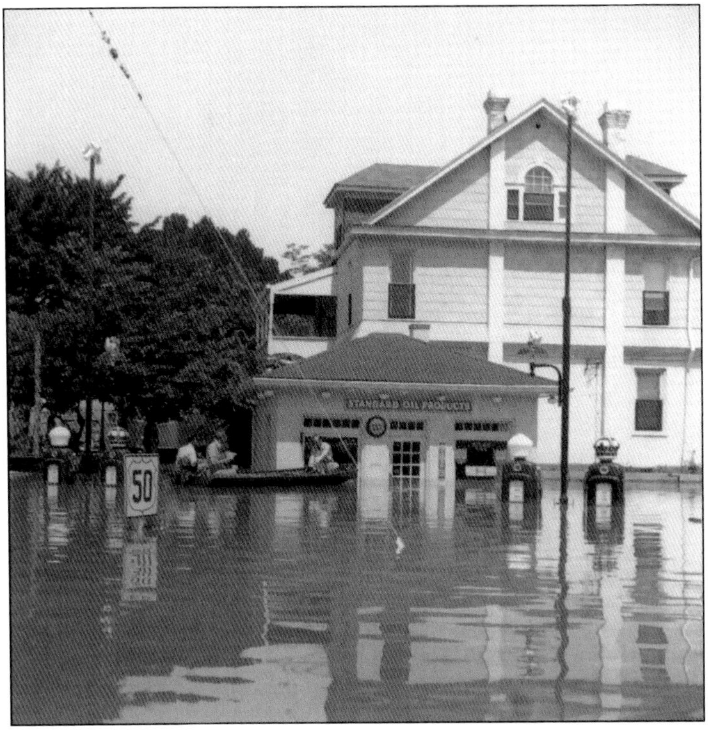

The 1951 flood at Five Points got up to mid-window at Harry Kallenbach's Standard Oil Service Station. The rooming house in back is up on a hill and was high enough so that it looked like a small island. Note the Highway 50 sign and men in the boat. (Joe Kroeger)

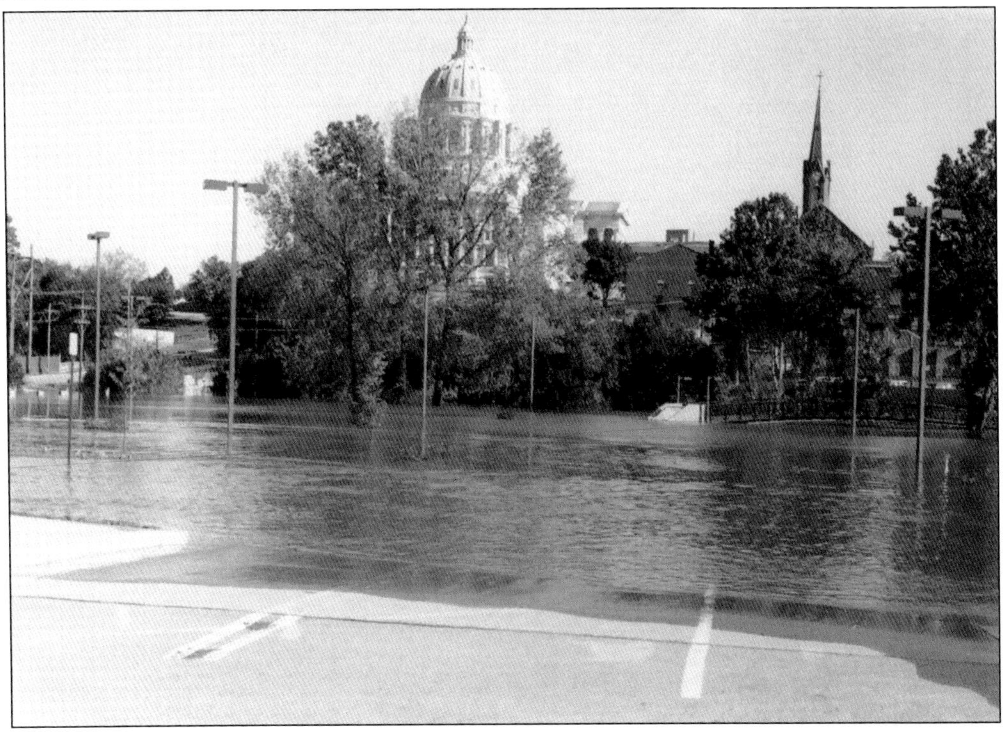

The flood of 1986 showing Millbottom looking west to east. The buildings that characterized Millbottom are now gone in favor of surface parking for state workers. On the hill above is the present capitol, as well as St. Peter's School and Church. (Joe Kroeger.)

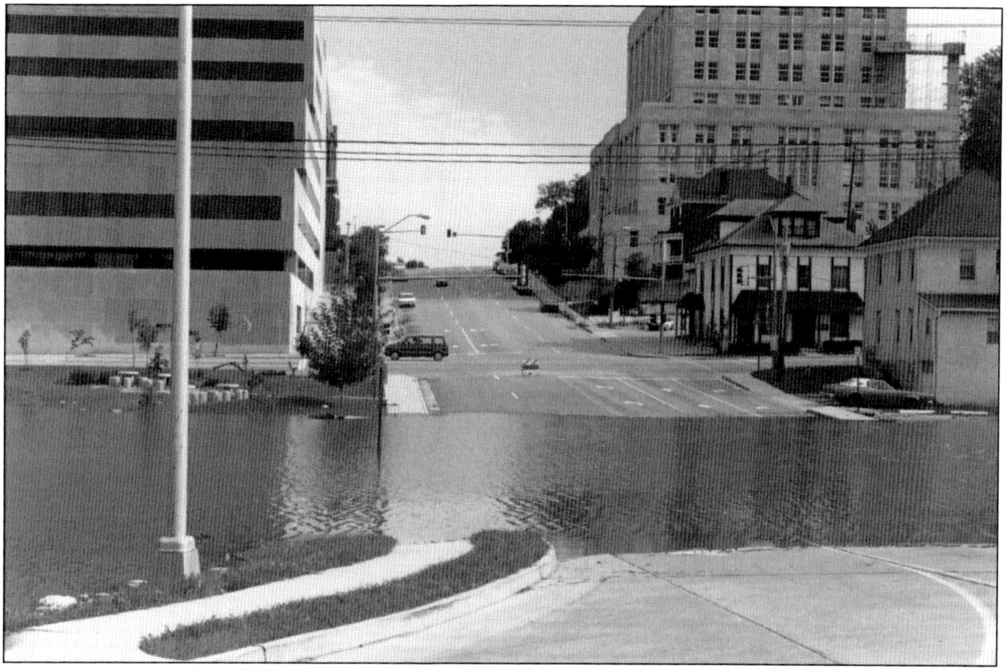

Another view of the 1986 flood, with Wears Creek overflowing enough to cover the Rex M. Whitten Expressway. This was taken from the corner of Broadway and Miller Streets looking to McCarty and High Streets. To the left of Broadway is the new Truman State Office Building and St. Peter's Church. To the right of Broadway is the Broadway State Office Building. (Joe Kroeger.)

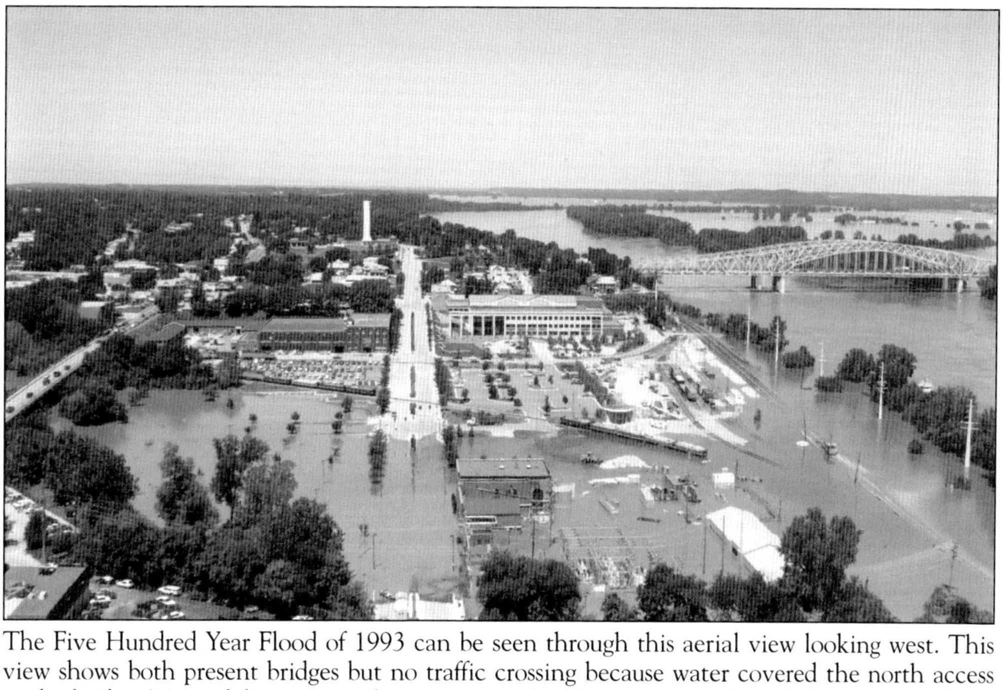

The Five Hundred Year Flood of 1993 can be seen through this aerial view looking west. This view shows both present bridges but no traffic crossing because water covered the north access to the bridge. Most of the train tracks were covered with water. Note how Millbottom has been changed. Very little of its original character is left. (Randy Z. Wright; Missouri State Archives.)

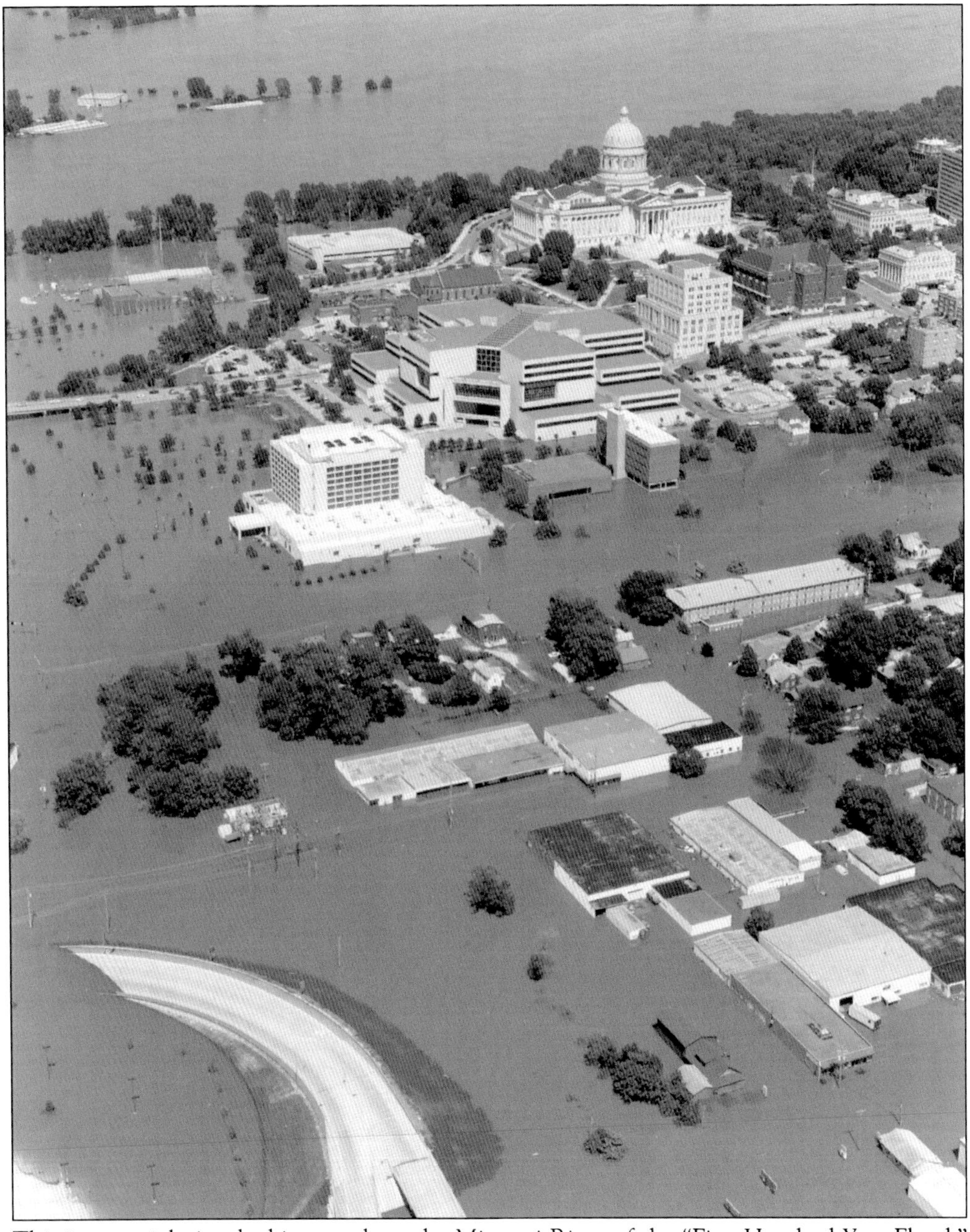

This is an aerial view looking north to the Missouri River of the "Five Hundred Year Flood." Wears Creek has covered Millbottom, Five Points, and much more south and east than ever before in the memory of citizens. Buildings of interest are the Hotel DeVille, State Health Laboratory, Capitol Plaza Hotel, Truman State Office Building, Broadway Office Building, Supreme Court Building, United States Post Office, St. Peter's School and Church, and the Capitol. (Michael Wright; Missouri State Archives)

Six

City of Jefferson Street Scenes

The City of Jefferson was once known as "Brick Town" because most of the buildings were of brick and stone from local brickyards and quarries. There is a unique feel to the city, as a result of its mixed heritage as a river town, the "Old South" English and Scot, with slaves of the original settlers, the frontier, the German immigrants, the state government buildings, the railroad buildings, influence of the prison on the economy, and Lincoln University. We hope to convey some of the feeling of the city through these street scenes.

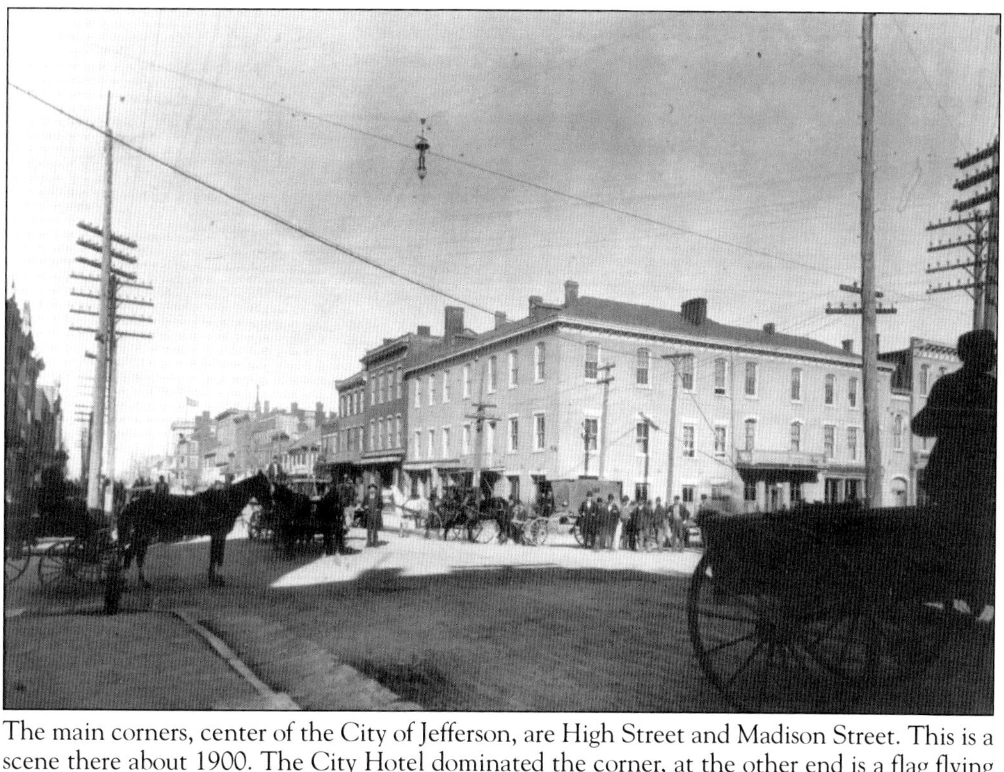

The main corners, center of the City of Jefferson, are High Street and Madison Street. This is a scene there about 1900. The City Hotel dominated the corner, at the other end is a flag flying on the United States Post Office and Courts Building. This photo is looking west along High Street. (Summers Collection; Missouri State Archives.)

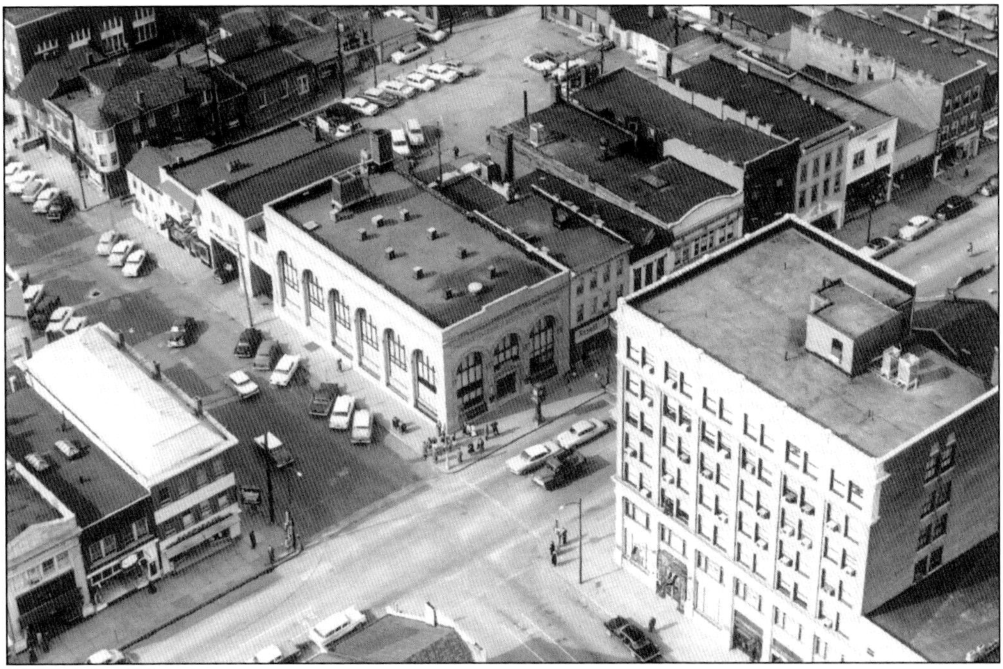

This aerial view of the corner of High and Madison in the 1960s shows the Central Trust Building on the northwest corner, the Hope Building on the northeast corner, Schneiders Clothing on the southeast corner, and the Exchange Bank Building on the southwest corner. (Summers Collection; Missouri State Archives.)

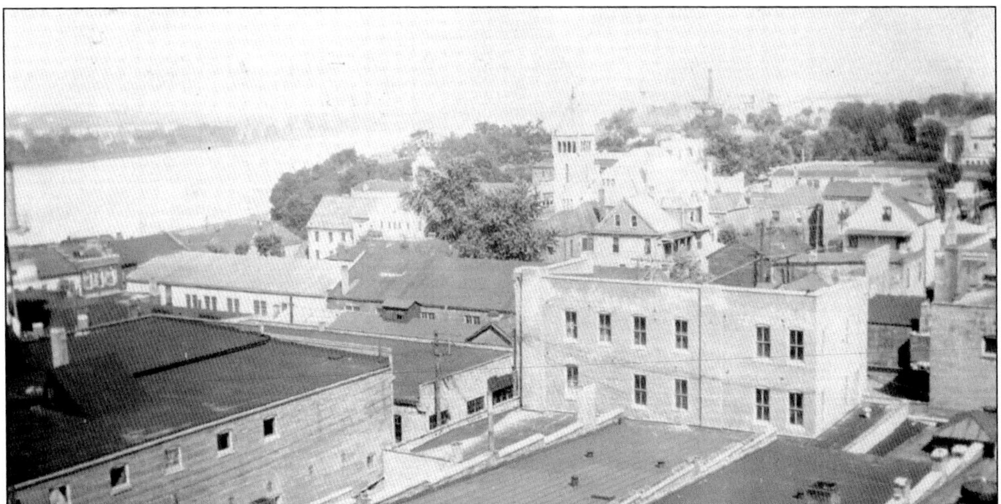

This view looking east from the 7th floor of the Central Trust Building was taken in the 1920s. Of note is the alley, traditionally called Hog Alley, now Commercial Street, the water tower from Hugh Stevens Press, Shryack-Hirst Wholesale Grocery Company, Vetter's Machine Shop, and the Methodist and Baptist Churches on Capitol Avenue. The back of the large house to center right was built for Ally Heskett as a rooming house, later the author's father bought it and raised young Joseph Summers there. In the background note the Missouri River and the Missouri State Prison. (Summers Collection; Missouri State Archives.)

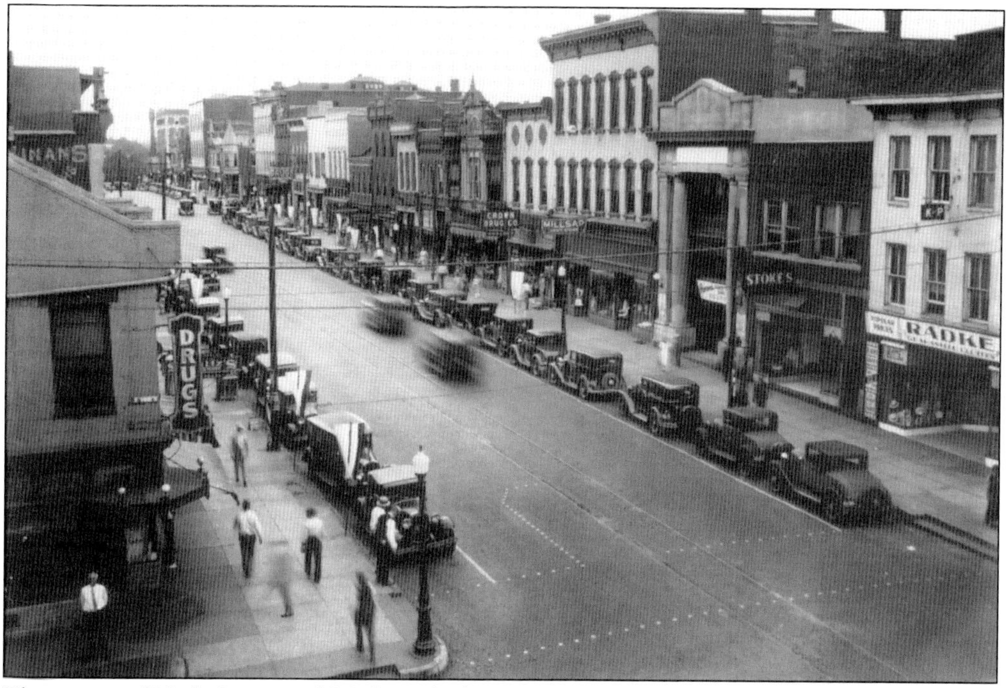

The corner of High Street and Madison looking east in the late 1920s, showing the merchants of the time. (Summers Collection; Missouri State Archives.)

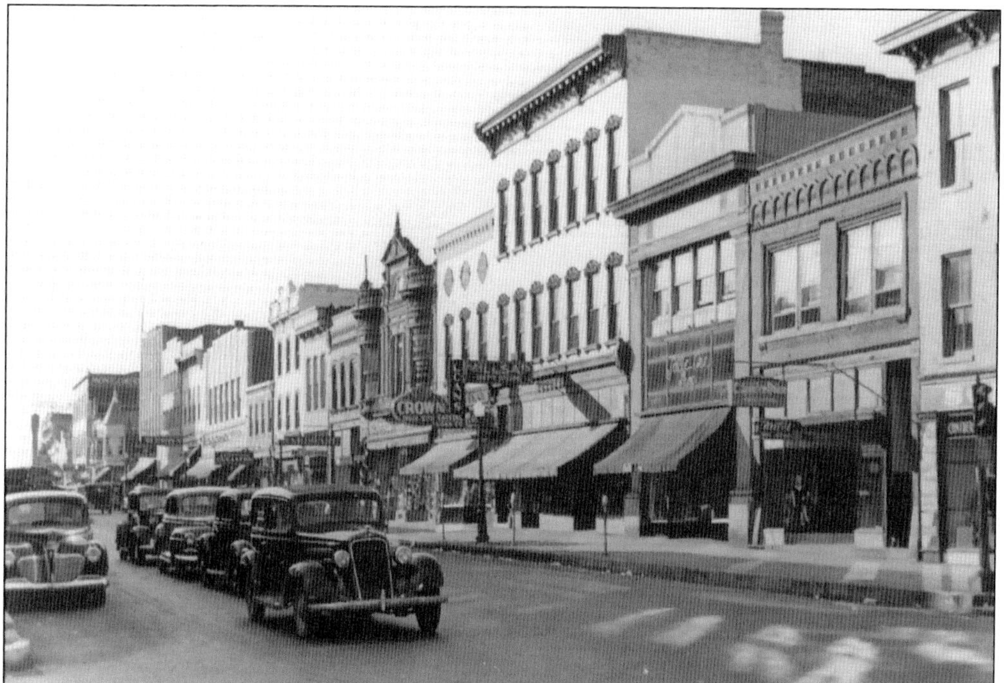
The 200 block East High Street looked like this in the early 1940s. This scene is of the south side of the street. Note the detail of the brick buildings. (Summers Collection; Missouri State Archives.)

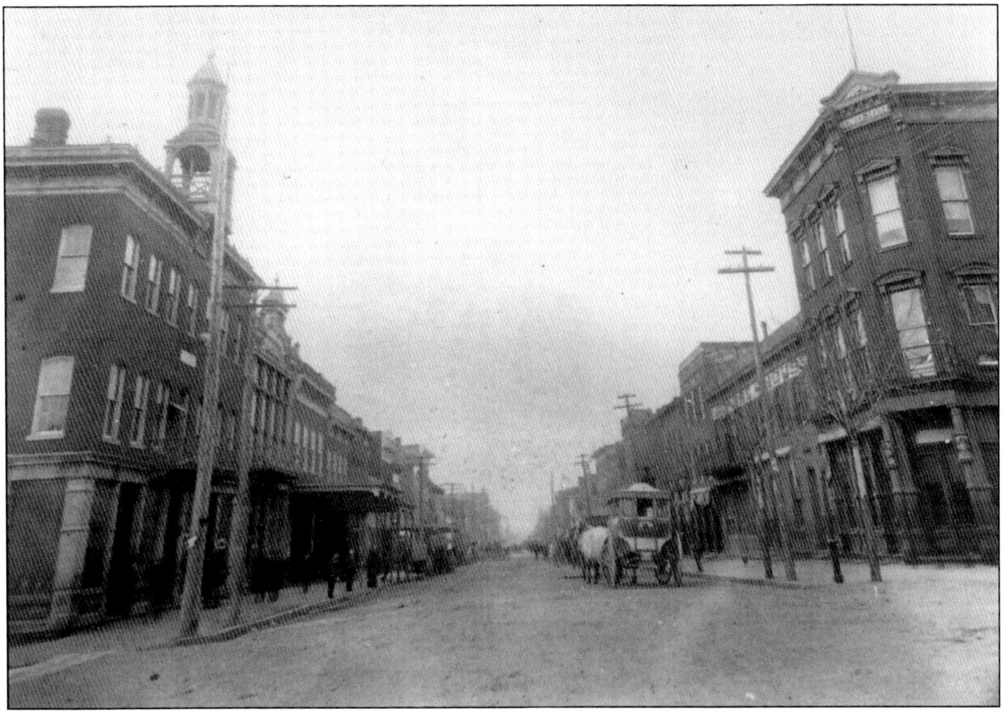

From the east looking west in the 200 block of East High Street, this photo was taken in 1891. It shows a horse-drawn 'bus" showing the back entrance. This was taken from the corner of Monroe Street. Bragg Hall is on the left corner and the Monroe House Hotel as it looked, incomplete, for nearly 100 years. (Summers Collection; Missouri State Archives.)

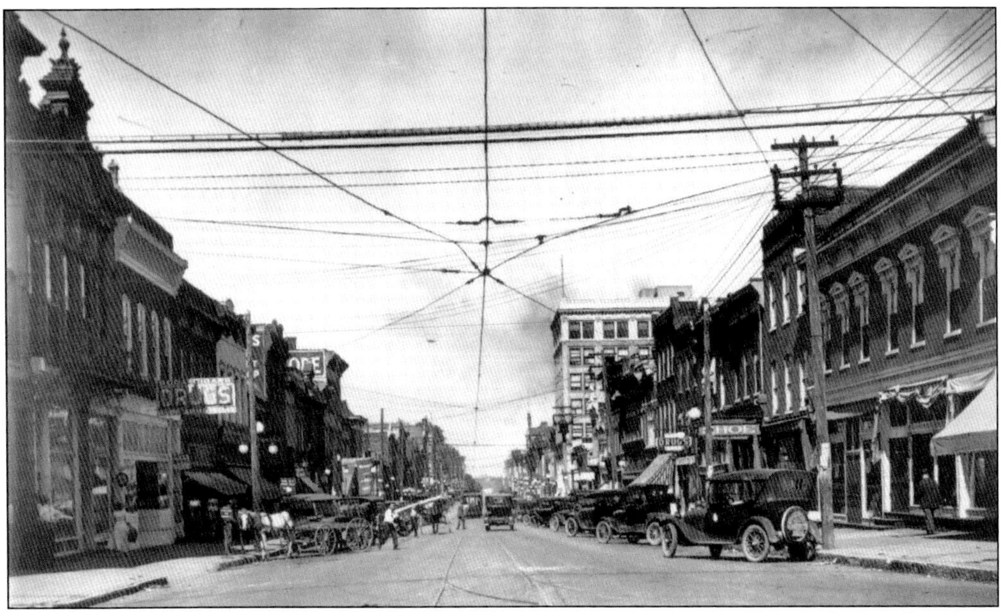

Looking west down the 200 block of East High Street in about 1924 shows diagonal parking and still horse drawn wagons. The Central Trust is the tallest building uptown. (Summers Collection; Missouri State Archives.)

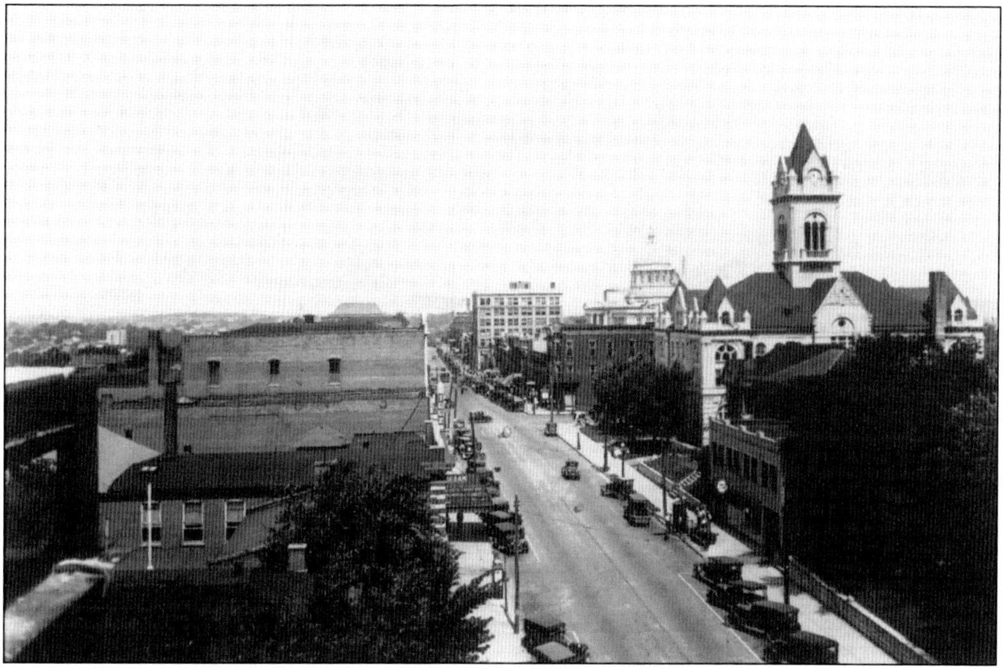

This view was taken from the Missouri Hotel on High Street looking west, the 300 and 200 blocks of High Street. Note the Cole County Court House, Monroe House, Central Trust Building, and the Capitol. This was taken in the late 1920s.

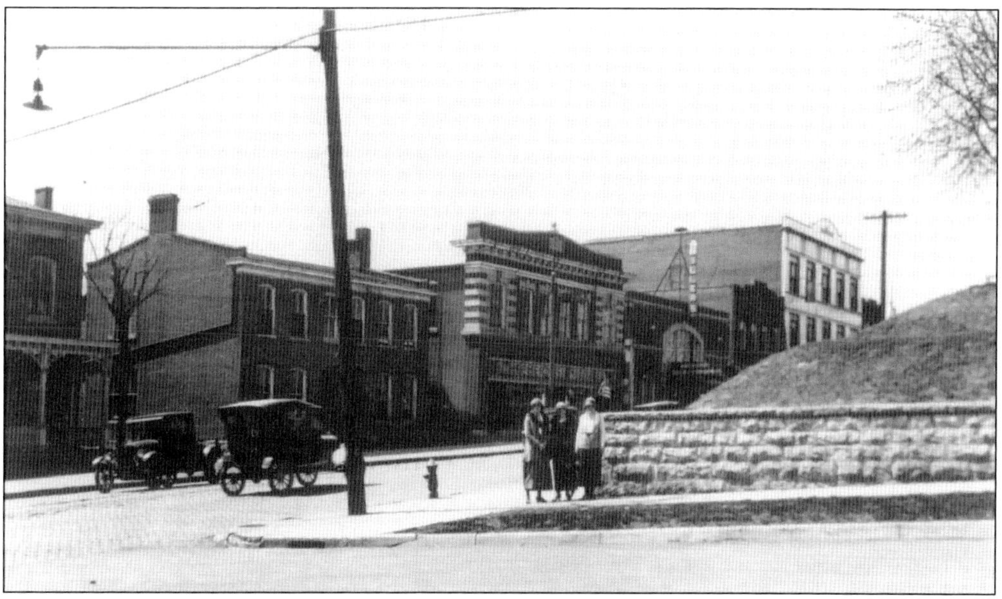

The corner of High Street and Adams taken April 15, 1924, shows the Schott House, the Masonic Hall, Miller Theatre, and the rock wall around the Dallmeyer family home Maple Terrace. (Summers Collection; Missouri State Archives.)

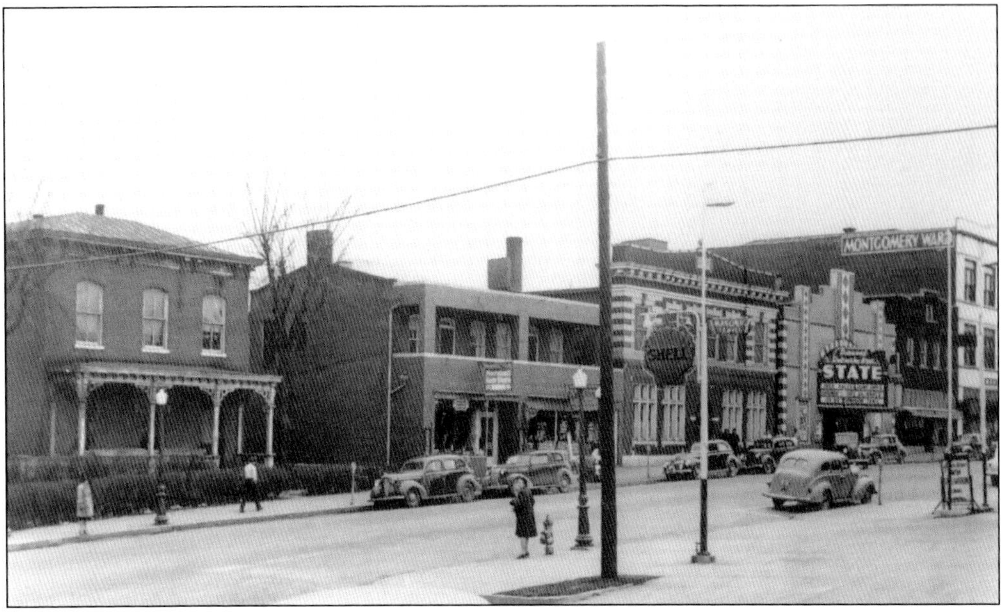

The corner of High Street and Adams looking west in the 1940s. The buildings on the south side of the street are about the same, the theater is now the State, but on the north, unfortunately "Maple Terrace" has been destroyed and replaced with a gas station and rooming house. The terrace on the north side was removed in 1937. (Summers Collection; Missouri State Archives.)

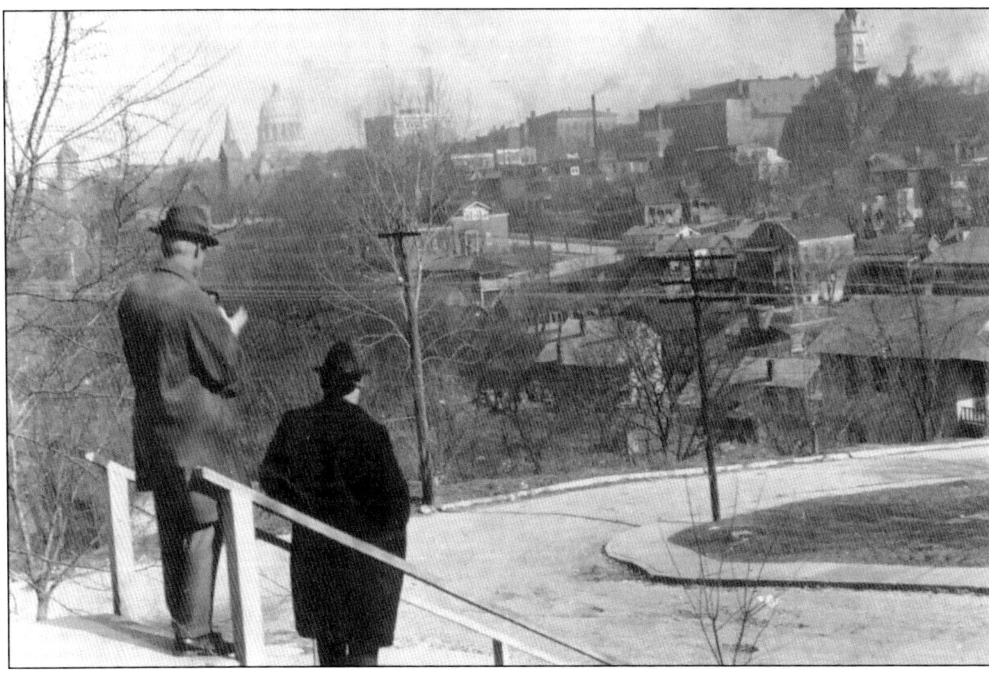

View of the cityscape from Pauline and Bill Hoefer's front steps at the corner of the 500 block of East Miller Street and the 500 block of Jackson Street in the late 1920s. Of note are the Cole County Court House, the Central Trust Building, and the Capitol.(Dottie Dallmeyer.)

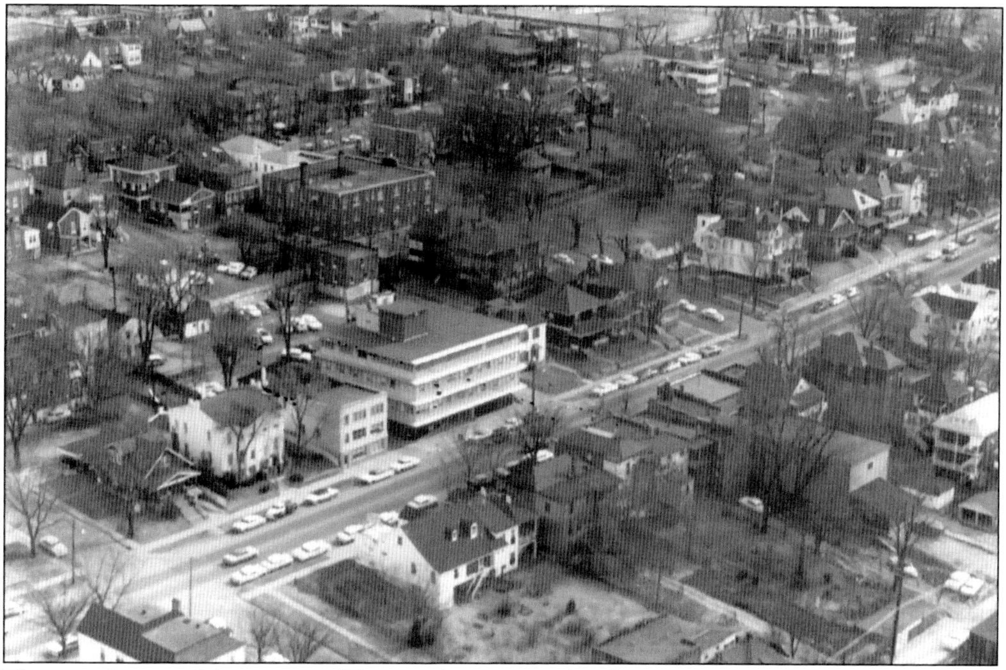

This aerial view of the corner of East High Street and Jackson was taken about 1957. Of note, in the center of the photo, is the Medical Arts Building—the only building built in the area using the "lift slab construction." (Summers Collection; Missouri State Archives.)

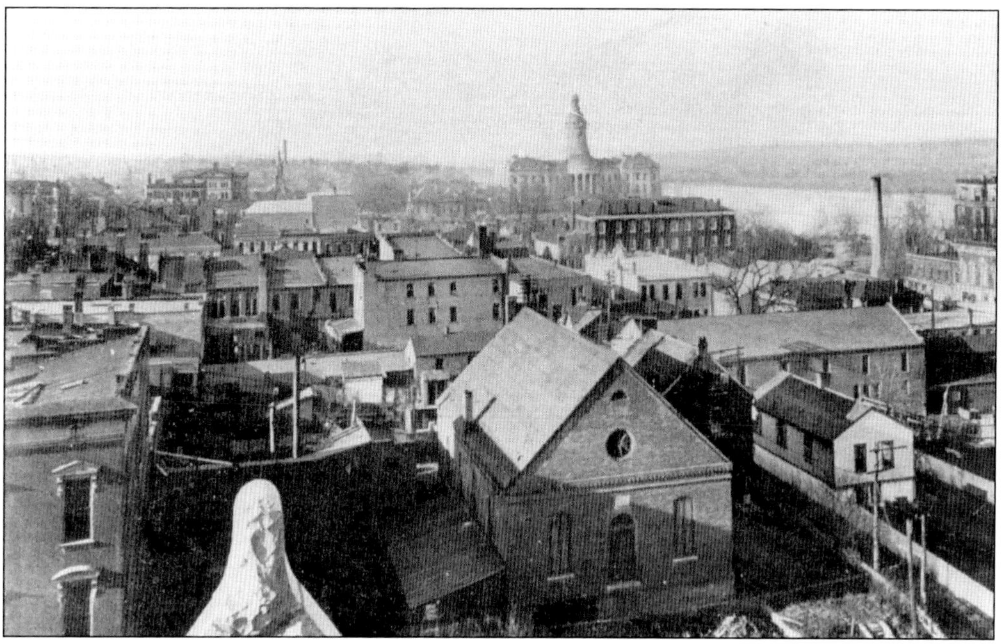

This view of the City of Jefferson is from the Cole County Court House looking northwest. Buildings to note are the corner of the Monroe House Hotel, The Madison Hotel, the Governor's Mansion, and the Capitol by the river. This was taken about 1900. (Summers Collection; Missouri State Archives.)

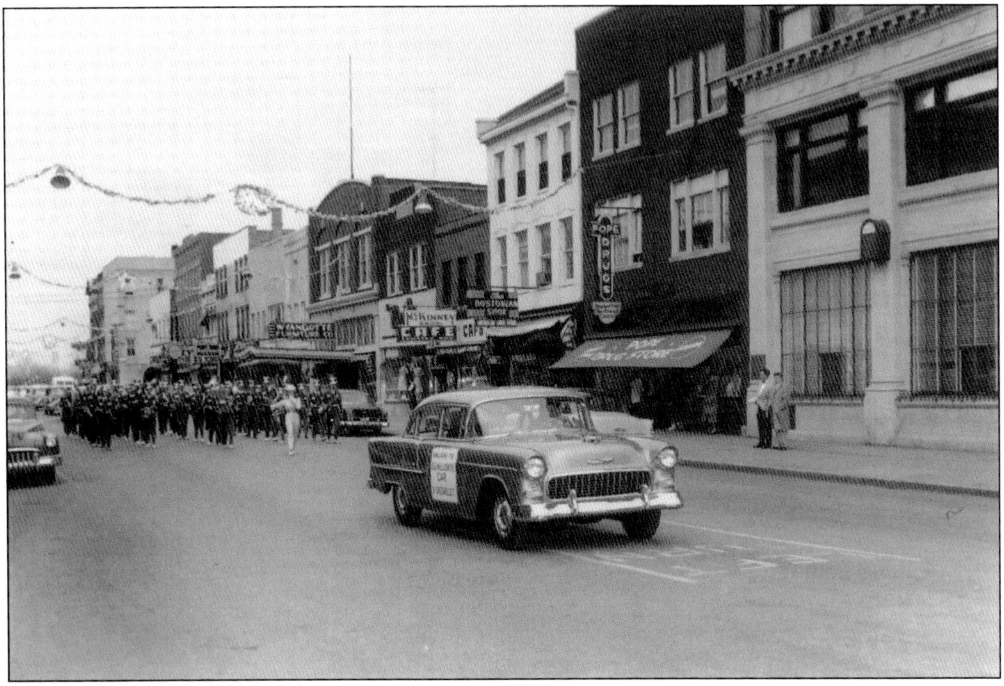

The 100 block of East High Street about 1958, showing the Christmas parade and the shops of the time. Wyandotte burned down soon after this photo was taken. (Summers Collection; Missouri State Archives.)

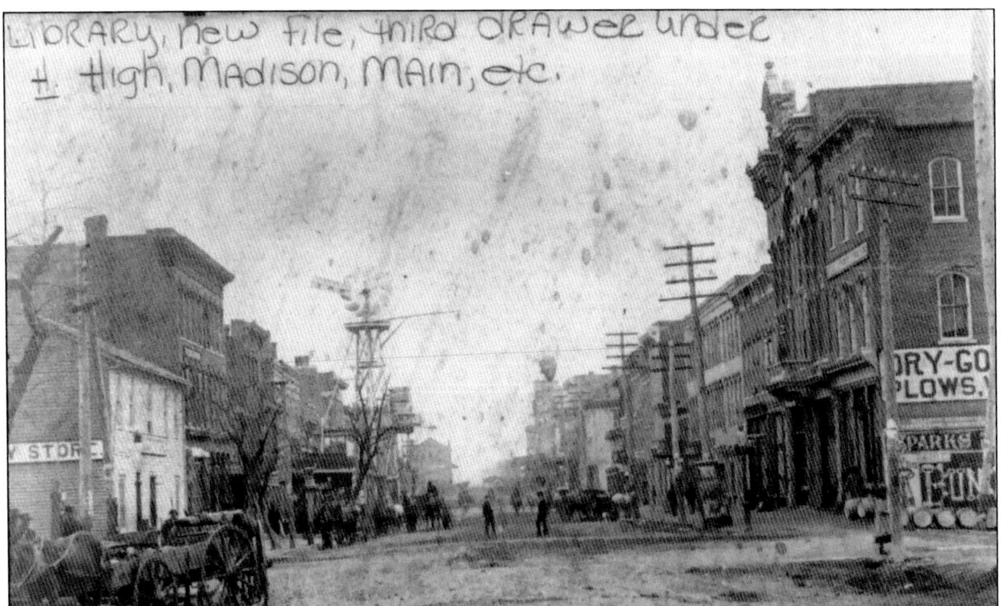

Pictured is the corner of High and Jefferson Streets in 1890 looking east. Note that the streets are still dirt, the windmill pumped and supplied the city water for horses. L.C. Lohman's building is on the left next to the Opera House. (Cole County Historical Society.)

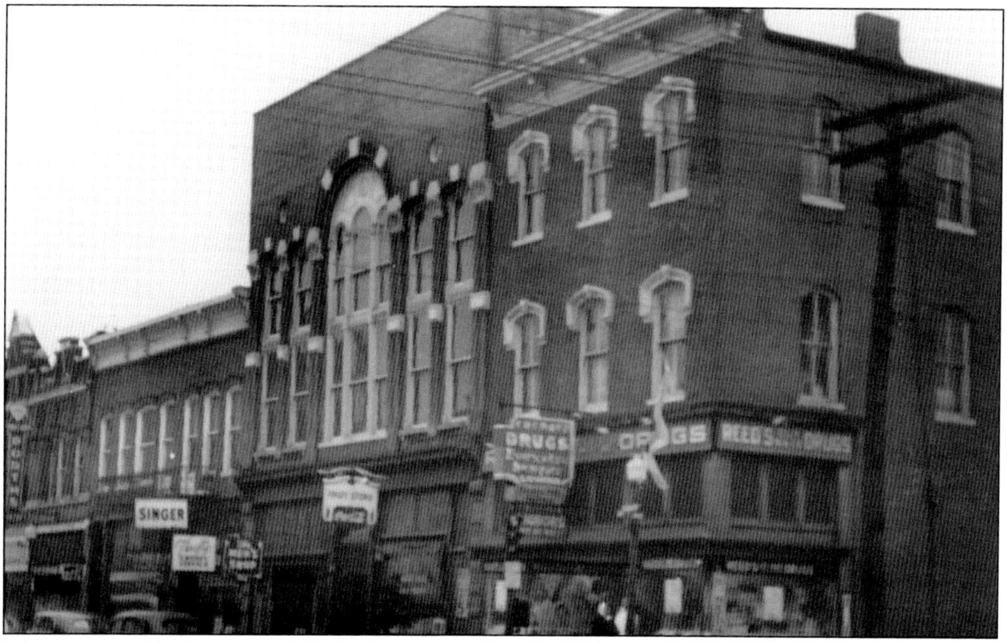

The corner of Jefferson and High Streets, south side, looking east, shows the Lohman Building at 100 East High in about 1947. (Summers Collection; Missouri State Archives.)

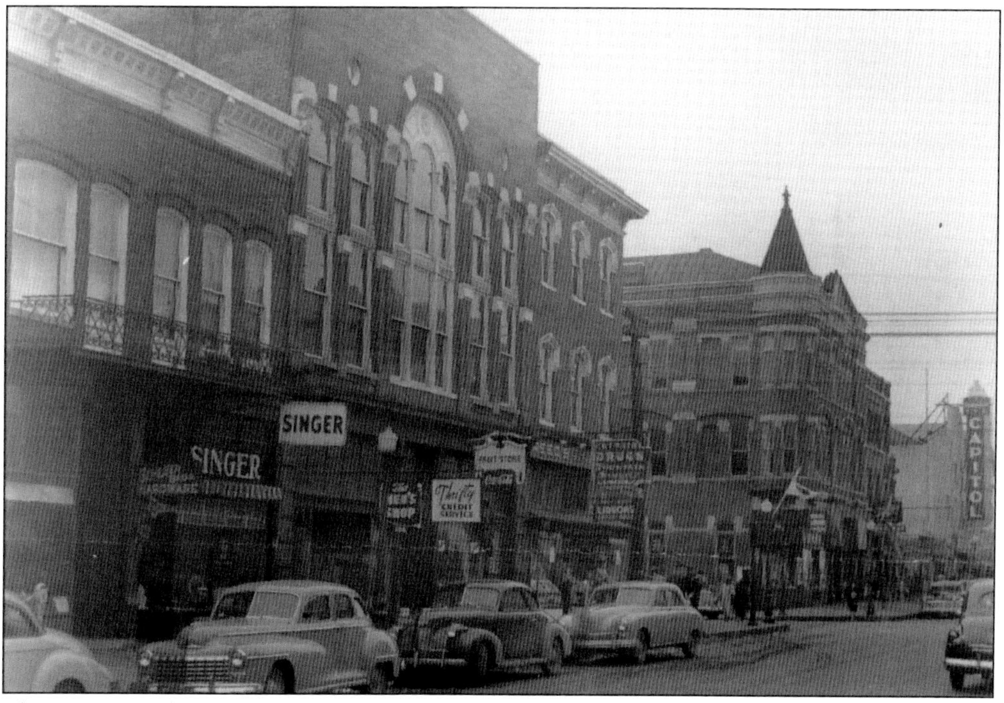

The corner High and Jefferson looking west in the 100 block, on the south side of the street, about 1947. Jefferson Street is the east-west divider in the city. Of note are the Opera House, Lohman Building, Merchants Bank Building, and the Capitol Theatre. (Summers Collection; Missouri State Archives.)

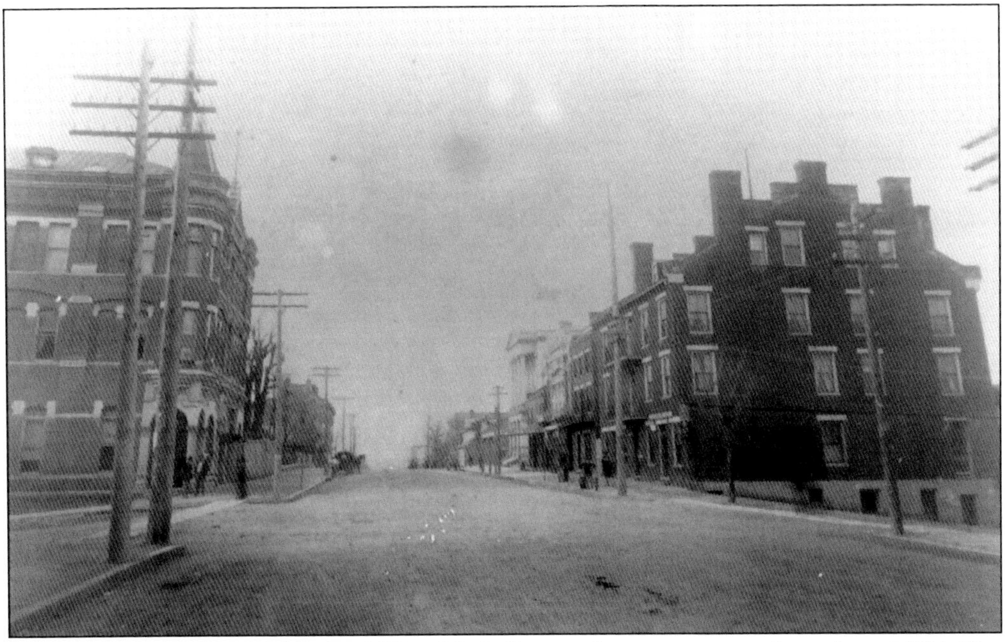

Looking west in the 100 block of West High Street, this image was taken about 1890. The buildings of note are the Merchants Bank, Central Hotel, and the United States Post Office and Courts Building. (Summers Collection; Missouri State Archives.)

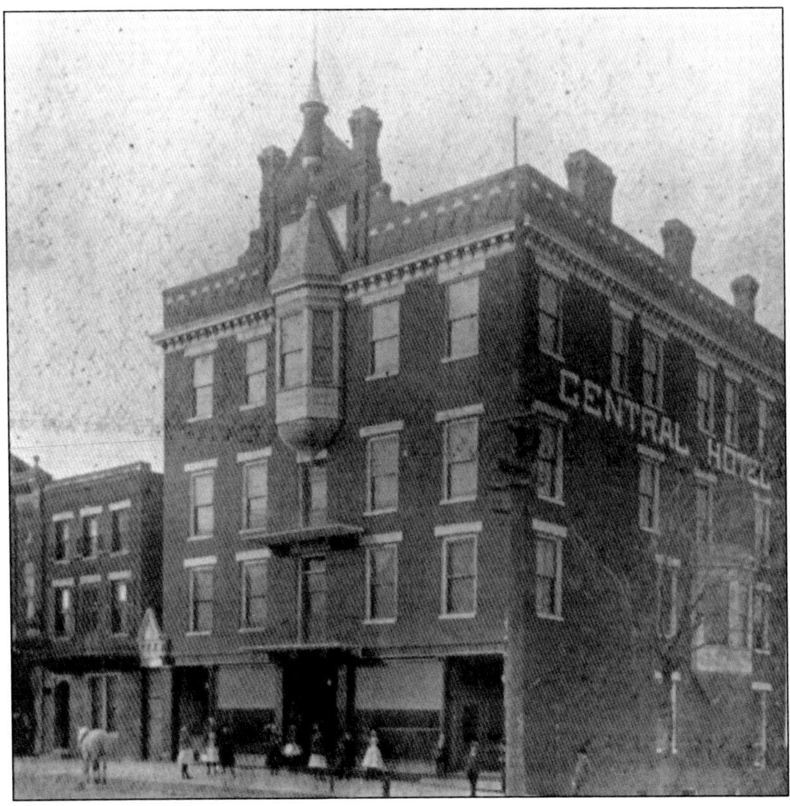

The north side of the 100 block west of High Street, taken in about 1900, shows the remodeled Central Hotel. (Summers Collection; Missouri State Archives.)

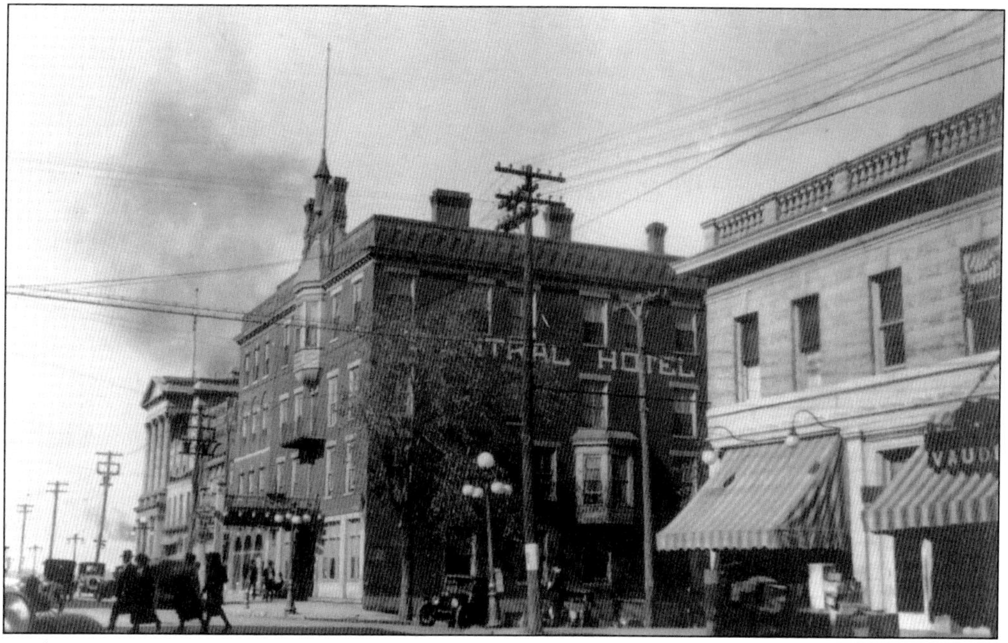

Looking west on High Street—the north side, in the 1920s . The Central Hotel and the Post Office are prominent. (Summers Collection; Missouri State Archives.)

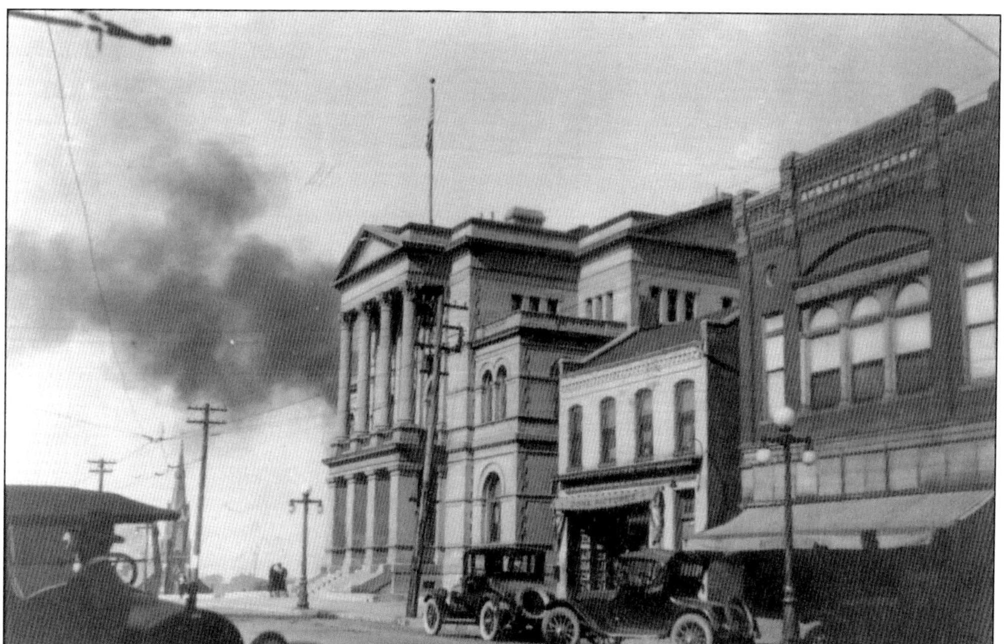
Looking west on the north side of High Street, 100 block, shows the Missouri Power and Light Building and the Post Office. (Summers Collection; Missouri State Archives.)

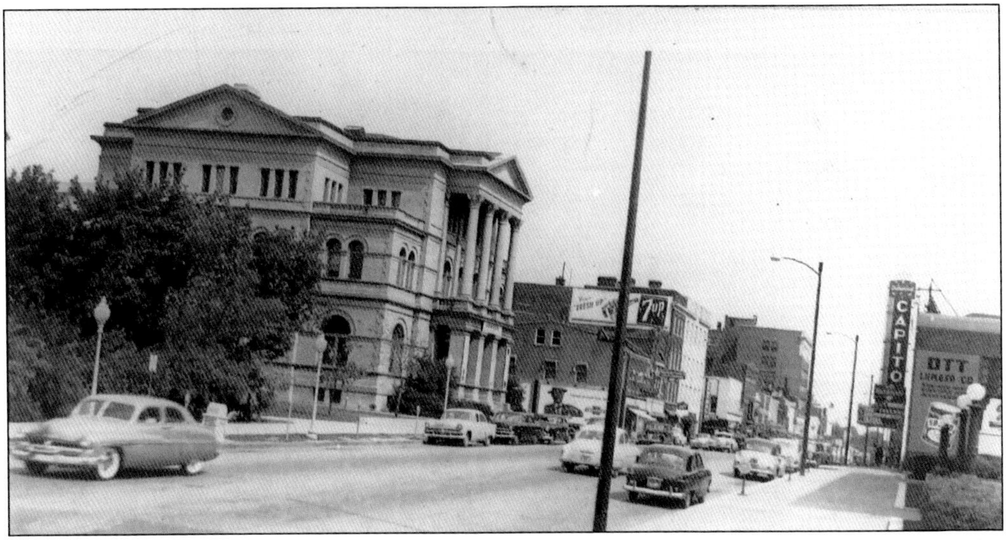

Looking from west to east in the 100 block of West High Street in the early 1950s shows the old Post Office, the Capitol Theatre, and the Central Hotel. (Summers Collection; Missouri State Archives.)

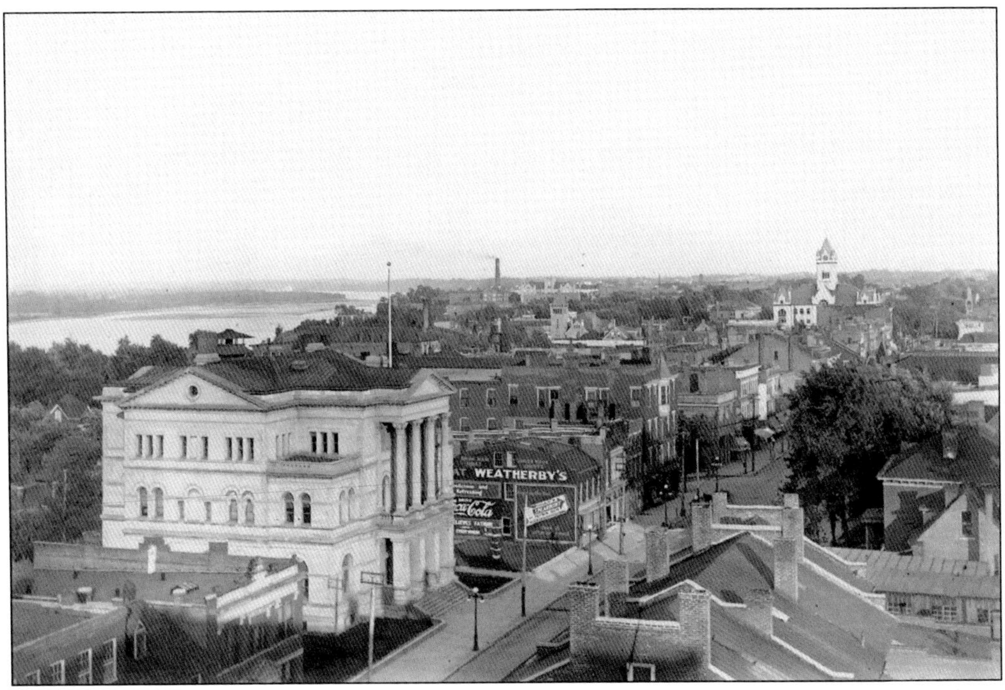

This view from the top of the Supreme Court Building looks northeast on High Street, in about 1916. Of note in the foreground is the Bruns house, on the south side of High Street the United States Post Office, and Court Building on the north side. Going down the street is the Central Hotel, Dallmeyer's "Big Store," and Bragg Hall on the south side of the street. Going toward the river is the Cole County Court House, the Methodist and Baptist Churches, and in the background, the Missouri State Penitentiary. (K.W. Gadd.)

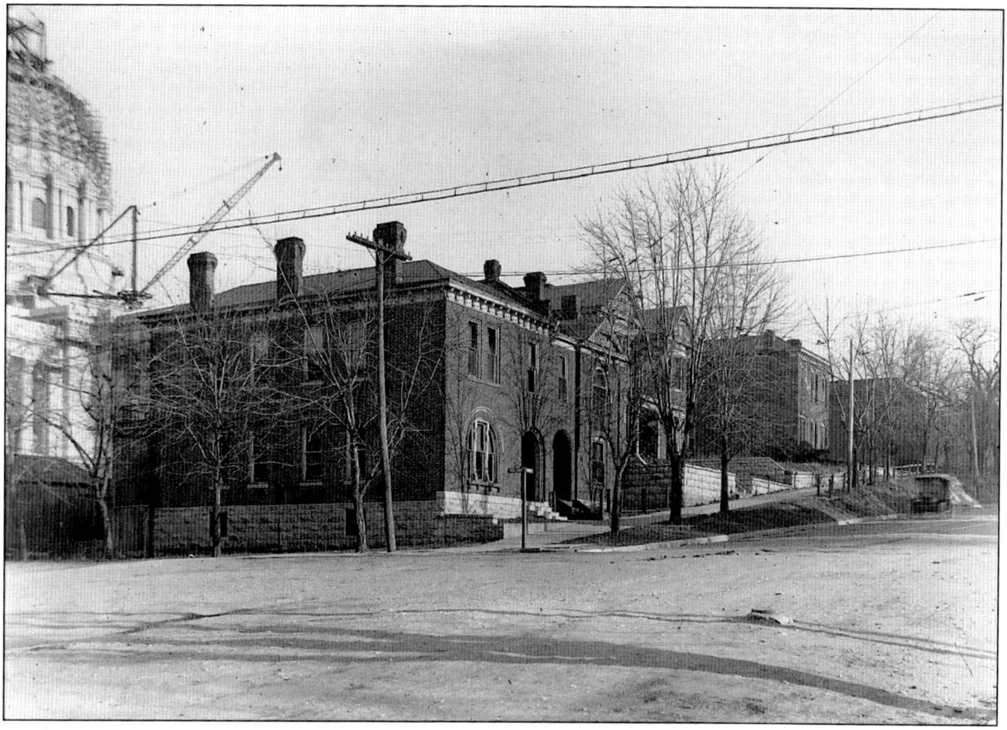

Looking northeast on the corner of Broadway and West High Street about 1916. The present capitol is being constructed in the background, houses are in the foreground. (H.W.Gadd.)

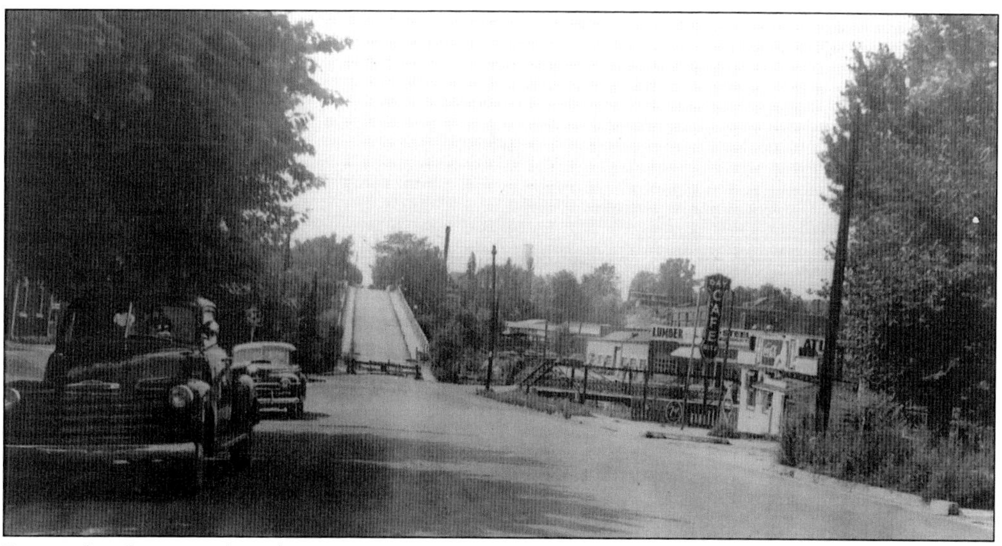

Pictured is the second viaduct on West High Street under construction about 1951. This shows some of the businesses at the foot of the viaduct in Millbottom at the time. (Bryan Pope.)

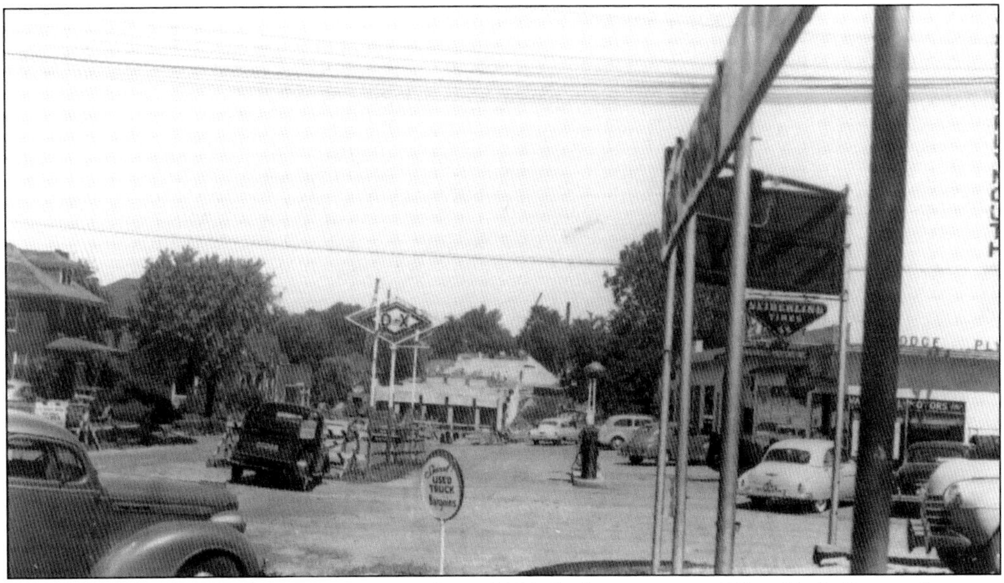

The second viaduct under construction, about 1951, looking west on West High Street, showing houses and businesses at the time. All are gone now. The Truman State Office Building is now on the south side of the street and parking lots are on the north side of the street. (Bryan Pope.)

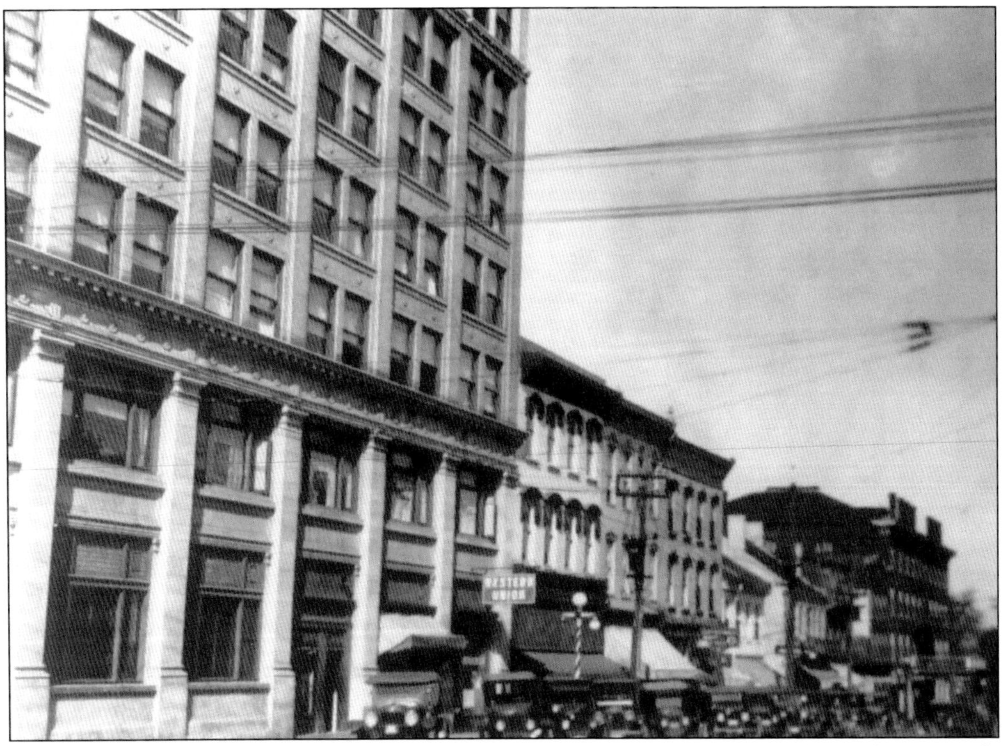

The corner of High Street and Madison Street looking north in the 1920s. This is the west side of the 200 block of Madison. The first building is the Central Trust Building and at the end of the block is the Madison Hotel. (Summers Collection; Missouri State Archives.)

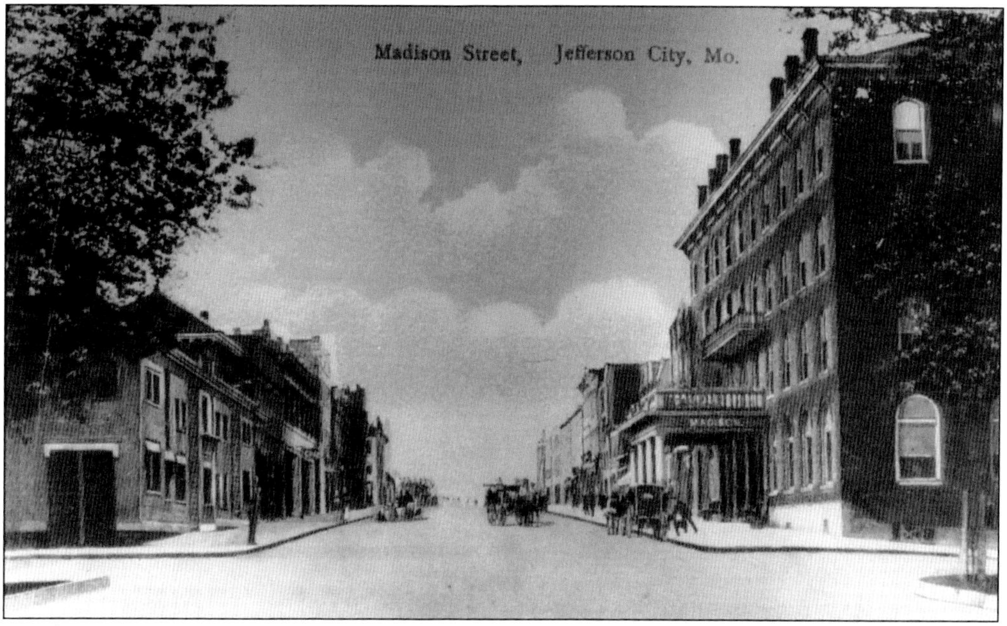

On the corner of East Main and Madison Streets, the predominant building is the Madison Hotel in 1900. This is the 200 block of Madison looking south. (Summers Collection; Missouri State Archives.)

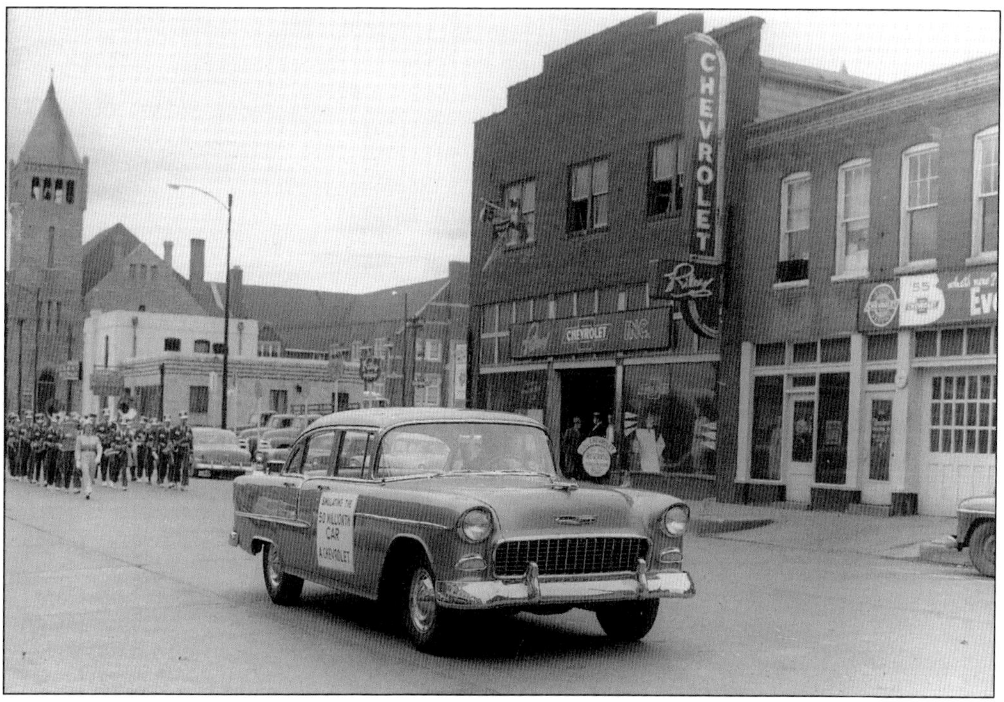

The 1958 Christmas parade showing the 200 block of East Capitol. The buildings to note going down the south side of the street are Riley Chevrolet, Greyhound Bus Station, the Jefferson City Water Company, and the Methodist Church. The Chevrolet in the parade was the 50,000th sold. (Summers Collection; Missouri State Archives.)

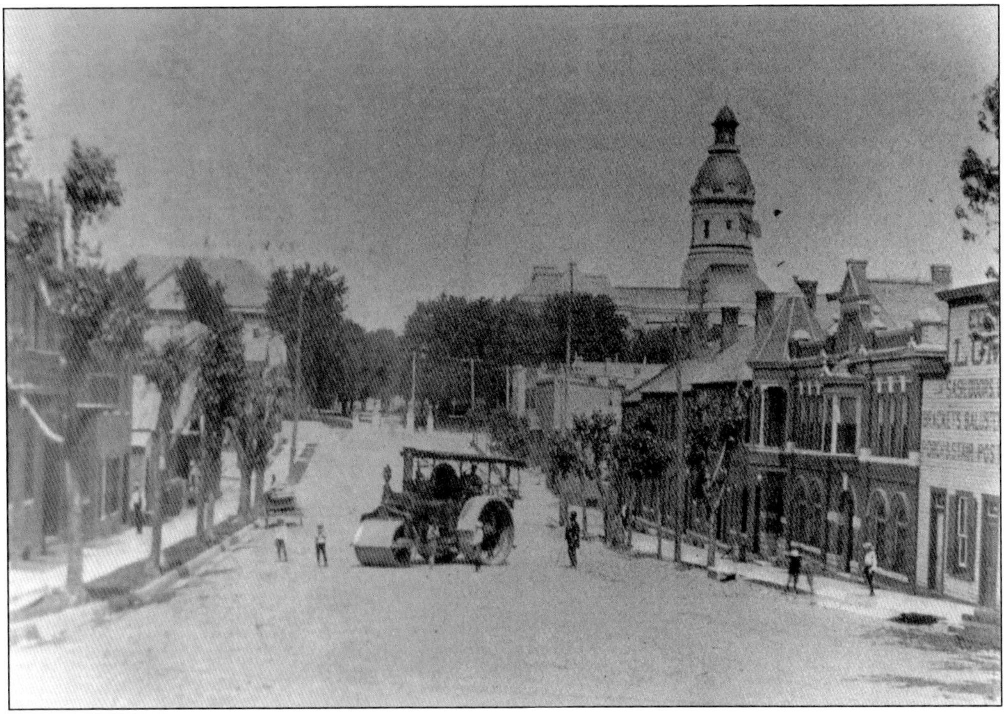

Joe Pope's street paving crew on East Main Street (now called Capital Avenue) is shown in this view, taken about 1910, looking west toward the Capitol. All the buildings along this street are gone and replaced by state office buildings and the Governor's Garden. (Summers Collection; Missouri State Archives.)

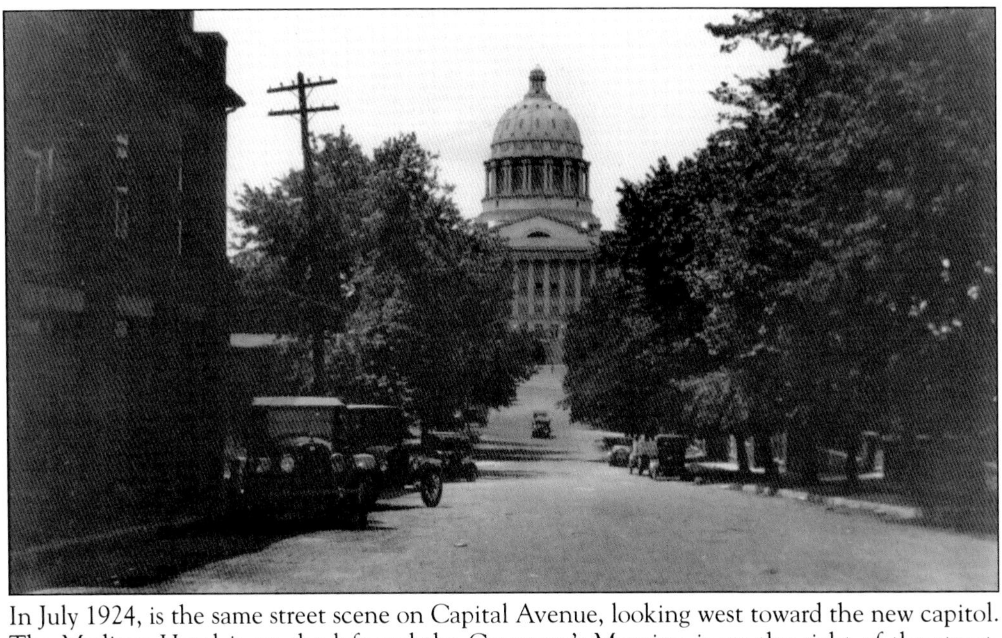

In July 1924, is the same street scene on Capital Avenue, looking west toward the new capitol. The Madison Hotel is on the left and the Governor's Mansion is on the right of the street. (Summers Collection; Missouri State Archives.)

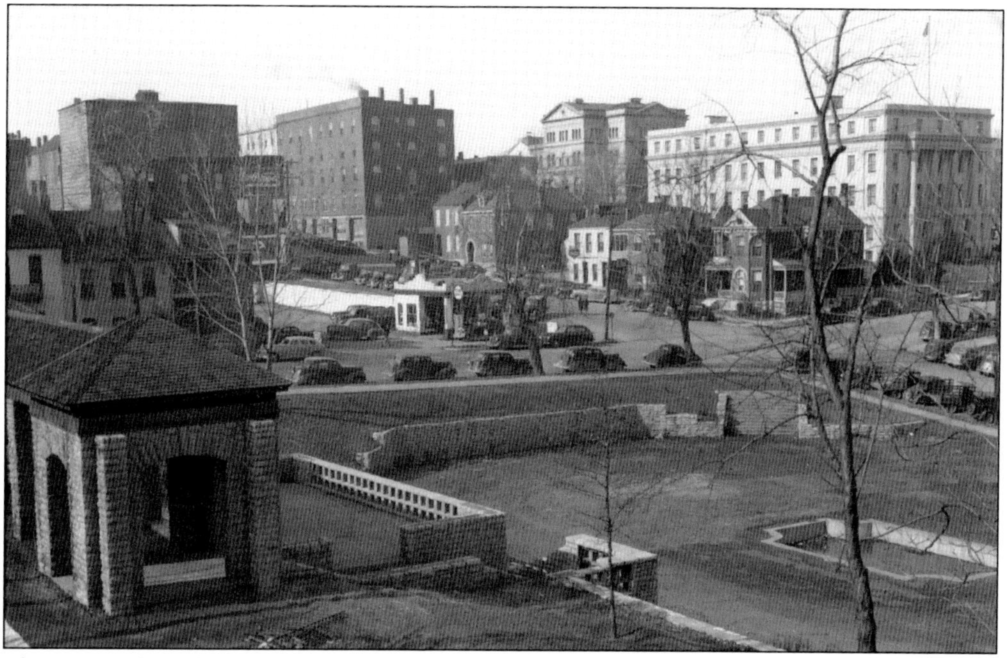

This view is from the backyard of the Governor's Mansion in 1946. The Governor's Garden is in the foreground, Missouri Highway Department Building is the building with columns and behind it is the United States Post Office and Courts. To the left, on the corner of High and Jefferson Streets, is the Central Hotel. (Historic City of Jefferson Archives; at the Missouri State Archives.)

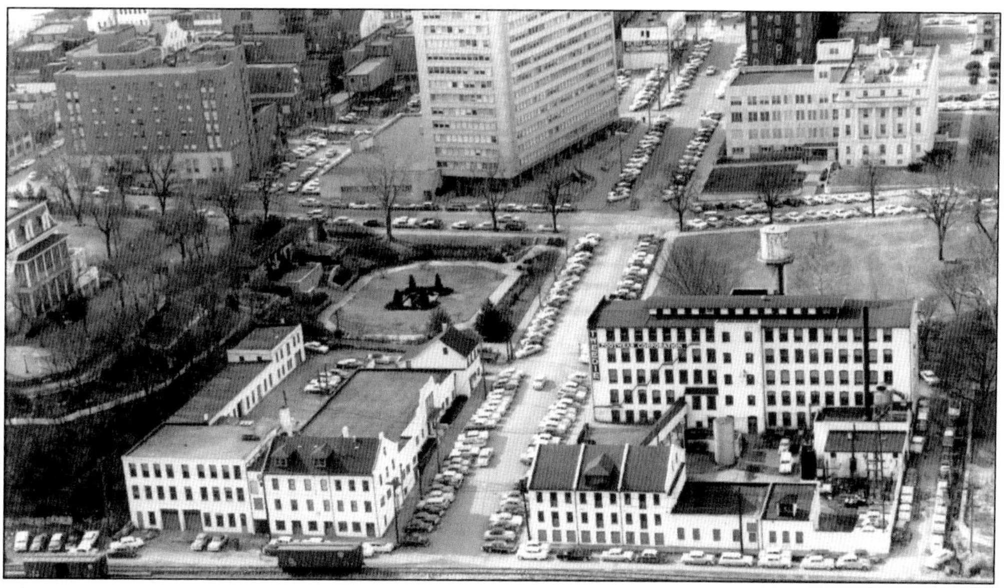

This aerial view shows the 100 and 200 blocks of Jefferson Street looking south, the 100 block of East Capitol, and the 100 block of West Capitol, about 1958. By the railroad tracks is Tweedie's Shoe Factory, the Governor's Mansion is to the left, across Capitol Avenue from the Mansion is the Hotel Governor and south of that is the Central Trust Building. In the center of the photo is the Jefferson Building, the State Highway Department is across the street from that, and the Central Hotel just behind. (Summers Collection; Missouri State Archives.)

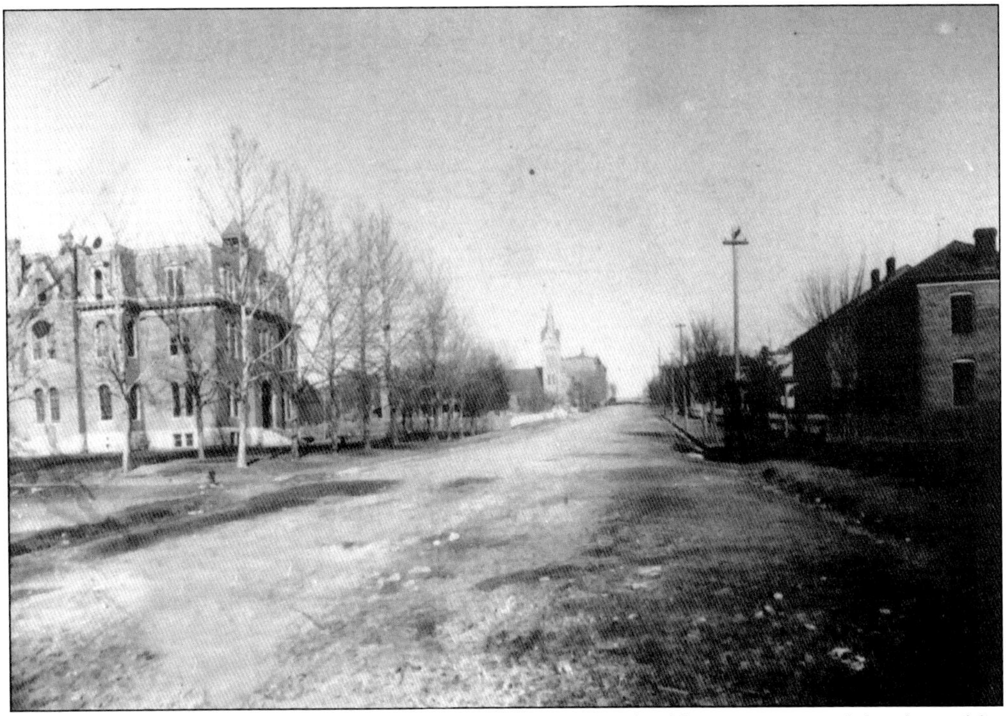

Monroe Street about 1900 shows Central School, the first building constructed for the public schools. The top floor was for the high school. Up the street is the Lutheran Church. (Summers Collection; Missouri State Archives.)

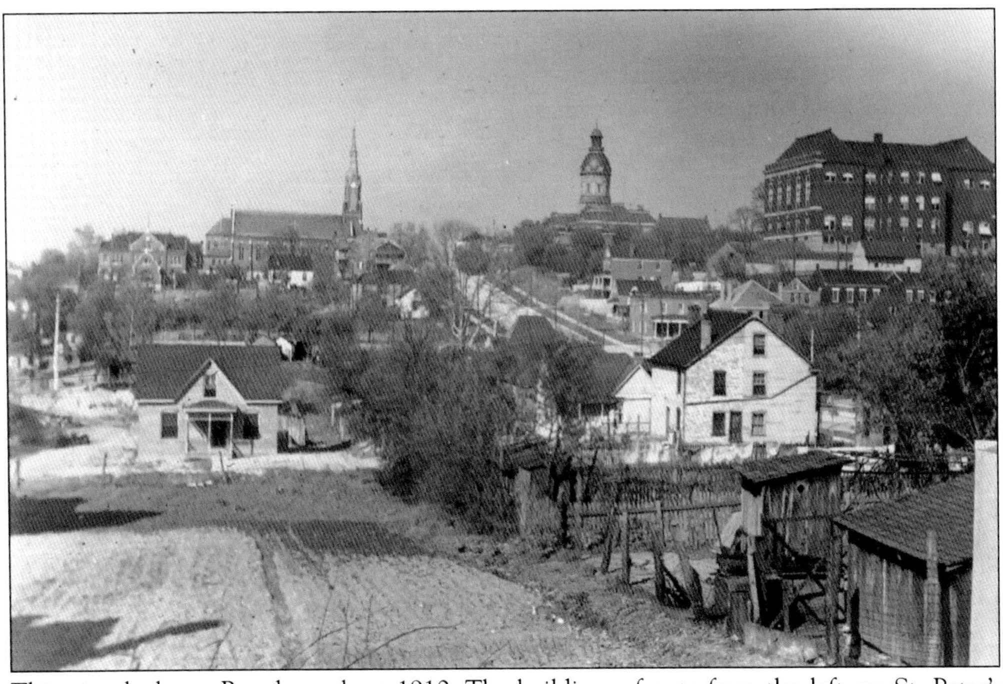

This view looks up Broadway about 1910. The buildings of note from the left are St. Peter's School and Church, the Capitol, and the Supreme Court Building. (H.G. Gadd.)

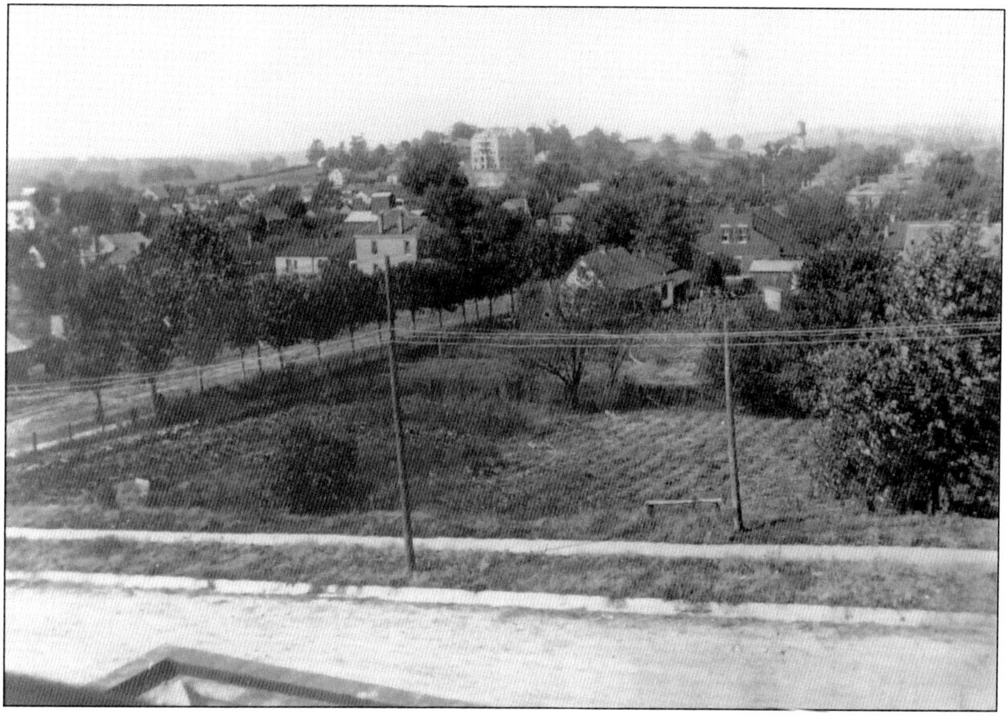

From the Supreme Court, this *c.* 1910 image looks southwest towards St. Mary's Hospital. Also note the water tower of the shoe factory on the horizon. (Summers Collection; Missouri State Archives.)

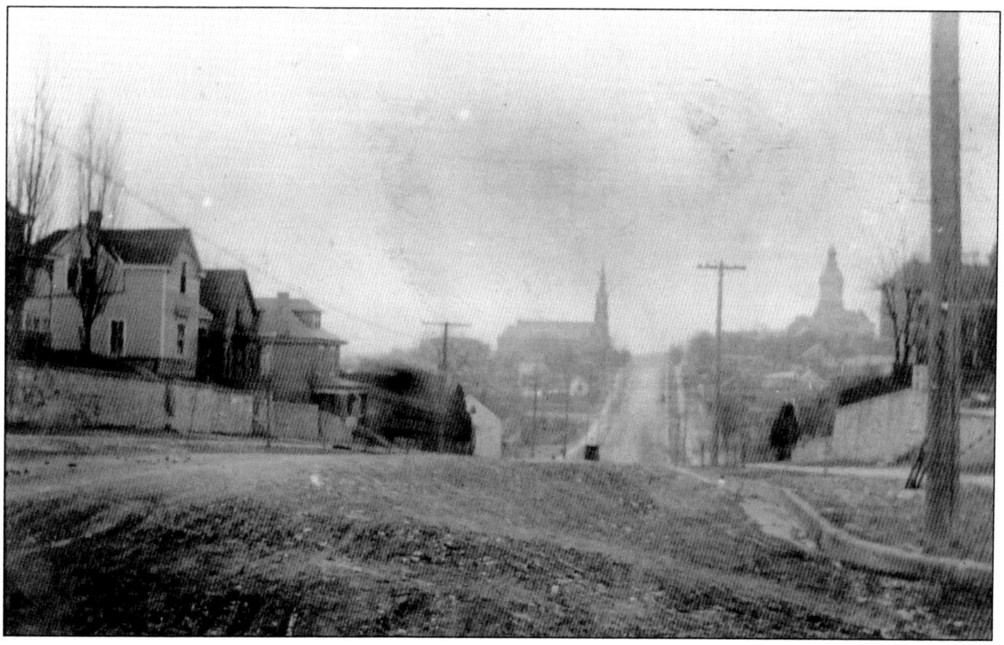

This view north on Broadway from the Munichburg area, at the corner of Broadway and Elm, was taken about 1900. Note St. Peter's School and Church and the Capitol on the horizon. (Summers Collection; Missouri State Archives.)

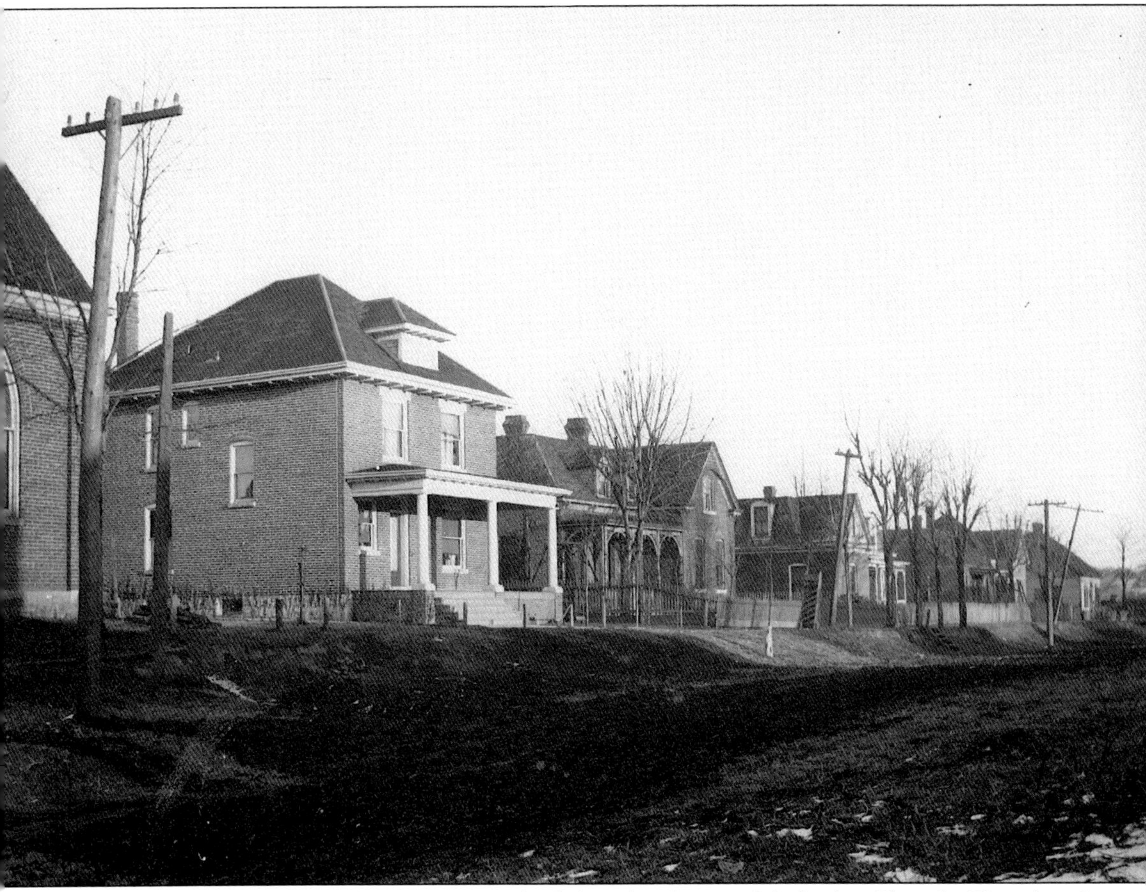

Pictured is Elm Street, about 1900. At the left is the German Methodist Church. This church disbanded during World War I rather than have their services in English. It was a totally German-speaking church before that time. (Summers Collection; Missouri State Archives.)

Seven

THE EVOLUTION OF THE CITY

The photos in this chapter were taken from the dome of the second and third capitols built in the City of Jefferson. They start in 1891 and go to 1987, showing the evolution of the streets during those years.

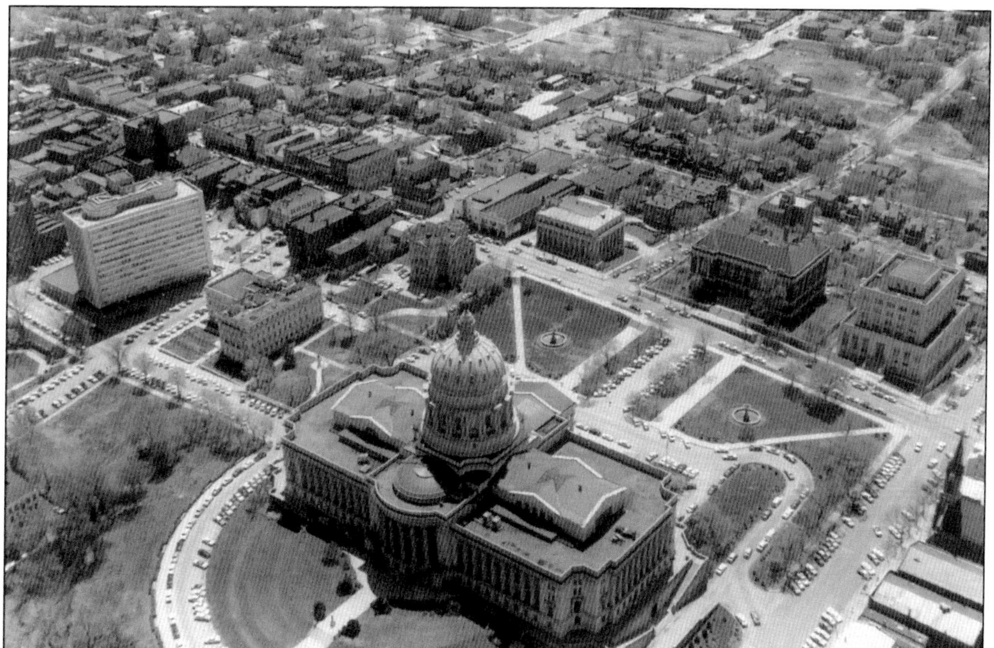

Aerial view of the Capitol and buildings around it in about 1958. To the left of the Capitol is the Missouri Highway Department Building, the Jefferson State Office Building, clockwise around is the Central Hotel, the Old Post Office, the new Post Office, Supreme Court, Broadway State Office Building, and St. Peter's Church. (Summers Collection; Missouri State Archives.)

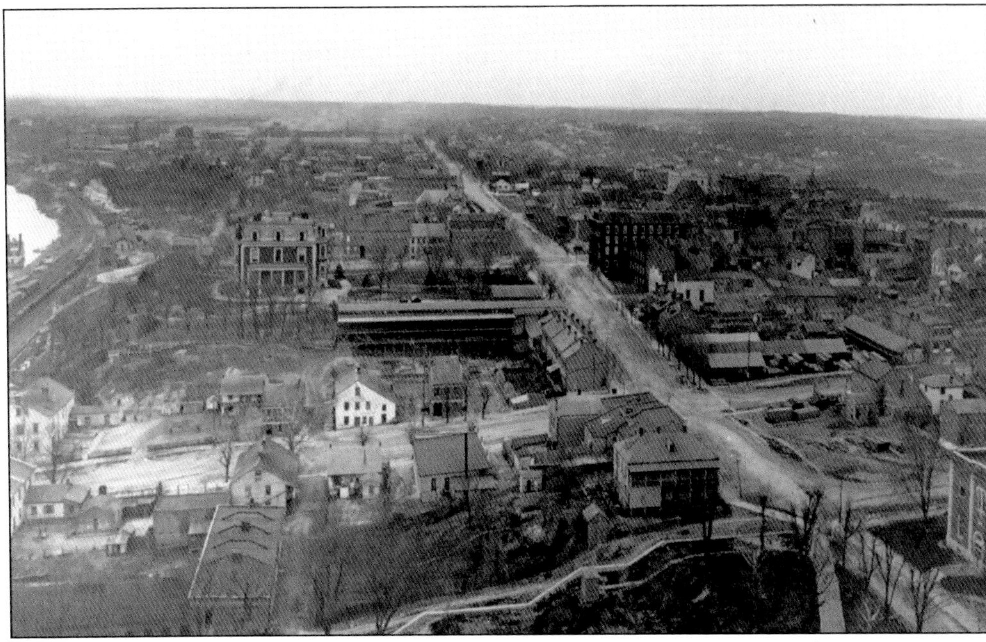

Looking east from the dome of the second capitol in 1891 shows steamboats on the Missouri River, Lohman's Landing at the foot of Jefferson Street, the Governor's Mansion, and the Penitentiary in background at the bend of the river. The white stone building just right of the center of the photo is the old Cole County Court House. The buildings in the right foreground are the old Missouri Supreme Court Building and the State Library. (Cole County Historical Society.)

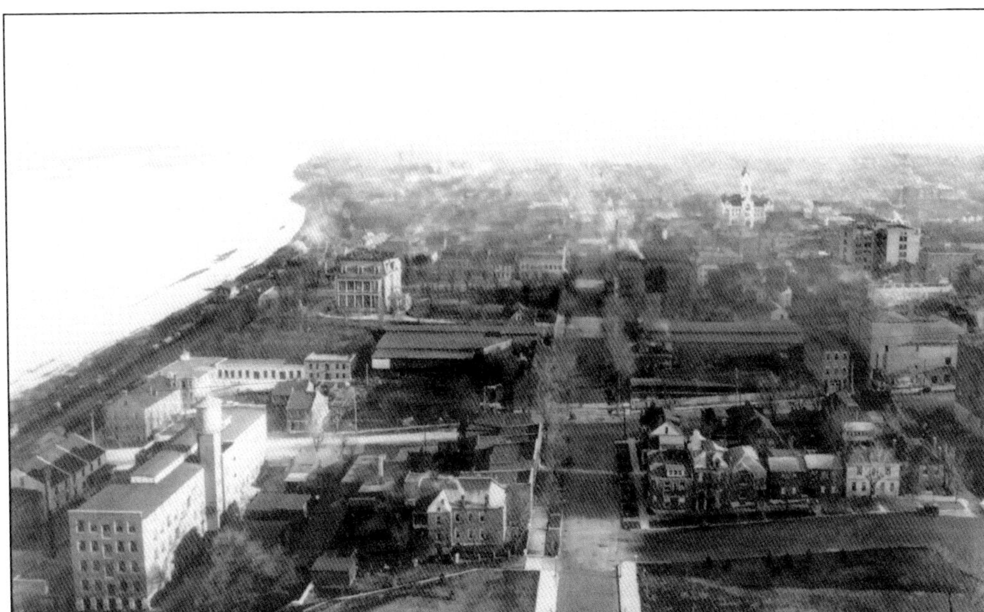

This view looks east from the dome of the present capitol, about 1925. Lohman's Landing has become Tweedie Foot Wear Corporation. The new Cole County Court House dominates the center of the photo, the Supreme Court Building and State Library are gone, and there seems to be no river traffic. (Jim Twyman.)

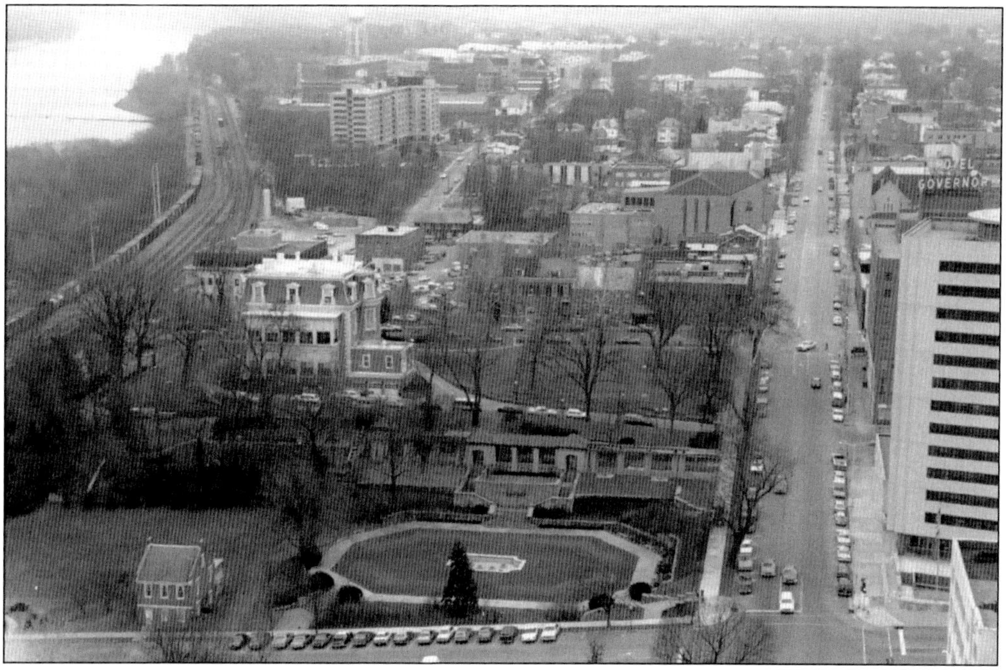

The same view in January 1987, looking east, shows the Christopher Maus House, the Governor's Garden, Governor's Mansion, new Baptist Church, and the Methodist Church in the center of the photo, close to the river, in front of the Penitentiary is Dulle Towers. On the right side of the photo in the foreground is the Hotel Governor, the Jefferson State Office Building, and the Missouri State Highway Department Building. (Joe Kroeger.)

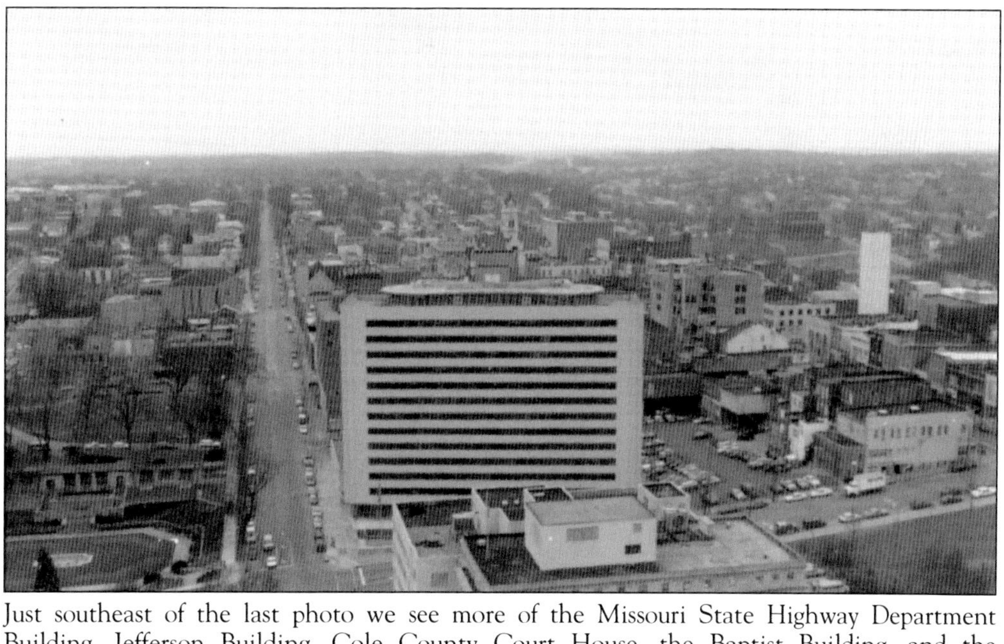

Just southeast of the last photo we see more of the Missouri State Highway Department Building, Jefferson Building, Cole County Court House, the Baptist Building, and the Central Trust Building. This view was taken in January 1987. (Summers Collection; Missouri State Archives.)

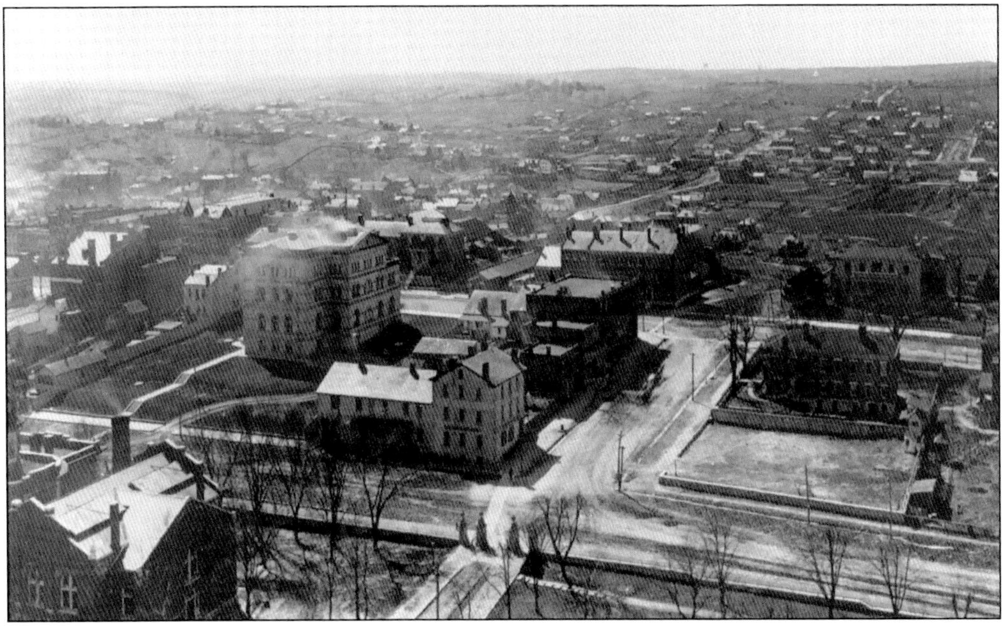

Looking south from the second capitol, in 1891, shows the State Library, Supreme Court Building, Central Hotel, the Post Office, and the Bruns house. Carl Deeg, a local photographer, took this photo. (Cole County Historical Society.)

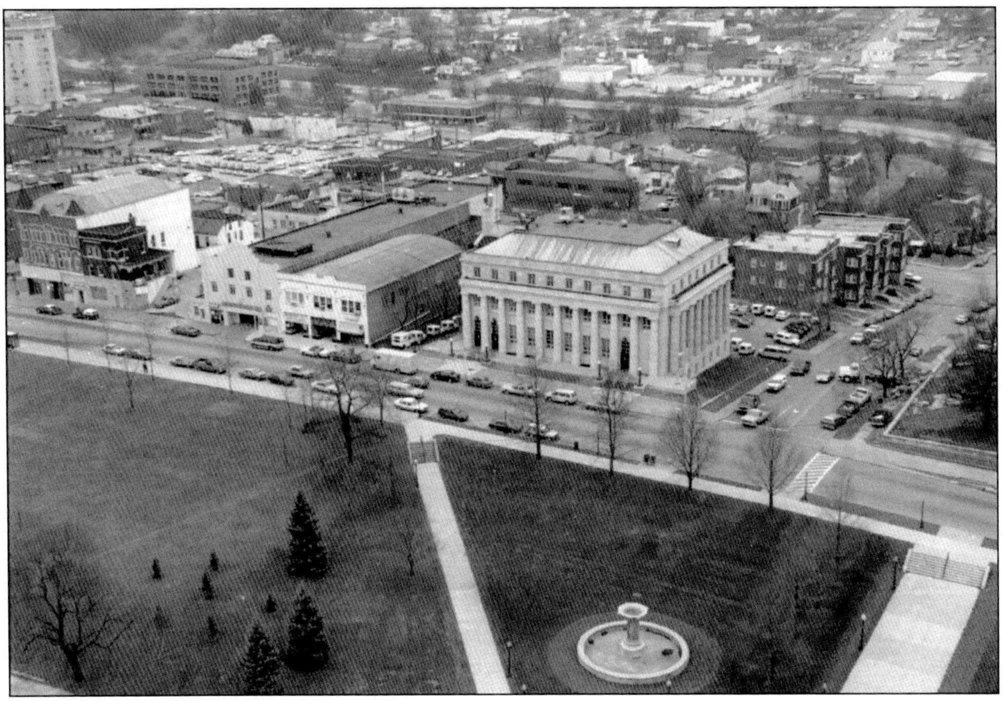

The view south in January 1987. No buildings remain on the immediate block in front of the Capitol. On the south side of High Street is, from Jefferson Street, the Merchants Bank Building, the current United States Post Office, and behind it the Washington Apartments. (Joe Kroeger.)

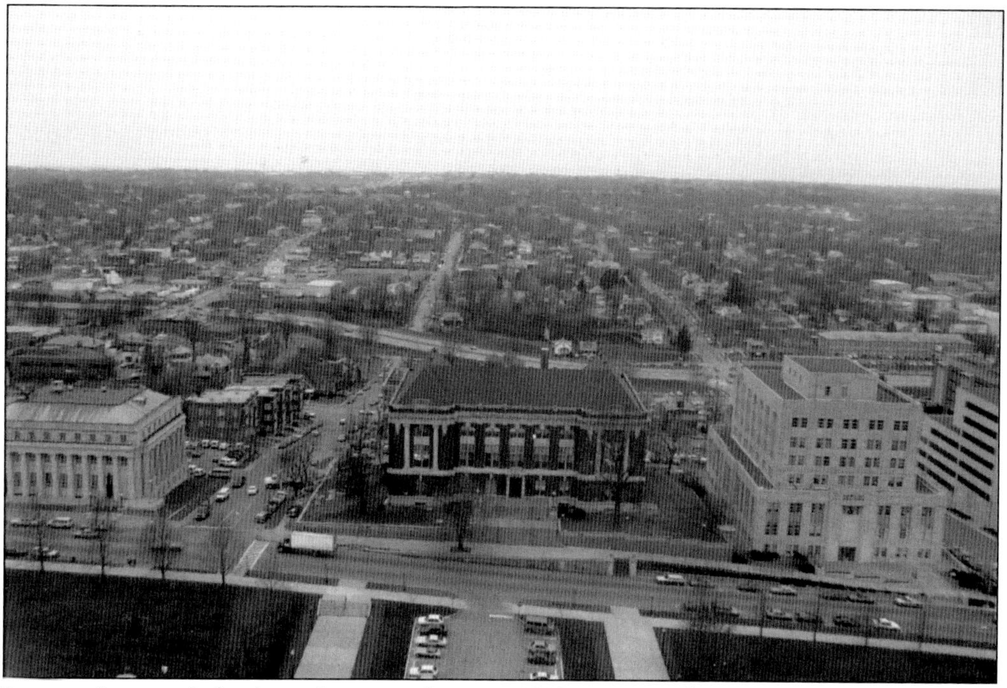

Just southwest of the last photo, in January 1987, we see the Post Office, Washington Apartments, Supreme Court Building, Broadway State Office Building, Truman State Office Building, and the Rex M. Whitten Expressway. (Joe Kroeger.)

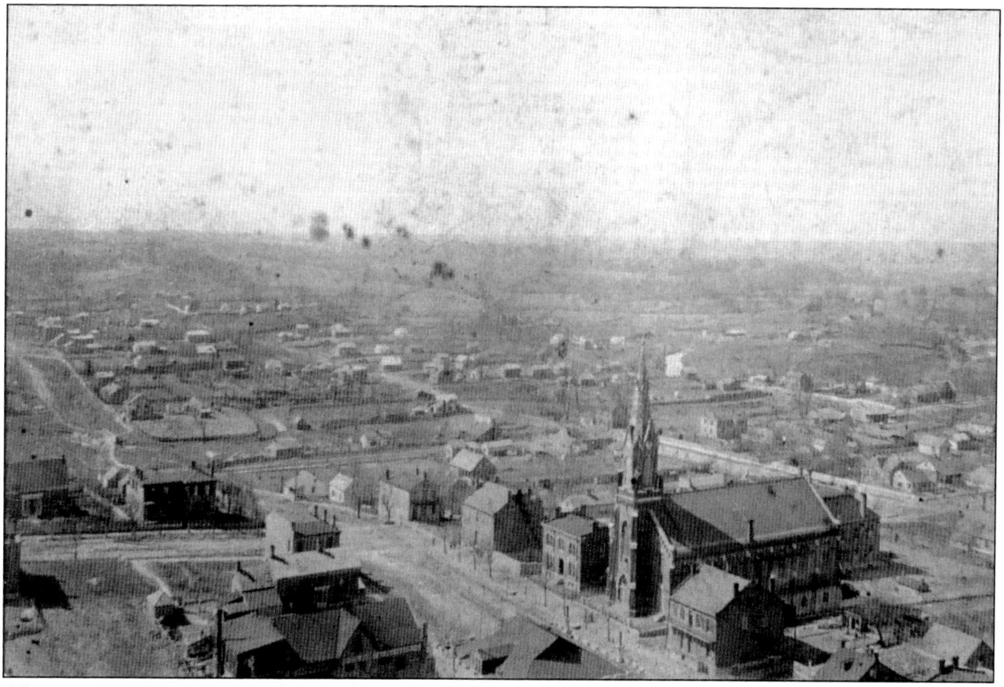

About 1890 the view southwest from the capitol dome shows, in center foreground, the State Armory, St. Peter's Church, and homes. (Cole County Historical Society.)

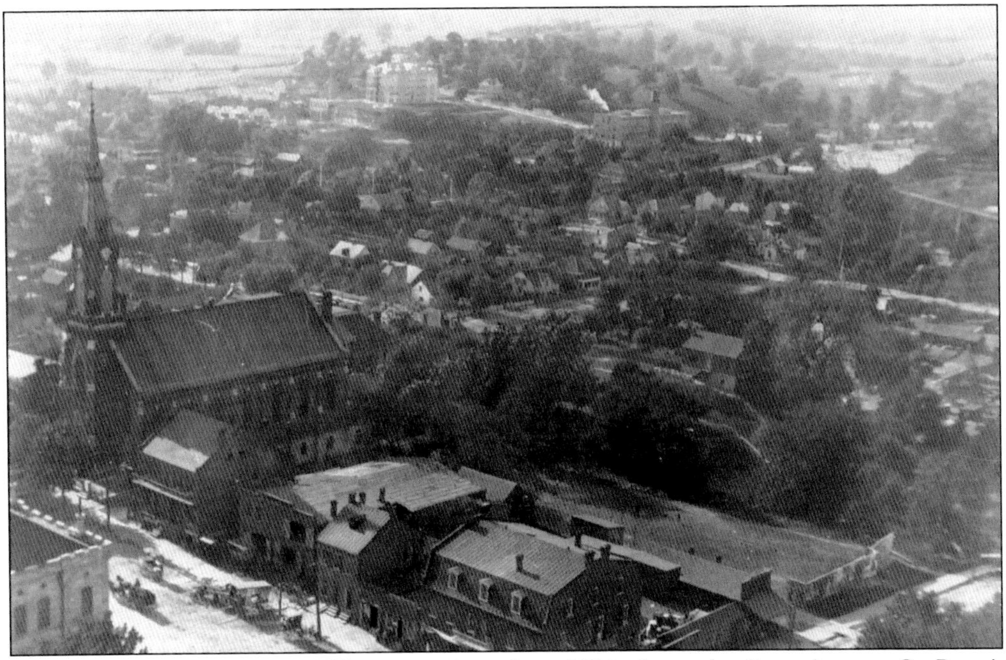

View just south, going into Millbottom, taken about 1910, shows the State Armory, St. Peter's Church, and in background is St. Mary's Hospital. (Cole County Historical Society.)

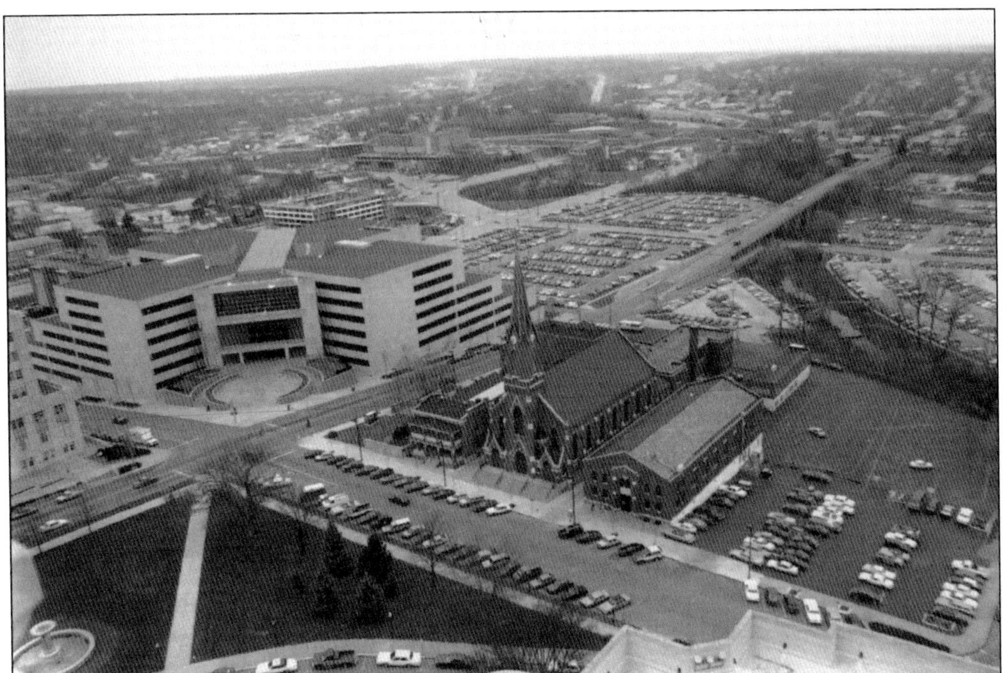

The 1987 view southwest of the City of Jefferson shows, from left, the Broadway Building, the Truman Building, the Capitol Plaza Hotel behind it, and a much larger St. Mary's Hospital. Also seen are St. Peter's Church and lots of surface parking.

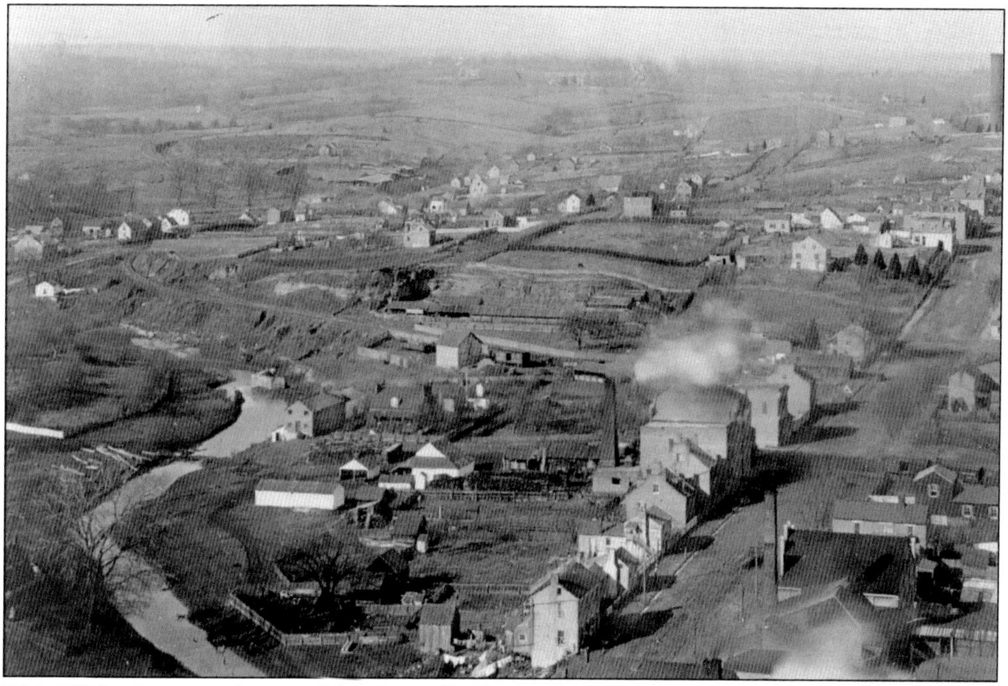

This 1890s photo southwest of the City of Jefferson shows Wears Creek in its banks, the houses and businesses in Millbottom at the time, the water tower and farm land in the background.

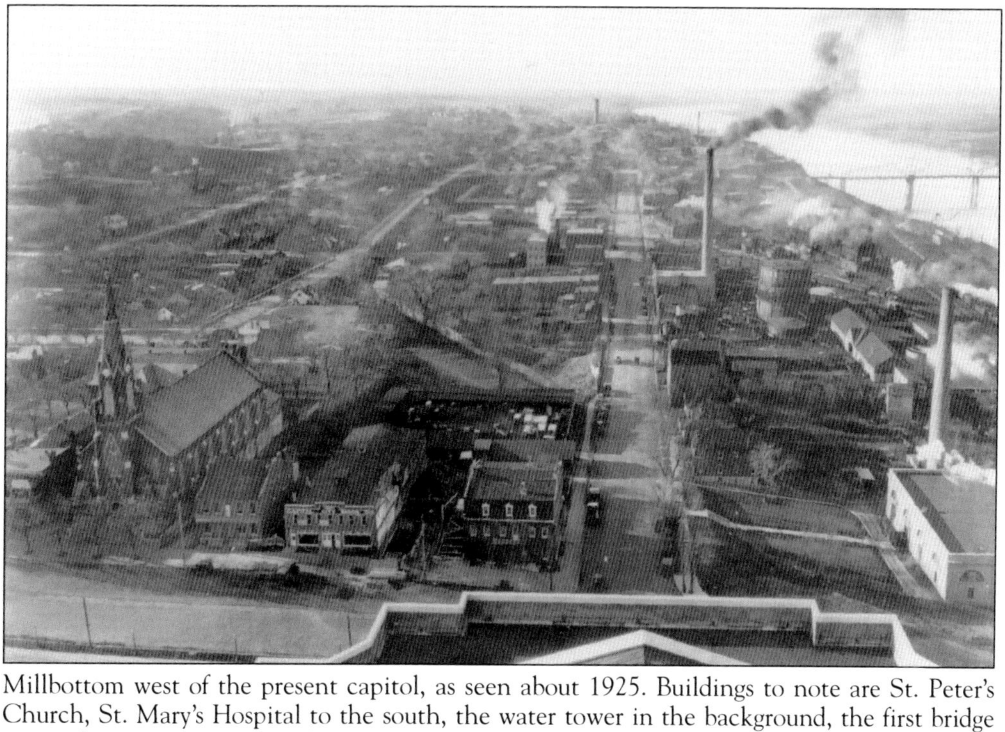

Millbottom west of the present capitol, as seen about 1925. Buildings to note are St. Peter's Church, St. Mary's Hospital to the south, the water tower in the background, the first bridge across the Missouri River at the City of Jefferson, the train round house, the trains, Dulle Mills, and the Missouri Power and Light Company. (Jim Twyman.)

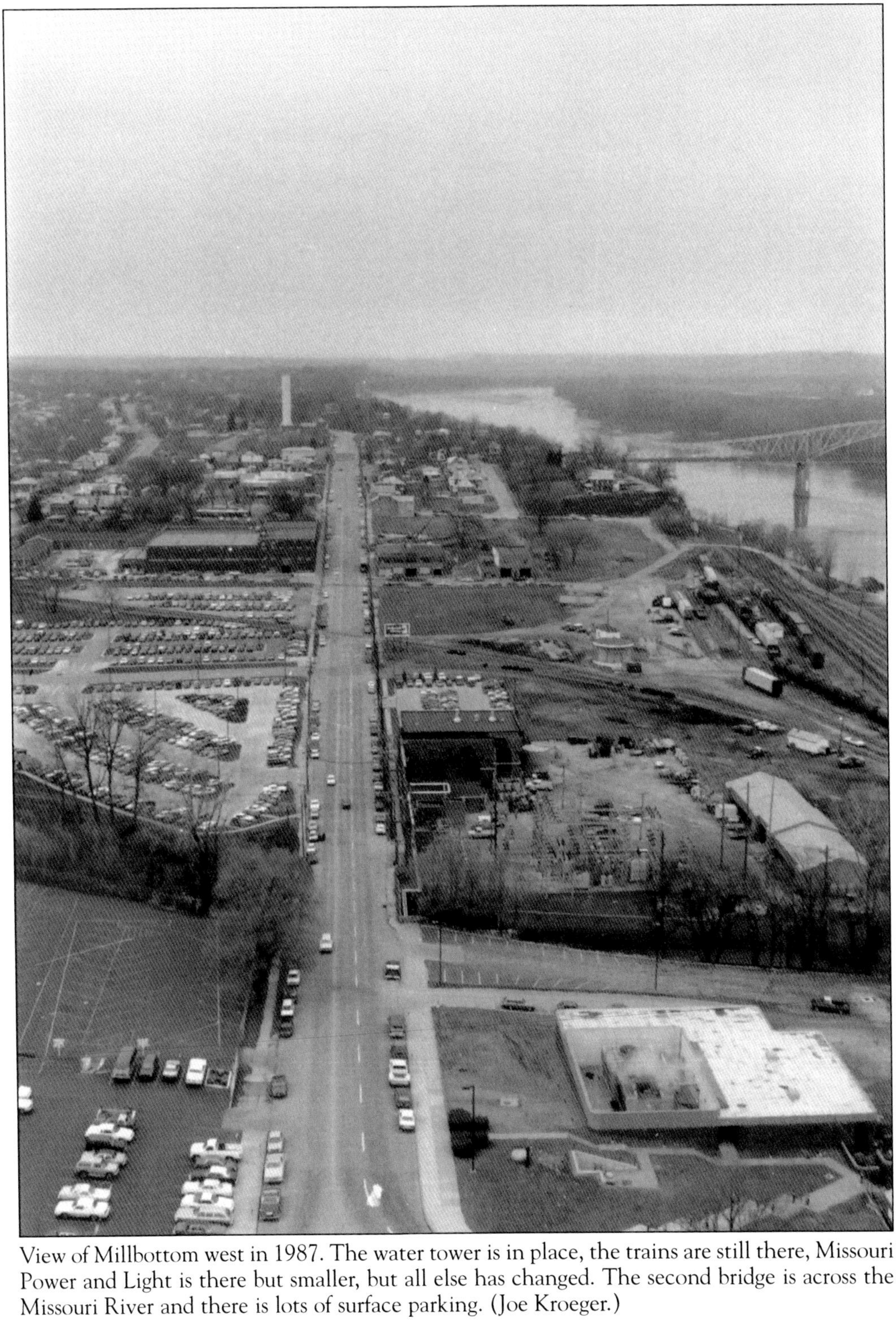

View of Millbottom west in 1987. The water tower is in place, the trains are still there, Missouri Power and Light is there but smaller, but all else has changed. The second bridge is across the Missouri River and there is lots of surface parking. (Joe Kroeger.)

Eight

Life and Times in the City of Jefferson

This will show, briefly, some of the cultural traditions that have been established in the City of Jefferson over the years, some of the people and their places. The City of Jefferson is a unique place with unique people. It also has an attractive appearance and history. Everyone feels that way about their "home town," but we feel that our "home town" is special and hope we were able to convey some of its uniqueness to you in this book.

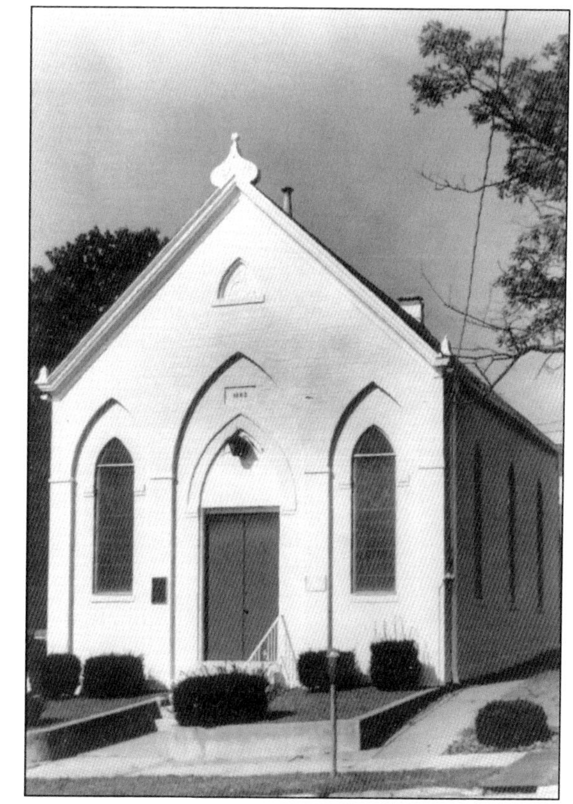

Temple Beth-El at 318 Monroe Street was built in 1883 and is one of the oldest reformed synagogues west of the Mississippi River. The City of Jefferson has a great many churches which are important to the community. We have space only to show a few. (Summers Collection; Missouri State Archives.)

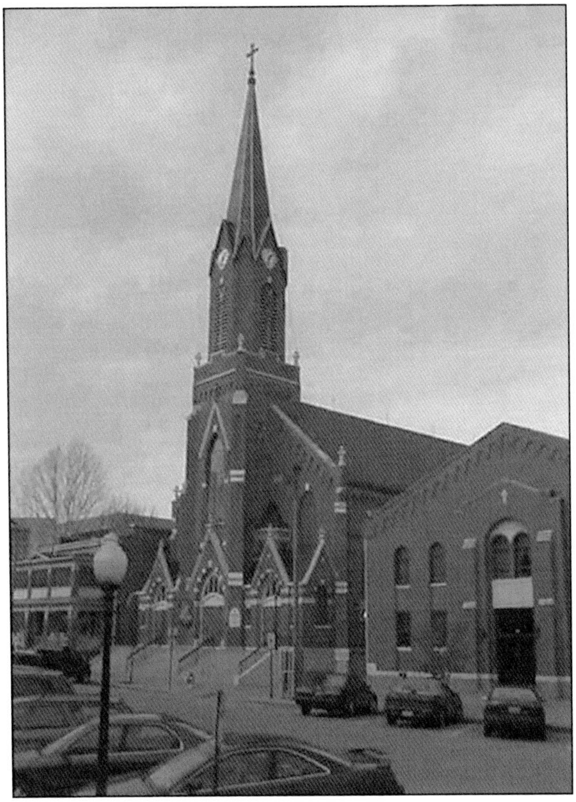

St. Peter's Catholic Church at 216 Broadway was built between 1881 and 1883 by Frederick H. Binder, a local architect and builder. (Dottie Dallmeyer.)

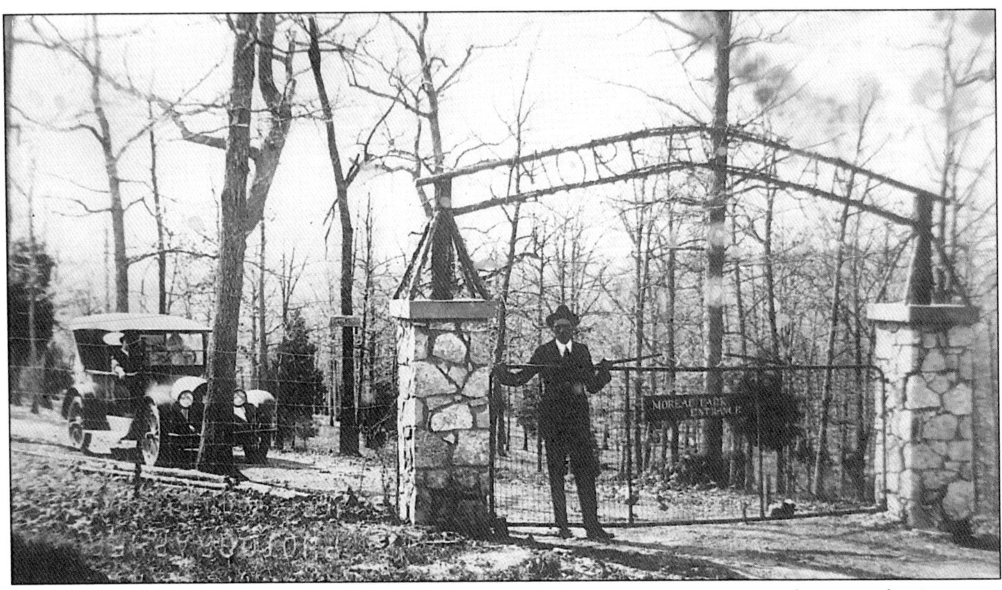

This image shows the gateway to Moreau Park in the 1920s. Moreau Park is on the Moreau River and was the place to swim and picnic before there were swimming pools in the City of Jefferson. There is also a lodge for dancing and family gatherings. (Rudi Dallmeyer.)

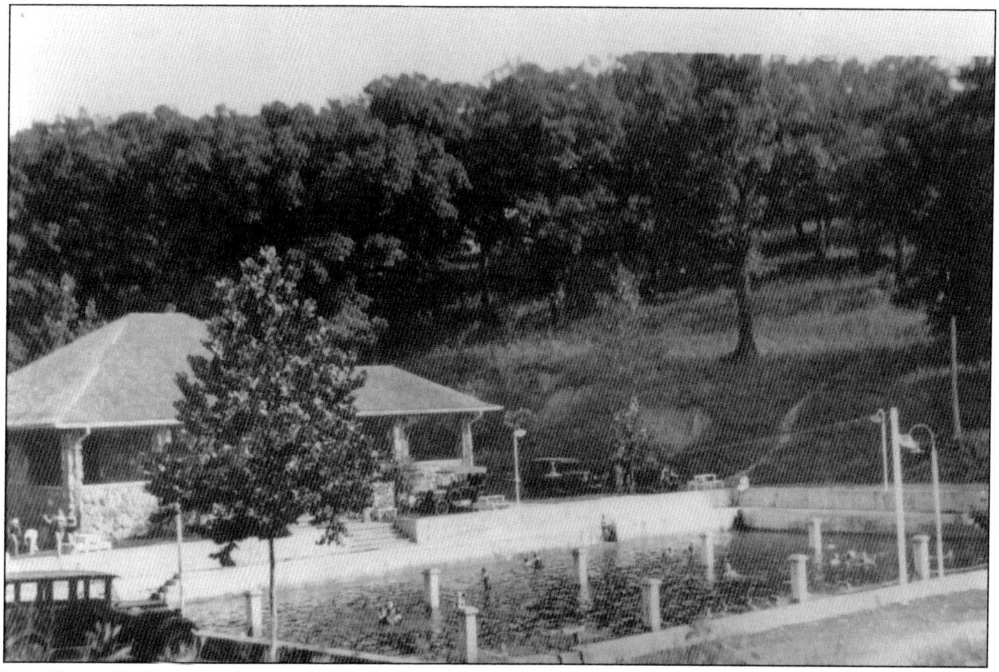

McClung Park swimming pool was the first swimming pool in town. This photo is from about 1928.

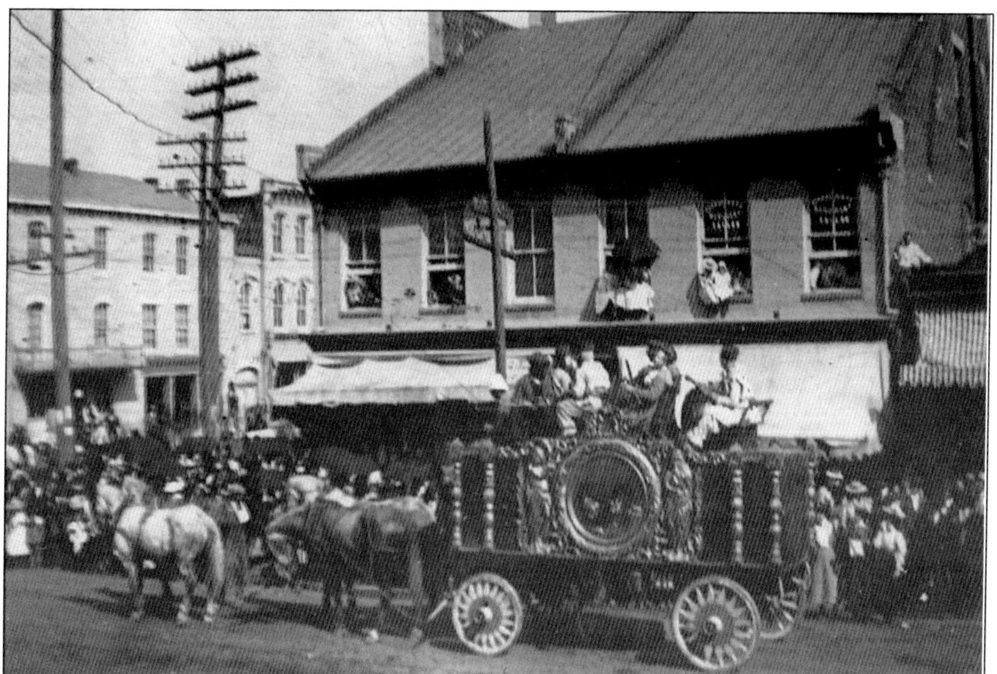

The City of Jefferson has always done parades well. This circus parade from the 1890s is shown on the corner of High Street and Madison in front of the Hope Building with the City Hotel across the street. (Phil Dallmeyer.)

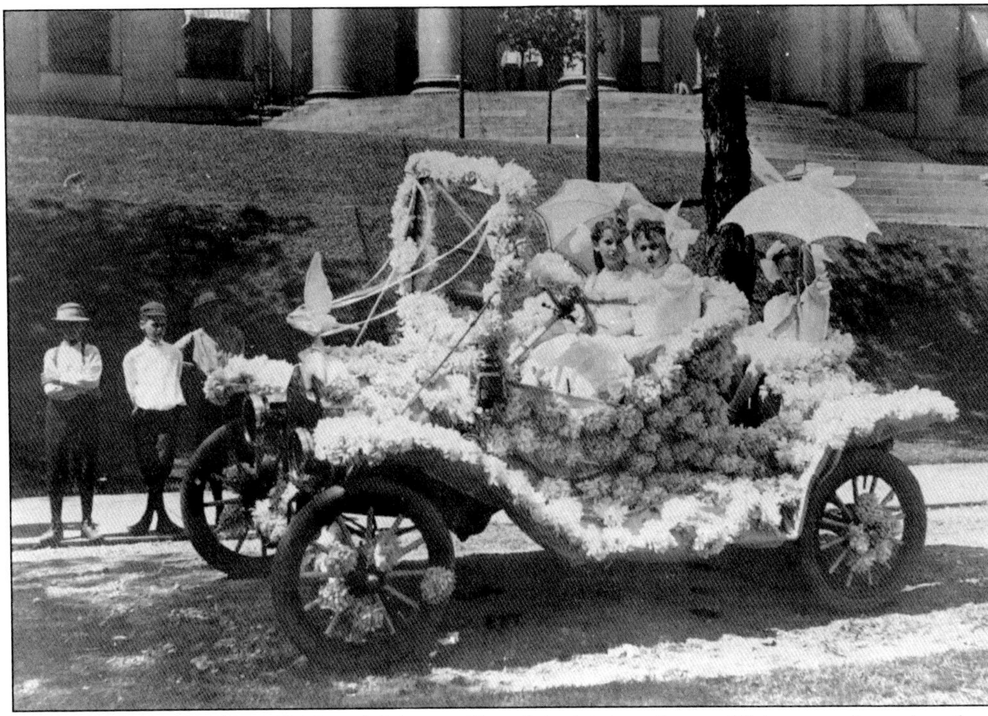

The flower parade about 1910 with Myrene Houchin driving the car. This seemed to take place in the summer and was associated with the local horse racing track. (Mary Gamble.)

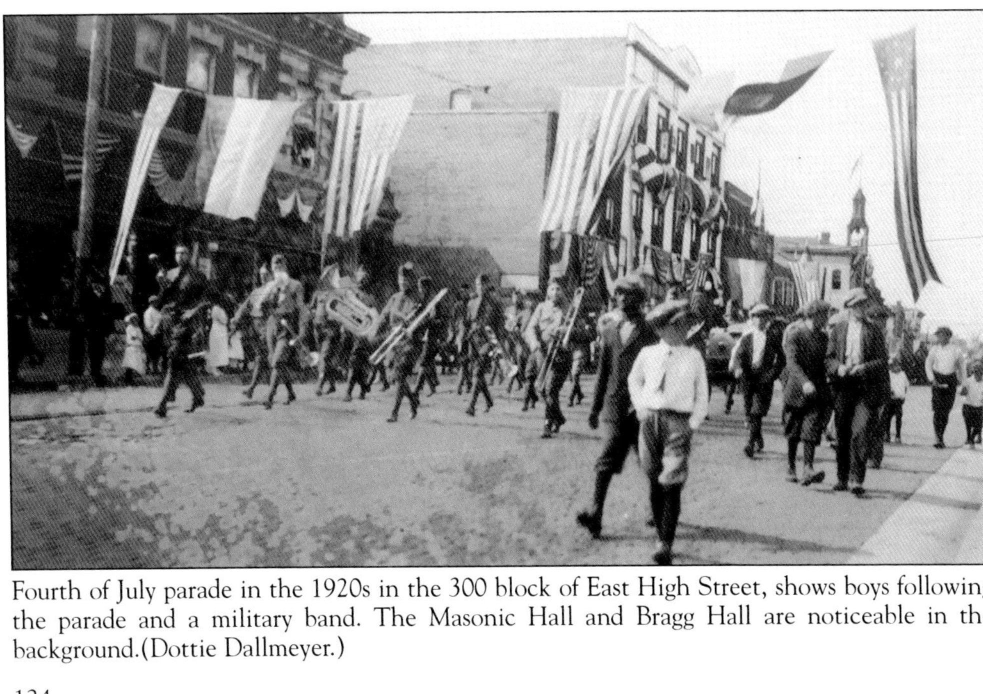

Fourth of July parade in the 1920s in the 300 block of East High Street, shows boys following the parade and a military band. The Masonic Hall and Bragg Hall are noticeable in the background.(Dottie Dallmeyer.)

"John the Baptist," shown leading the parade in the early 1950s, established a 50-year tradition of leading parades in the City of Jefferson and a much beloved character in our city. There are many "John the Baptist" stories that float about the town. (Summers Collection; Missouri State Archives.)

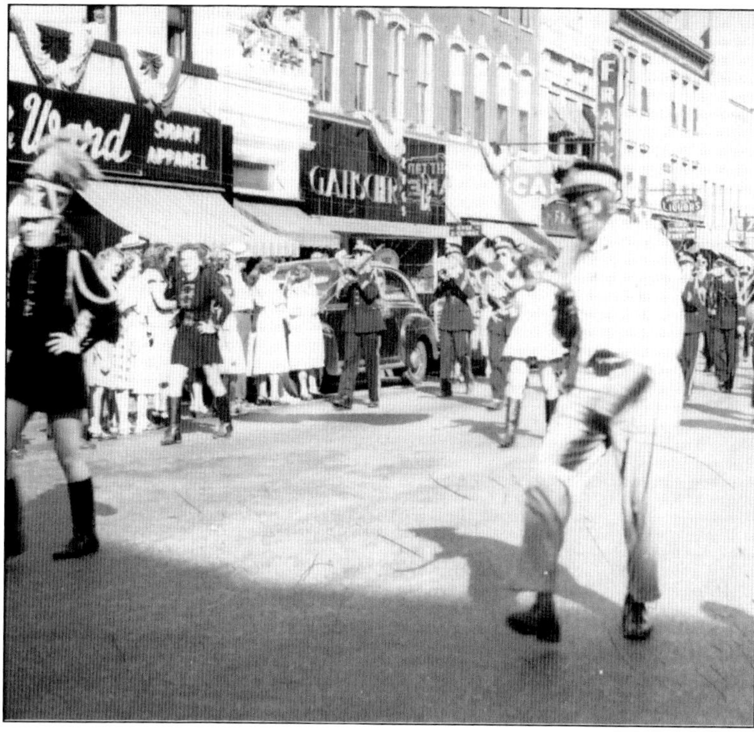

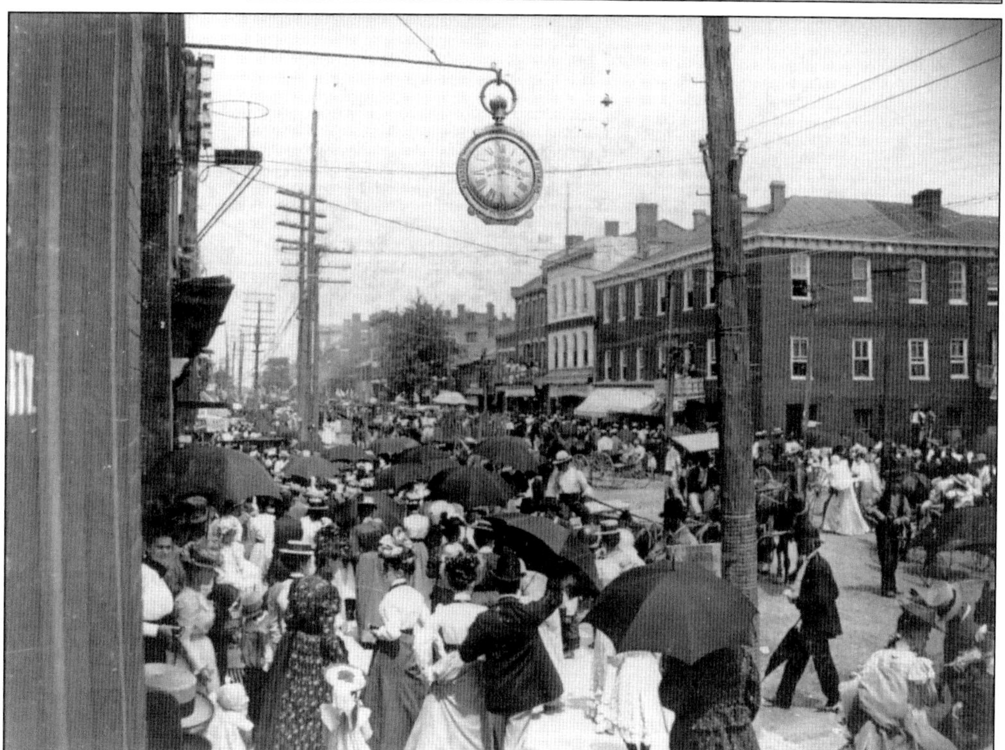

This street scene in the 1890s at the corner of High Street and Madison shows the City Hotel is in the background. (Summers Collection; Missouri State Archives.)

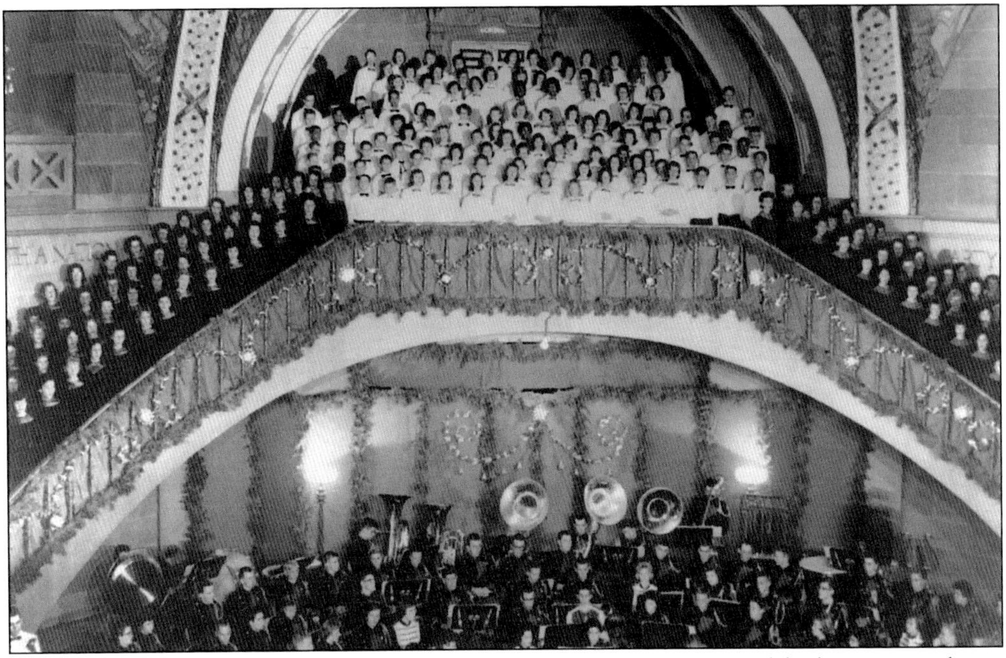

Capitol Caroling has been a tradition here since the 1930s. It is a beautiful Christmas tradition joining the high school band and choir in the rotunda of the capitol to sing Christmas music. This photo is from the 1958 Christmas Caroling Concert. (Joe Kroeger.)

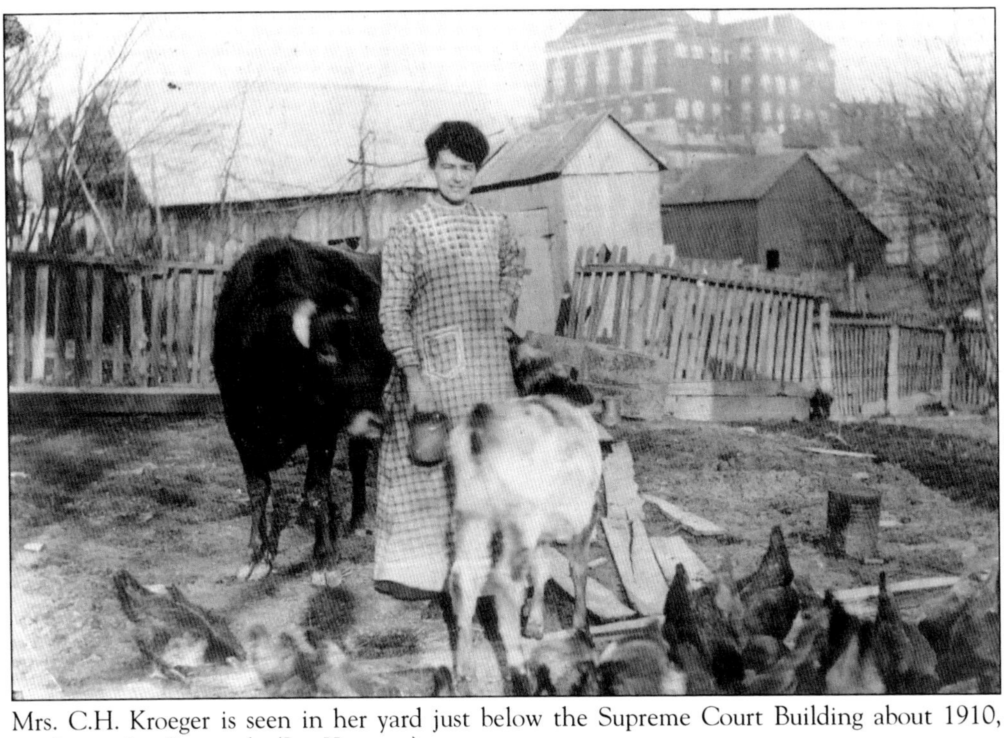

Mrs. C.H. Kroeger is seen in her yard just below the Supreme Court Building about 1910, tending to her livestock. (Joe Kroeger.)

Sunday tours of the prison were popular for awhile around the turn of the last century. The prisoners would parade, provide entertainment, and there would be a picnic type feeling on Sunday afternoon. (Dottie Dallmeyer.)

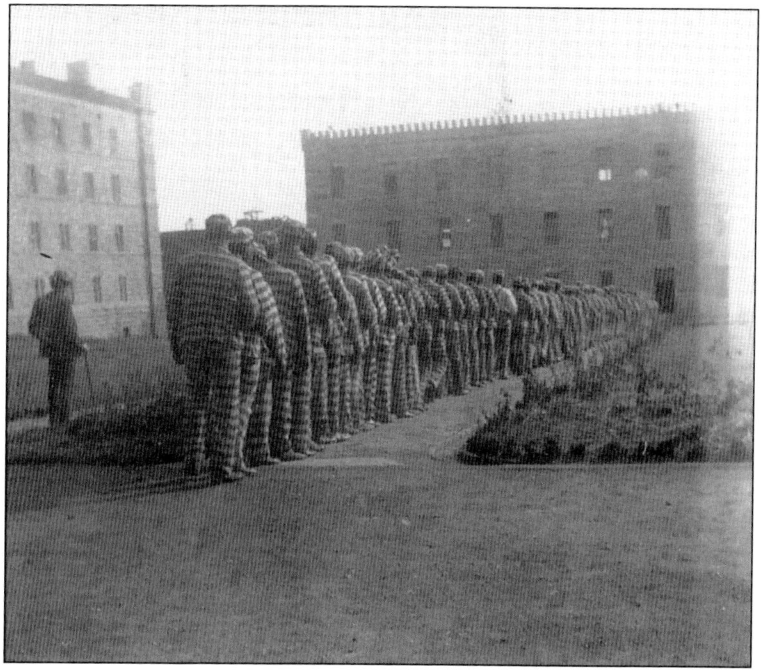

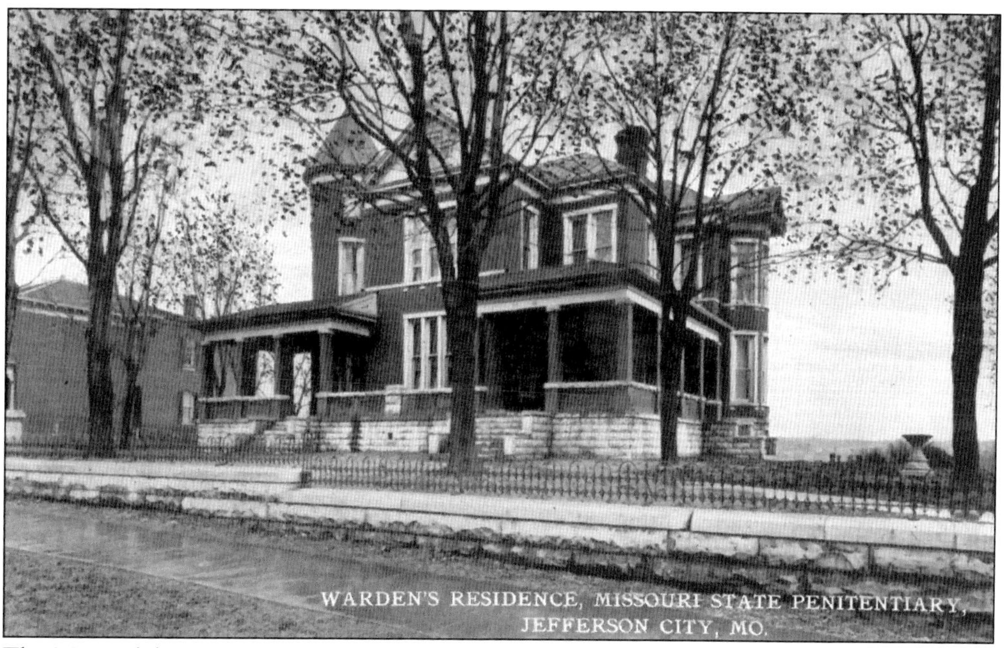

The Marmaduke House at 700 East Capital was built in the 1880s as a prison warden's house by prison labor, as many houses in that neighborhood were. It has recently been beautifully restored. (Summers Collection; Missouri State Archives.)

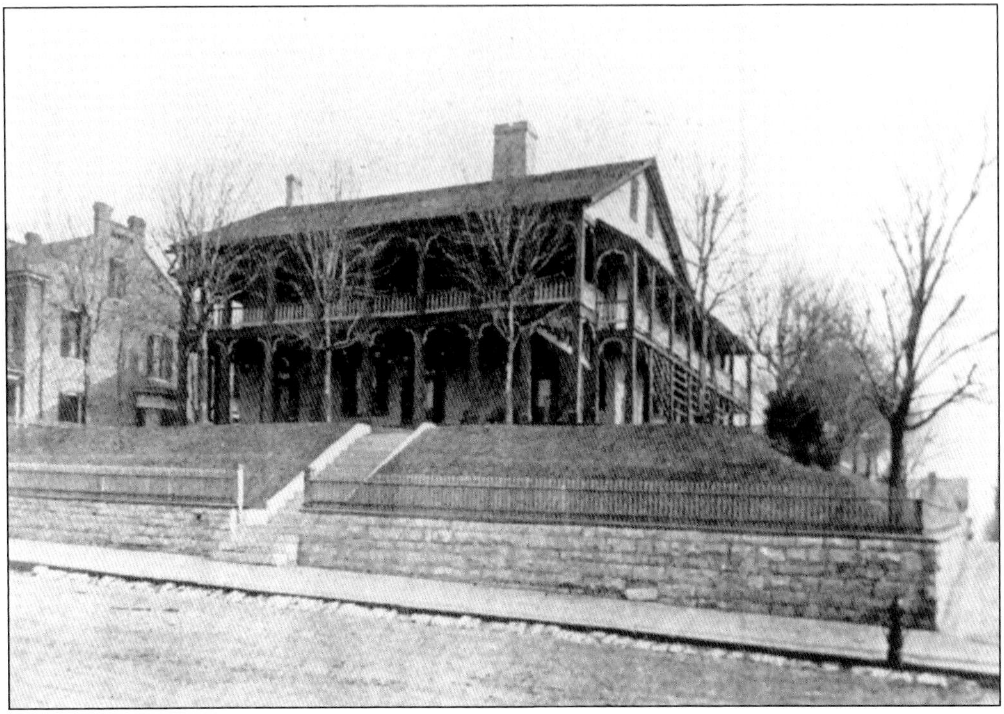

Maple Terrace, at the corner of High Street and Adams, was built by Robert Wells to look like a steamboat. For many years it was lived in by the Rudolph Dallmeyer family. It was destroyed in the late 1930s. (Summers Collection; Missouri State Archives.)

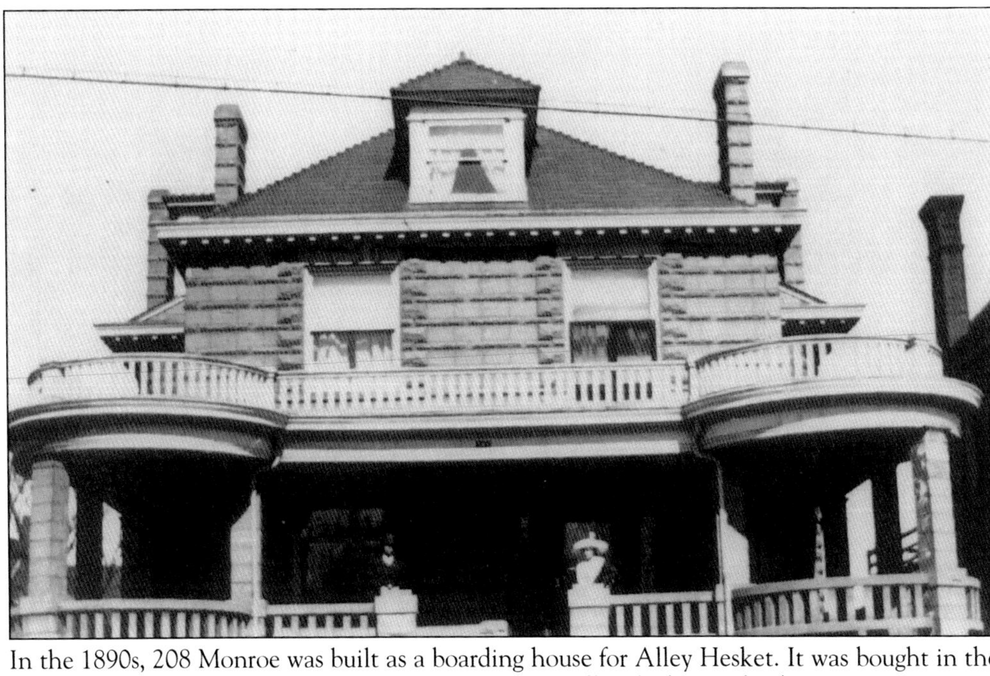

In the 1890s, 208 Monroe was built as a boarding house for Alley Hesket. It was bought in the early 1920s by Dr. J.S. Summers for use as a home and office for his medical practice. It was torn down in the 1940s. (Dottie Dallmeyer.)